Introduction to Chemistry

interactive SCIENCE

PEARSON

Boston, Massachusetts
Chandler, Arizona
Glenview, Illinois
Upper Saddle River, New Jersey

AUTHORS

You're an author!

As you write in this science book, your answers and personal discoveries will be recorded for you to keep, making this book unique to you. That is why you are one of the primary authors of this book.

✎ **In the space below, print your name, school, town, and state. Then write a short autobiography that includes your interests and accomplishments.**

YOUR NAME _____

SCHOOL _____

TOWN, STATE _____

AUTOBIOGRAPHY _____

_____

_____

_____

_____

_____

_____

_____

_____

Your Photo

Acknowledgments appear on pages 247–249, which constitute an extension of this copyright page.

ISBN-13: 978-0-13-368479-7
ISBN-10: 0-13-368479-2
12 13 V011 16 15 14

ON THE COVER
Liquid Metal
Because mercury is a heavy, silvery liquid at room temperature, it is sometimes called quicksilver. Mercury is poisonous if swallowed or inhaled and must be handled carefully. In the past, people used mercury-filled thermometers to take their temperatures. Today, most people use digital or other safer thermometers at home.

Program Authors

DON BUCKLEY, M.Sc.
*Information and Communications Technology Director,
The School at Columbia University, New York, New York*
Mr. Buckley has been at the forefront of K–12 educational
technology for nearly two decades. A founder of New York City
Independent School Technologists (NYCIST) and long-time chair
of New York Association of Independent Schools' annual IT
conference, he has taught students on two continents and
created multimedia and Internet-based instructional systems
for schools worldwide.

ZIPPORAH MILLER, M.A.Ed.
*Associate Executive Director for Professional Programs
and Conferences, National Science Teachers Association,
Arlington, Virginia*
Associate executive director for professional programs and
conferences at NSTA, Ms. Zipporah Miller is a former K–12 science
supervisor and STEM coordinator for the Prince George's County
Public School District in Maryland. She is a science education
consultant who has overseen curriculum development and staff
training for more than 150 district science coordinators.

MICHAEL J. PADILLA, Ph.D.
*Associate Dean and Director, Eugene P. Moore School of
Education, Clemson University, Clemson, South Carolina*
A former middle school teacher and a leader in middle school
science education, Dr. Michael Padilla has served as president of
the National Science Teachers Association and as a writer of the
National Science Education Standards. He is professor of science
education at Clemson University. As lead author of the *Science
Explorer* series, Dr. Padilla has inspired the team in developing a
program that promotes student inquiry and meets the needs of
today's students.

KATHRYN THORNTON, Ph.D.
*Professor and Associate Dean, School of Engineering
and Applied Science, University of Virginia,
Charlottesville, Virginia*
Selected by NASA in May 1984, Dr. Kathryn Thornton is a veteran
of four space flights. She has logged over 975 hours in space,
including more than 21 hours of extravehicular activity. As an
author on the *Scott Foresman Science* series, Dr. Thornton's
enthusiasm for science has inspired teachers around the globe.

MICHAEL E. WYSESSION, Ph.D.
*Associate Professor of Earth and Planetary Science,
Washington University, St. Louis, Missouri*
An author on more than 50 scientific publications, Dr. Wysession
was awarded the prestigious Packard Foundation Fellowship and
Presidential Faculty Fellowship for his research in geophysics. Dr.
Wysession is an expert on Earth's inner structure and has mapped
various regions of Earth using seismic tomography. He is known
internationally for his work in geoscience education and outreach.

Instructional Design Author

GRANT WIGGINS, Ed.D.
*President, Authentic Education,
Hopewell, New Jersey*
Dr. Wiggins is a co-author with
Jay McTighe of *Understanding by Design,
2nd Edition* (ASCD 2005). His approach
to instructional design provides teachers
with a disciplined way of thinking about
curriculum design, assessment, and instruction that moves teaching from covering
content to ensuring understanding.
    UNDERSTANDING BY DESIGN® and
UbD™ are trademarks of ASCD, and are
used under license.

Planet Diary Author

JACK HANKIN
*Science/Mathematics Teacher,
The Hilldale School, Daly City, California
Founder, Planet Diary Web site*
Mr. Hankin is the creator and writer of
Planet Diary, a science current events
Web site. He is passionate about bringing
science news and environmental awareness
into classrooms and offers numerous Planet
Diary workshops at NSTA and other events
to train middle and high school teachers.

ELL Consultant

JIM CUMMINS, Ph.D.
*Professor and Canada Research Chair,
Curriculum, Teaching and Learning
department at the University of Toronto*
Dr. Cummins focuses on literacy development in multilingual schools and the role of
technology in promoting student learning
across the curriculum. *Interactive Science*
incorporates essential research-based
principles for integrating language with the
teaching of academic content based on his
instructional framework.

Reading Consultant

HARVEY DANIELS, Ph.D.
*Professor of Secondary Education,
University of New Mexico,
Albuquerque, New Mexico*
Dr. Daniels is an international consultant
to schools, districts, and educational
agencies. He has authored or coauthored
13 books on language, literacy, and education. His most recent works are *Compre-
hension and Collaboration: Inquiry Circles
in Action* and *Subjects Matter: Every
Teacher's Guide to Content-Area Reading.*

REVIEWERS

Contributing Writers

Edward Aguado, Ph.D.
Professor, Department of Geography
San Diego State University
San Diego, California

Elizabeth Coolidge-Stolz, M.D.
Medical Writer
North Reading, Massachusetts

Donald L. Cronkite, Ph.D.
Professor of Biology
Hope College
Holland, Michigan

Jan Jenner, Ph.D.
Science Writer
Talladega, Alabama

Linda Cronin Jones, Ph.D.
Associate Professor of Science and
    Environmental Education
University of Florida
Gainesville, Florida

T. Griffith Jones, Ph.D.
Clinical Associate Professor
    of Science Education
College of Education
University of Florida
Gainesville, Florida

Andrew C. Kemp, Ph.D.
Teacher
Jefferson County Public Schools
Louisville, Kentucky

Matthew Stoneking, Ph.D.
Associate Professor of Physics
Lawrence University
Appleton, Wisconsin

R. Bruce Ward, Ed.D.
Senior Research Associate
Science Education Department
Harvard-Smithsonian Center for
    Astrophysics
Cambridge, Massachusetts

Content Reviewers

Paul D. Beale, Ph.D.
Department of Physics
University of Colorado at Boulder
Boulder, Colorado

Jeff R. Bodart, Ph.D.
Professor of Physical Sciences
Chipola College
Marianna, Florida

Joy Branlund, Ph.D.
Department of Earth Science
Southwestern Illinois College
Granite City, Illinois

Marguerite Brickman, Ph.D.
Division of Biological Sciences
University of Georgia
Athens, Georgia

Bonnie J. Brunkhorst, Ph.D.
Science Education and Geological
    Sciences
California State University
San Bernardino, California

Michael Castellani, Ph.D.
Department of Chemistry
Marshall University
Huntington, West Virginia

Charles C. Curtis, Ph.D.
Research Associate Professor
    of Physics
University of Arizona
Tucson, Arizona

Diane I. Doser, Ph.D.
Department of Geological
    Sciences
University of Texas
El Paso, Texas

Rick Duhrkopf, Ph.D.
Department of Biology
Baylor University
Waco, Texas

Alice K. Hankla, Ph.D.
The Galloway School
Atlanta, Georgia

Mark Henriksen, Ph.D.
Physics Department
University of Maryland
Baltimore, Maryland

Chad Hershock, Ph.D.
Center for Research on Learning
    and Teaching
University of Michigan
Ann Arbor, Michigan

Jeremiah N. Jarrett, Ph.D.
Department of Biology
Central Connecticut State
    University
New Britain, Connecticut

Scott L. Kight, Ph.D.
Department of Biology
Montclair State University
Montclair, New Jersey

Jennifer O. Liang, Ph.D.
Department of Biology
University of Minnesota–Duluth
Duluth, Minnesota

Candace Lutzow-Felling, Ph.D.
Director of Education
The State Arboretum of Virginia
University of Virginia
Boyce, Virginia

Cortney V. Martin, Ph.D.
Virginia Polytechnic Institute
Blacksburg, Virginia

Joseph F. McCullough, Ph.D.
Physics Program Chair
Cabrillo College
Aptos, California

Heather Mernitz, Ph.D.
Department of Physical Science
Alverno College
Milwaukee, Wisconsin

Sadredin C. Moosavi, Ph.D.
Department of Earth and
    Environmental Sciences
Tulane University
New Orleans, Louisiana

David L. Reid, Ph.D.
Department of Biology
Blackburn College
Carlinville, Illinois

Scott M. Rochette, Ph.D.
Department of the Earth Sciences
SUNY College at Brockport
Brockport, New York

Karyn L. Rogers, Ph.D.
Department of Geological
    Sciences
University of Missouri
Columbia, Missouri

Laurence Rosenhein, Ph.D.
Department of Chemistry
Indiana State University
Terre Haute, Indiana

Sara Seager, Ph.D.
Department of Planetary Sciences
    and Physics
Massachusetts Institute of
    Technology
Cambridge, Massachusetts

Tom Shoberg, Ph.D.
Missouri University of Science
    and Technology
Rolla, Missouri

Patricia Simmons, Ph.D.
North Carolina State University
Raleigh, North Carolina

William H. Steinecker, Ph.D.
Research Scholar
Miami University
Oxford, Ohio

Paul R. Stoddard, Ph.D.
Department of Geology and
    Environmental Geosciences
Northern Illinois University
DeKalb, Illinois

John R. Villarreal, Ph.D.
Department of Chemistry
The University of Texas–Pan
    American
Edinburg, Texas

John R. Wagner, Ph.D.
Department of Geology
Clemson University
Clemson, South Carolina

Jerry Waldvogel, Ph.D.
Department of Biological Sciences
Clemson University
Clemson, South Carolina

Donna L. Witter, Ph.D.
Department of Geology
Kent State University
Kent, Ohio

Edward J. Zalisko, Ph.D.
Department of Biology
Blackburn College
Carlinville, Illinois

Museum of Science.

Special thanks to the Museum of Science,
Boston, Massachusetts, and Ioannis Miaoulis,
the Museum's president and director, for
serving as content advisors for the technology
and design strand in this program.

CONTENTS

CHAPTER 1 Introduction to Matter

Enter the Lab zone for hands-on inquiry.

Chapter Lab Investigation:
• Directed Inquiry: Making Sense of Density
• Open Inquiry: Making Sense of Density

Inquiry Warm-Ups: • How Do You Describe Matter? • What Is a Mixture? • Which Has More Mass? • Is a New Substance Formed?

Quick Labs: • Observing Physical Properties • Modeling Atoms and Molecules • Separating Mixtures • Calculating Volume • What Is a Physical Change? • Demonstrating Tarnishing • Where Was the Energy?

my science online.com

Go to MyScienceOnline.com to interact with this chapter's content.
Keyword: Introduction to Matter

> **UNTAMED SCIENCE**
• What's the Matter?

> **PLANET DIARY**
• Introduction to Matter

> **INTERACTIVE ART**
• Conservation of Matter • Properties of Matter

> **ART IN MOTION**
• What Makes Up Matter?

> **VIRTUAL LAB**
• How Do You Measure Weight and Volume?
• Will It Float? Density of Solids and Liquids

Lab zone® Enter the Lab zone
for hands-on inquiry.

Chapter Lab Investigation:
    • Directed Inquiry: Melting Ice
    • Open Inquiry: Melting Ice

Inquiry Warm-Ups: • What Are Solids,
Liquids, and Gases? • What Happens When
You Breathe on a Mirror? • How Can Air Keep
Chalk From Breaking?

Quick Labs: • Modeling Particles • As
Thick as Honey • How Do the Particles in
a Gas Move? • Keeping Cool • Observing
Sublimation • How Are Pressure and
Temperature Related? • Hot and Cold
Balloons • It's a Gas

my science online.com

**Go to MyScienceOnline.com to
interact with this chapter's content.
Keyword:** Solids, Liquids, and Gases

> **UNTAMED SCIENCE**
• Building a House of Snow

> **PLANET DIARY**
• Solids, Liquids, and Gases

> **INTERACTIVE ART**
• Gas Laws • States of Matter

> **VIRTUAL LAB**
• Solid to Liquid to Gas: Changes of State

CONTENTS

Enter the Lab zone for hands-on inquiry.

Chapter Lab Investigation:
• Directed Inquiry: Copper or Carbon? That Is the Question
• Open Inquiry: Copper or Carbon? That Is the Question

Inquiry Warm-Ups: • What's in the Box?
• What Is Easier? • Why Use Aluminum?
• What Are the Properties of Charcoal? • How Much Goes Away?

Quick Labs: • Visualizing an Electron Cloud
• How Far Away Is the Electron? • Classifying
• Using the Periodic Table • Expanding the Periodic Table • Finding Metals • Carbon—A Nonmetal • Finding Nonmetals • What Happens When an Atom Decays? • Modeling Beta Decay • Designing Experiments Using Radioactive Tracers

my science online.com

Go to MyScienceOnline.com to interact with this chapter's content.
Keyword: Elements and the Periodic Table

> **PLANET DIARY**
• Elements and the Periodic Table

> **INTERACTIVE ART**
• Periodic Table • Investigate an Atom

> **ART IN MOTION**
• Types of Radioactive Decay

> **VIRTUAL LAB**
• Which Element Is This?

CHAPTER
4

Atoms and Bonding

Lab zone® **Enter the Lab zone
for hands-on inquiry.**

Chapter Lab Investigation:
• Directed Inquiry: Shedding Light on Ions
• Open Inquiry: Shedding Light on Ions

Inquiry Warm-Ups: • What Are the Trends
in the Periodic Table? • How Do Ions Form?
• Covalent Bonds • Are They "Steel" the
Same?

Quick Labs: • Element Chemistry • Ion
Formation • How Do You Write Ionic
Names and Formulas? • Sharing Electrons
• Properties of Molecular Compounds
• Attraction Between Polar Molecules • Metal
Crystals • What Do Metals Do?

my science ONLINE .com

**Go to MyScienceOnline.com to
interact with this chapter's content.
Keyword:** Atoms and Bonding

> **UNTAMED SCIENCE**
• The Elements of Hockey

> **PLANET DIARY**
• Atoms and Bonding

> **INTERACTIVE ART**
• Periodic Table • Investigate Ionic
Compounds • Table Salt Dissolving in Water

> **ART IN MOTION**
• Bonding in Polar Molecules

> **VIRTUAL LAB**
• Will It React?

CONTENTS

 **Enter the Lab zone for hands-on inquiry.**

Chapter Lab Investigation:
• Directed Inquiry: Where's the Evidence?
• Open Inquiry: Where's the Evidence?

Inquiry Warm-Ups: • What Happens When Chemicals React? • Did You Lose Anything? • Can You Speed Up or Slow Down a Reaction?

Quick Labs: • Observing Change • Information in a Chemical Equation • Is Matter Conserved? • Categories of Chemical Reactions • Modeling Activation Energy • Effect of Temperature on Chemical Reactions

my science online.com

Go to MyScienceOnline.com to interact with this chapter's content.
Keyword: **Chemical Reactions**

> **UNTAMED SCIENCE**
• Chemical Reactions to the Rescue

> **PLANET DIARY**
• Chemical Reactions

> **INTERACTIVE ART**
• Physical or Chemical Change? • Conservation of Matter • Balancing Equations

> **ART IN MOTION**
• Activation Energy

> **VIRTUAL LAB**
• Energy and Chemical Changes

Lab zone® Enter the Lab zone for hands-on inquiry.

Chapter Lab Investigation:
• Directed Inquiry: Speedy Solutions
• Open Inquiry: Speedy Solutions

Inquiry Warm-Ups: • What Makes a Mixture a Solution? • Does It Dissolve? • What Color Does Litmus Paper Turn? • What Can Cabbage Juice Tell You?

Quick Labs: • Scattered Light • Measuring Concentration • Predicting Rates of Solubility • Properties of Acids • Properties of Bases • pHone Home • The Antacid Test

my science online.com

Go to MyScienceOnline.com to interact with this chapter's content. Keyword: Acids, Bases, and Solutions

> **UNTAMED SCIENCE**
• What's the Solution?

> **PLANET DIARY**
• Acids, Bases, and Solutions

> **INTERACTIVE ART**
• Table Salt Dissolving in Water • Classifying Solutions • The pH Scale

> **VIRTUAL LAB**
• Acid, Base, or Neutral?

interactive SCIENCE

This is your book.
You can write in it!

Get Engaged!

At the start of each chapter, you will see two questions: an Engaging Question and the Big Question. Each chapter's Big Question will help you start thinking about the Big Ideas of Science. Look for the Big Q symbol throughout the chapter!

HOW CAN WIND KEEP YOUR LIGHTS ON?

THE BIG ? What are some of Earth's energy sources?

This man is repairing a wind turbine at a wind farm in Texas. Most wind turbines are at least 30 meters off the ground where the winds are fast. Wind speed and blade length help determine the best way to capture the wind and turn it into power. Develop Hypotheses Why do you think people are working to increase the amount of power we get from wind?

Wind energy collected by the turbine does not cause air pollution.

> UNTAMED SCIENCE Watch the **Untamed Science** video to learn more about energy resources.

174 Energy Resources

Untamed Science™

Follow the Untamed Science video crew as they travel the globe exploring the Big Ideas of Science.

Interact with your textbook.   **Interact with inquiry.**   **Interact online.**

Build Reading, Inquiry, and Vocabulary Skills

In every lesson you will learn new ↻ Reading and ▲ Inquiry skills. These skills will help you read and think like a scientist. Vocabulary skills will help you communicate effectively and uncover the meaning of words.

my SCIENCE **online.com**

Go Online!

Look for the MyScienceOnline.com technology options. At MyScienceOnline.com you can immerse yourself in amazing virtual environments, get extra practice, and even blog about current events in science.

Explore the Key Concepts.

Each lesson begins with a series of Key Concept questions. The interactivities in each lesson will help you understand these concepts and Unlock the Big Question.

my planet diary

At the start of each lesson, My Planet Diary will introduce you to amazing events, significant people, and important discoveries in science or help you to overcome common misconceptions about science concepts.

Desertification If the soil of moisture and nutrients, advance of desertlike condi fertile is called **desertificat**

One cause of desertifica is a period when less rain t droughts, crops fail. Witho blows away. Overgrazing o cutting down trees for firev

Desertification is a serio and graze livestock where people may face famine an central Africa. Millions of cities because they can no

apply it!

Desertification affects man areas around the world.

1 Name Which continen has the most existing dese

2 Interpret Maps Where the United States is the gr risk of desertification?

3 Infer Is desertificatio is existing desert? Explain your answer.

4 CHALLENGE If an area things people could do to

132 Land, Air, and Wat

Explain what you know.

Look for the pencil. When you see it, it's time to interact with your book and demonstrate what you have learned.

Elaborate further with the Apply It activities.

This is your opportunity to take what you've learned and apply those skills to new situations.

Lab Zone

Look for the Lab zone triangle. This means it's time to do a hands-on inquiry lab. In every lesson, you'll have the opportunity to do a hands-on inquiry activity that will help reinforce your understanding of the lesson topic.

area becomes depleted
me a desert. The
hat previously were
fih KAY shun).
or example, a **drought**
n an area. During
exposed soil easily
tle and sheep and
sertification, too.
le cannot grow crops
occurred. As a result,
rtification is severe in
are moving to the
mselves on the land.

Key
- Existing desert
- High-risk area
- Moderate-risk area

s where there
e map to support

n, what are some
ts?

Land Reclamation Fortunately, it is possible to replace land damaged by erosion or mining. The process of restoring an area of land to a more productive state is called **land reclamation.** In addition to restoring land for agriculture, land reclamation can restore habitats for wildlife. Many different types of land reclamation projects are currently underway all over the world. But it is generally more difficult and expensive to restore damaged land and soil than it is to protect those resources in the first place. In some cases, the land may not return to its original state.

FIGURE 4
Land Reclamation
These pictures show land before and after it was mined.

✎ **Communicate** Below the pictures, write a story about what happened to the land.

_____
_____
_____

Lab zone Do the Quick Lab
Modeling S

🔑 Assess Your Understanding

1a. Review Subsoil has (less/more) plant and animal matter than topsoil.

b. Explain What can happen to soil if plants are removed?

_____
_____

c. Apply Concepts
that could prev
land reclam

got it?

○ **I get it!** Now I know that soil management is important becau

○ **I need extra help with** _____

Go to MY SCIENCE COACH online for help with this subject.

got it?

Evaluate Your Progress.

After answering the Got It question, think about how you're doing. Did you get it or do you need a little help? Remember, MY SCIENCE COACH is there for you if you need extra help.

Explore the Big Question.

At one point in the chapter, you'll have the opportunity to take all that you've learned to further explore the Big Question.

Pollution and Solutions

What can people do to use resources wisely?

FIGURE 4 ....

▶ REAL-WORLD INQUIRY All living things depend on land, air, and water. Conserving these resources for the future is important. Part of resource conservation is identifying and limiting sources of pollution.

✏ Interpret Photos On the photograph, write the letter from the key into the circle that best identifies the source of pollution.

Land
Describe at least one thing your community could do to reduce pollution on land.

_____
_____
_____
_____
_____

Air
Describe at least one thing your community could do to reduce air pollution.

_____
_____
_____
_____
_____
_____

Water
Describe at least one thing your community could do to reduce water pollution.

_____
_____
_____
_____
_____

Pollution Sources
A. Sediments
B. Municipal solid waste
C. Runoff from development

Lab zone

▭ **Assess Your U**

1a. Define What are sedim

_____
_____

b. Explain How can bacte spill in the ocean?

_____
_____

c. ANSWER What can peop resources wise

_____
_____
_____

d. CHALLENGE Why mig to recycle the waste would reduce water

_____
_____
_____

got it? ....

○ I get it! Now I kno can be reduced by

_____

○ I need extra help

Go to MY SCIENCE with this subject.

Answer the Big Question.

Now it's time to show what you know and answer the Big Question.

Review What You've Learned.

Use the Chapter Study Guide to review the
Big Question and prepare for the test.

Practice Taking Tests.

Apply the Big Question and take
a practice test in standardized
test format.

INTERACT... WITH YOUR TEXTBOOK...

Go to <u>MyScienceOnline.com</u> and immerse yourself in amazing virtual environments.

▶ THE BIG QUESTION

Each online chapter starts with a Big Question. Your mission is to unlock the meaning of this Big Question as each science lesson unfolds.

Unit 4 > Chapter 1 > Lesson 1

<< The Big Question | Unlock the Big Question | Explore the Big Question | >>
The Big Question | Check Your Understanding | Vocabulary Skill

Populations and Communities

Tools

? The Big Question

Unit 2 > Chapter 4 > Lesson 1

Engage & Explore | Exp
Planet Diary

my planet diary

▶ VOCAB FLASH CARDS

Practice chapter vocabulary with interactive flash cards. Each card has an image, definitions in English and Spanish, and space for your own notes.

Unit 4 > Chapter 1 > Lesson 1

<< The Big Question | Unlock the Big Question | Explore the Big Question | >>
The Big Question | Untamed Science | Check Your Understanding | Vocabulary Skill | Vocabulary Flashcards

Vocabulary Flashcards

Tools

Card List | Create-a-Card | 10 Cards Left | Test Me
Lesson Cards | My Cards

Birth Rate
Carrying Capacity
Commensalism
Community
Competition
Death Rate
Ecology
Ecosystem
Emigration
Habitat
Host
Immigration
Limiting Factor

Science Vocabulary

Term: Community

Definition: All the different populations that live together in a particular area.

View Spanish

Add Notes

Card 5 of

Unit 6 > Chapter 1 >

Engage & Explore
Apply It | Directed Vi

Color in Light

Unit 6 > Chapter 1 > Lesson 1

Engage & Explore | Explain | Elaborate | Evaluate
Apply It | Do the Math | Art in Motion | Interactive Art | Real World Inquiry

The Nebraska Plains

▶ Bald Eagle
Information | Media

Haliaeetus leucocephalus
Bald Eagles are 80-95 cm tall with a wingspan of 180-230 cm. These birds are born with all brown feathers but grow white feathers on their head, neck, and tail.

Layers List | ▲ Show

Next
22 of 22
Back

▶ INTERACTIVE ART

At MyScienceOnline.com, many of the beautiful visuals in your book become interactive so you can extend your learning.

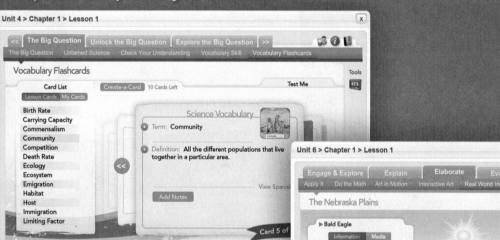

interactive SCIENCE
GO ONLINE

 Populations and Communities ▷ PLANET DIARY ▷ LAB ZONE ▷ VIRTUAL LAB

⟳ ＋ ⊕ http://www.myscienceonline.com/

▷ PLANET DIARY

My Planet Diary online is the place to find more information and activities related to the topic in the lesson.

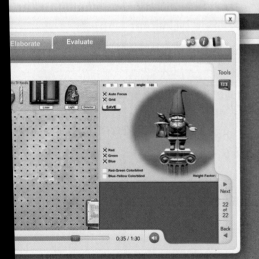

Elaborate | Evaluate | 🛠 ⓘ 📖 ✕

...erest | Tools [123]

Still Growing! Mount Everest in the Himalayas is the highest mountain on Earth. Climbers who reach the peak stand 8,850 meters above sea level. You might think that mountains never change. But forces inside Earth push Mount Everest at least several millimeters higher each year. Over time, Earth's forces slowly but constantly lift, stretch, bend, and break Earth's crust in dramatic ways!

▷ Planet Diary Go to Planet Diary to learn more about forces in the Earth's crust.

▶ Next 22 of 22 Back ◀

0:35 / 1:30 🔊

▷ VIRTUAL LAB

Get more practice with realistic virtual labs. Manipulate the variables on-screen and test your hypothesis.

Find Your Chapter

1 Go to www.myscienceonline.com.

2 Log in with username and password.

3 Click on your program and select your chapter.

Keyword Search

1 Go to www.myscienceonline.com.

2 Log in with username and password.

3 Click on your program and select Search.

4 Enter the keyword (from your book) in the search box.

Other Content Available Online

▷ UNTAMED SCIENCE Follow these young scientists through their amazing online video blogs as they travel the globe in search of answers to the Big Questions of Science.

▷ MY SCIENCE COACH Need extra help? My Science Coach is your personal online study partner. My Science Coach is a chance for you to get more practice on key science concepts. There you can choose from a variety of tools that will help guide you through each science lesson.

▷ MY READING WEB Need extra reading help on a particular science topic? At My Reading Web you will find a choice of reading selections targeted to your specific reading level.

Have you ever worked on a jigsaw puzzle? Usually a puzzle has a theme that leads you to group the pieces by what they have in common. But until you put all the pieces together you can't solve the puzzle. Studying science is similar to solving a puzzle. The big ideas of science are like puzzle themes. To understand big ideas, scientists ask questions. The answers to those questions are like pieces of a puzzle. Each chapter in this book asks a big question to help you think about a big idea of science. By answering the big questions, you will get closer to understanding the big idea.

✎ **Before you read each chapter, write about what you know and what more you'd like to know.**

This DNA molecule consists of billions of individual atoms. Atoms make up every kind of matter, including living things like you.

BIGIDEA

Atoms are the building blocks of matter.

If the building blocks of matter are the same, then what makes everything different?
✎ **What more would you like to know?**

_____

_____

_____

_____

Big Questions:

? How is matter described? Chapter 1

? How is the periodic table organized? Chapter 3

? How can bonding determine the properties of a substance? Chapter 4

? What determines the properties of a solution? Chapter 6

✎ **After reading the chapters, write what you have learned about the Big Idea.**

_____

_____

_____

_____

Mass and energy are conserved during physical and chemical changes.

If you burn a candle, gradually the candle becomes smaller. What happens to the part of the candle that burns away? Does it cease to exist?

✎ **What more would you like to know?**

_____

_____

_____

_____

_____

Big Questions:

❓ Why does a substance change states? Chapter 2

❓ How is matter conserved in a chemical reaction? Chapter 5

✎ **After reading the chapters, write what you have learned about the Big Idea.**

_____

_____

_____

_____

_____

_____

_____

Over the years, the Statue of Liberty has changed from a shiny copper to this bluish-green color because of its exposure to oxygen in the air. During these changes, the total mass and energy of the statue's atoms have been conserved.

WHAT ARE ALL OF THESE THINGS MADE OF?

How is matter described?

Imagine a warm day at Waikiki Beach on the island of Oahu, Hawaii. You can feel the warm breeze, the hot sand, and the cool water. Palm trees, hotels, shops, and the volcanic crater called Diamond Head, are all a part of the scenery around you. People swimming, surfing, and sailing are enjoying the ocean.

Classify **Categorize the items found at Waikiki Beach by what they are made of.**

_____

_____

_____

_____

_____

_____

_____

> **UNTAMED SCIENCE** Watch the **Untamed Science** video to learn more about matter.

Introduction to Matter

 Getting Started

Check Your Understanding

1. **Background** Read the paragraph below and then answer the question.

On a hot day, Jorge decides to make a pitcher of cold lemonade. He combines pure water with lemon juice in a ratio of six to one. He adds sugar and ice and stirs all the ingredients together. The properties of the lemonade are that it is cold, yellow, and sweet.

A **pure** material is not mixed with any other matter.

A **ratio** tells you the relationship between two or more things.

A **property** is a characteristic that belongs to a person or thing.

- How would the properties of the lemonade change if the ratio of pure water to lemon juice were three to one? Assume the amount of sugar is the same.

_____

_____

> MY READING WEB If you had trouble completing the question above, visit **My Reading Web** and type in *Introduction to Matter.*

Vocabulary Skill

Prefixes A prefix is a word part that is added at the beginning of a root word to change the word's meaning. The prefixes below will help you understand some of the vocabulary in this chapter.

Prefix	Meaning	Example
endo-	in, within	endogenous, *adj.* describes something that arises from inside an organism's tissues or cells
exo-	out	exoskeleton, *n.* an outer shell or outer skeleton that protects animals, such as crustaceans

2. **Quick Check** The Greek root *therm* means "heat." Predict the meaning of the term *endothermic change.*

_____

_____

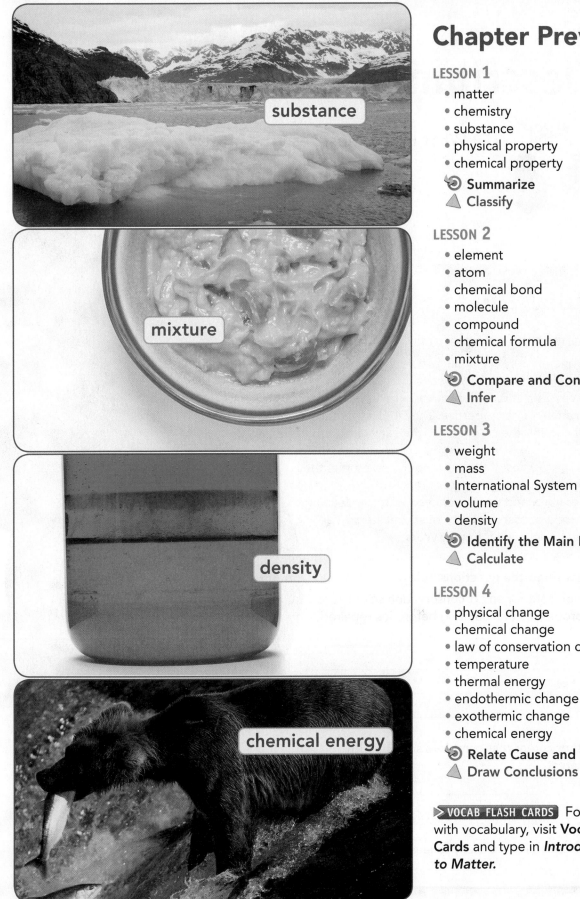

substance

mixture

density

chemical energy

Chapter Preview

LESSON 1
- matter
- chemistry
- substance
- physical property
- chemical property
- **Summarize**
- **Classify**

LESSON 2
- element
- atom
- chemical bond
- molecule
- compound
- chemical formula
- mixture
- **Compare and Contrast**
- **Infer**

LESSON 3
- weight
- mass
- International System of Units
- volume
- density
- **Identify the Main Idea**
- **Calculate**

LESSON 4
- physical change
- chemical change
- law of conservation of mass
- temperature
- thermal energy
- endothermic change
- exothermic change
- chemical energy
- **Relate Cause and Effect**
- **Draw Conclusions**

> VOCAB FLASH CARDS For extra help with vocabulary, visit **Vocab Flash Cards** and type in *Introduction to Matter.*

Describing Matter

UNLOCK THE BIG ?

🔑 **What Properties Describe Matter?**

MY PLANET DIARY

CAREER

Art Conservation Scientist

Science and art may seem like two very different interests, but they are both part of the job for an art conservation scientist. Over time, art can fade, decay, or get dirty. Conservation scientists find ways to restore art by examining its properties. They look at texture, color and age of the paint, the condition of the canvas, and materials used to make the paint. Then, the scientists can determine chemical properties of the painting. For example, they can predict how the painting will react to light, changes in temperature, and the use of chemicals for cleaning. Thanks to art conservation scientists, masterpieces of art can be enjoyed for many years.

Before

After

Write your answers to the questions below.

1. Why is it important for an art conservation scientist to study the properties of a painting before it's repaired?

   _____

   _____

   _____

   _____

2. Name another career that combines science with another interest.

   _____

   _____

Medusa by Caravaggio, about 1598. Uffizi Gallery, Florence, Italy

▶ **PLANET DIARY** Go to **Planet Diary** to learn more about matter.

Lab zone®

Do the Inquiry Warm-Up *How Do You Describe Matter?*

Vocabulary
- matter • chemistry
- substance • physical property
- chemical property

Skills
- Reading: Summarize
- Inquiry: Classify

What Properties Describe Matter?

You have probably heard the word *matter* used many times. "As a matter of fact…" or "Hey, what's the matter?" In science, **matter** is anything that has mass and takes up space. All the "stuff" around you is matter, and you are matter too. Air, plastic, metal, wood, glass, paper, and cloth are all matter.

Even though air and paper are both matter, you know they are different materials. Matter can have many different properties, or characteristics that can be used to identify and classify it. Materials can be hard or soft, hot or cold, liquid, solid, or gas. Some materials catch fire easily, but others do not burn. **Chemistry** is the study of matter and how matter changes.

Substances Some types of matter are substances and some are not. In chemistry, a **substance** is a single kind of matter that is pure, meaning it always has a specific makeup, or composition. For example, table salt has the same composition and properties whether it comes from seawater or a salt mine. **Figure 1** shows two examples of water that appear to be very different. Water is a substance. Pure water is always the same, whether it comes from a glacier or from a geyser.

Summarize How are matter and substances related?

_____
_____
_____
_____
_____
_____

FIGURE 1 ···

Properties of Matter

Compare and Contrast Complete the Venn diagram with the properties of water from a glacier and from a geyser.

Glacier   Geyser

_____   _____
_____   _____
_____   _____
_____   _____

Physical and Chemical Properties of Matter

Matter is described by its properties. 🗝️ **Every form of matter has two kinds of properties—physical properties and chemical properties.** A physical property is a characteristic of a substance that can be observed without changing it into another substance.

Some properties of matter can't be seen just by observation or touch. A **chemical property** is a characteristic of a substance that describes its ability to change into different substances. To observe the chemical properties of a substance, you must try to change it into another substance. Physical and chemical properties are used to classify matter.

Basketball Hoop Two physical properties of metals are luster, or shine, and the ability to conduct electric current and heat. Another physical property is flexibility, which is the ability to be bent into shapes.

Mark all the objects that are flexible.

- ⭘ Aluminum can
- ⭘ Copper sheeting
- ⭘ Brick house
- ⭘ Glass window
- ⭘ Silver spoon
- ⭘ Wood drumstick

What do all of the flexible objects have in common?

_____

What physical property makes metal pots good for cooking?

_____

Water A physical property of water is that it freezes at 0°C. When liquid water freezes, it changes to ice, but it is still water. The temperatures at which substances boil and melt are also physical properties.

Rusty Metal Chain A chemical property of iron is that it combines slowly with oxygen in the air to form a different substance, rust. Silver reacts with sulfur in the air to form tarnish. In contrast, a chemical property of gold is that it does not react easily with oxygen or sulfur.

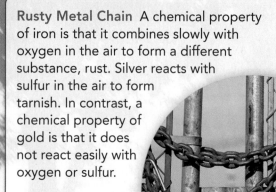

Frozen Fruit Bar Hardness, texture, temperature, and color are examples of physical properties. When you describe a material as a solid, a liquid, or a gas, you are describing its state of matter. State of matter is another physical property.

Describe three properties of a frozen fruit bar, including its state of matter.

_____

_____

Will any of these properties change after a couple of hours in the sun? Explain.

_____

_____

Charcoal Briquettes Fuels, like charcoal, can catch fire and burn. When a fuel burns, it combines with oxygen in the air and changes into the substances water and carbon dioxide. The ability to burn, or flammability, is a chemical property.

How do you know that flammability is a chemical property?

_____

_____

_____

_____

apply it!

The wax in a burning candle can be described by both physical and chemical properties.

❶ Describe What are the physical properties of the wax in a burning candle?

_____

_____

_____

_____

❷ CHALLENGE Why is melting a physical property of the wax, but flammability is a chemical property?

_____

_____

_____

_____

_____

_____

_____

Lab zone® Do the Quick Lab *Observing Physical Properties.*

🔑 Assess Your Understanding

1a. Classify The melting point of table salt is 801°C. Is this a physical or chemical property?

_____

b. Draw Conclusions Helium does not usually react with other substances. Does this mean that helium has no chemical properties? Explain.

_____

_____

got it?

○ **I get it!** Now I know that matter is described by its _____

_____

_____

○ **I need extra help with** _____

_____

Go to MY SCIENCE ⓢ COACH *online for help with this subject.*

2 Classifying Matter

UNLOCK THE BIG ?

🔑 **What Is Matter Made Of?**

🔑 **What Are Two Types of Mixtures?**

MY PLANET DIARY

SCIENCE STATS

Write your answers to the questions below.

1. A nickel is about 2 millimeters thick, or 2/1,000 of a meter. How many nanometers is this?

_____

_____

2. Imagine being the size of an atom. Describe how something like a red blood cell might look to you.

_____

_____

_____

▶ PLANET DIARY Go to **Planet Diary** to learn more about atoms.

Smaller Than Small

What's the smallest thing you can think of? A grain of sand? A speck of dust? If you look at these items under a powerful microscope, you'll see that they're made up of smaller and smaller pieces. All matter is made up of very tiny particles called atoms. Atoms are so small, there is a special unit of measure used to describe them called a nanometer (nm). A nanometer is equal to 1/1,000,000,000 or one-billionth of a meter!

At least 50,000 of these tiny compounds called nanobouquets could fit on the head of a pin.

Common Objects in Nanometers (nm)

Object	Approximate Size
Compact disc diameter	120,000,000 nm
Grain of sand	3,000,000 nm
Grain of pollen	500,000 nm
Human hair diameter	100,000 nm
Red blood cell	7000 nm
Length of 3–10 atoms lined up	1 nm

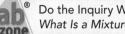

Lab® zone Do the Inquiry Warm-Up *What Is a Mixture?*

Vocabulary

- element • atom • chemical bond
- molecule • compound • chemical formula
- mixture

Skills

↻ **Reading: Compare and Contrast**

△ Inquiry: Infer

What Is Matter Made Of?

What is matter? Why is one kind of matter different from another kind of matter? Around 450 B.C., a Greek philosopher named Empedocles attempted to answer these questions. He proposed that all matter was made of four "elements"—air, earth, fire, and water. Empedocles thought that all other matter was a combination of these elements. The idea of four elements was so convincing that people believed it for more than 2,000 years.

Elements In the late 1600s, experiments by early chemists began to show that matter was made up of many more than four elements. ⚷ Scientists know that all matter in the universe is made of more than 100 different substances, called elements. An **element** is a substance that cannot be broken down into any other substances by chemical or physical means. Elements are the simplest substances. Each element can be identified by its specific physical and chemical properties. You may already be familiar with some elements such as aluminum or tin. Elements are represented by one- or two-letter symbols, such as C for carbon, O for oxygen, and Ca for calcium.

apply it!

The elements make up all the matter in the universe.

1 Explain How can you tell one element from another?

_____

_____

_____

2 △ Infer Match the pictures on this page of items containing common elements to the element's name.

A) helium   B) gold   C) copper
D) iron   E) neon

3 CHALLENGE Choose another element that you are familiar with and describe its properties.

_____

_____

_____

Atoms Imagine tearing a piece of aluminum foil in half over and over again. Would you reach a point where you had the smallest possible piece of aluminum? The answer is yes. The particle theory of matter explains that all matter is made of atoms. An **atom** is the basic particle from which all elements are made. An atom has a positively charged center, or nucleus, containing smaller particles. The nucleus is surrounded by a "cloud" of negative charge. The elements have different properties because their atoms are different.

Molecules Atoms of most elements are able to combine with other atoms. When atoms combine, they form a **chemical bond,** which is a force of attraction between two atoms. In many cases, atoms combine to form larger particles called molecules. A **molecule** (MAHL uh kyool) is a group of two or more atoms held together by chemical bonds. A molecule of water, for example, is made up of an oxygen atom chemically bonded to two hydrogen atoms. Two atoms of the same element can also combine to form a molecule. Oxygen molecules are made up of two oxygen atoms. **Figure 1** shows models of some common molecules.

⟳ **Compare and Contrast** How are atoms and molecules the same? How are they different?

_____
_____
_____
_____
_____
_____

FIGURE 1 ....

Atoms and Molecules
Molecules are made up of groups of atoms.

✎ **Use the molecule models to complete the activities.**

1. **Interpret Diagrams** Count the number of atoms of each element in the molecules and write it on the lines below.
2. CHALLENGE On the bottom line, write a representation for each molecule using letters and numbers.

Key
C = Carbon
H = Hydrogen
O = Oxygen
N = Nitrogen

Carbon dioxide

_____
_____
_____

CHALLENGE

_____

Water

_____
_____
_____

Oxygen

_____
_____
_____

Ammonia

_____
_____
_____

Compounds Water, ammonia, and carbon dioxide are all compounds. A **compound** is a substance made of two or more elements that are chemically combined in a set ratio. A compound is represented by a **chemical formula,** which shows the elements in the compound and the ratio of atoms. For example, the chemical formula for carbon dioxide is CO_2. The 2 below the O for oxygen tells you that the ratio of carbon atoms to oxygen atoms is 1 to 2. If there is no number after an element's symbol, it is understood that the number is 1. A different number of atoms in a formula represents a different compound. For example, the formula for carbon monoxide is CO. Here, the ratio of carbon atoms to oxygen atoms is 1 to 1.

When elements chemically combine, they form compounds with properties different from those of the elements. **Figure 2** shows that the element sulfur is a yellow solid and the element copper is a shiny metal. When copper and sulfur combine, they form a compound called copper sulfide. The new compound has different properties from both copper and sulfur.

FIGURE 2 ···

> **ART IN MOTION** **Compounds From Elements**
When elements combine, the compound that forms has different properties than the original elements.

✎ **Describe** List the properties of copper, sulfur, and copper sulfide.

Copper
_____
_____
_____
_____

Sulfur
_____
_____
_____
_____

Copper Sulfide
_____
_____
_____
_____

Lab zone® Do the Quick Lab *Modeling Atoms and Molecules.*

🔑 Assess Your Understanding

1a. Review What holds the hydrogen and oxygen atoms together in a water molecule?

_____

_____

b. Identify Table sugar has the chemical formula $C_{12}H_{22}O_{11}$. What is the ratio of carbon atoms to oxygen atoms in this compound?

_____

_____

c. Draw Conclusions Two formulas for compounds containing hydrogen and oxygen are H_2O and H_2O_2. Do these formulas represent the same compound? Explain.

_____

_____

_____

_____

_____

got it? ··

○ **I get it!** Now I know that all matter is made up of _____

_____

○ **I need extra help with** _____

Go to MY SCIENCE ⬤ COACH online for help with this subject.

What Are Two Types of Mixtures?

Elements and compounds are substances, but most materials are mixtures. **Figure 3** shows some common mixtures. A **mixture** is made of two or more substances that are together in the same place, but their atoms are not chemically bonded. Mixtures differ from compounds. Each substance in a mixture keeps its own properties. Also, the parts of a mixture are not combined in a set ratio.

Think of a handful of sand. If you look closely at the sand, you will see particles of rock, bits of shells, maybe even crystals of salt.

Heterogeneous Mixtures
There are two types of mixtures.  **A mixture can be heterogeneous or homogeneous.** In a heterogeneous mixture (het ur oh JEE nee us), you can usually see the different parts and they can easily be separated out. The sand described above is a heterogeneous mixture. So is a salad. Think of how easy it is to see the pieces of lettuce, tomatoes, onions, and other ingredients that can be mixed in countless ways.

Homogeneous Mixtures
The substances involved in a homogeneous mixture (hoh moh JEE nee us), are so evenly mixed that you can't see the different parts. It is difficult to separate the parts of a homogeneous mixture. Air is a homogeneous mixture of gases. You know that oxygen is present in the air because you are able to breathe, but you cannot identify where the oxygen is in the air. A solution is another example of a homogeneous mixture. Solutions can be liquids, gases, or even solids.

Vocabulary Prefixes The prefix *homo-* comes from a Greek word that means "the same or alike." Predict the meaning of the prefix *hetero-*.

○ more than one
○ different
○ equal

FIGURE 3 ·············

Mixtures

Many foods are mixtures.

✎ **Interpret Photos** Label each food as a heterogeneous or homogeneous mixture.

Honey

Guacamole

Soy sauce

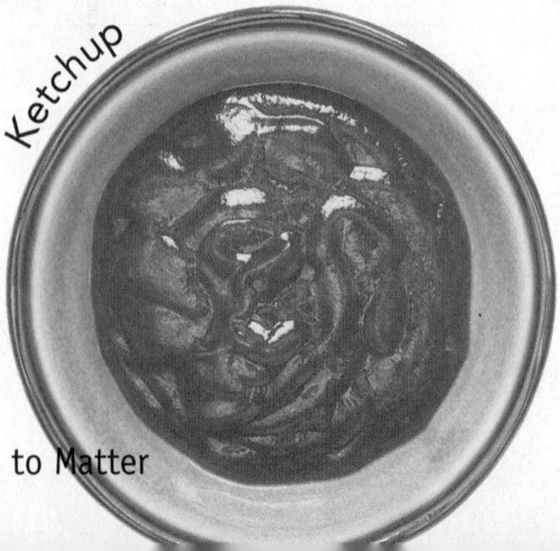

Ketchup

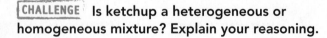 **CHALLENGE** Is ketchup a heterogeneous or homogeneous mixture? Explain your reasoning.

_____

_____

_____

_____

Separating Mixtures

Since the substances in a mixture keep their properties, you can use those properties to separate a mixture into its parts. Methods used to separate the parts of a mixture, including distillation, evaporation, filtration, and magnetic attraction, are shown in **Figure 4.**

FIGURE 4 ·······························

Separating a Mixture

Different methods can be used to separate mixtures.

✎ **Identify Name the type of separation method being used in each photo.**

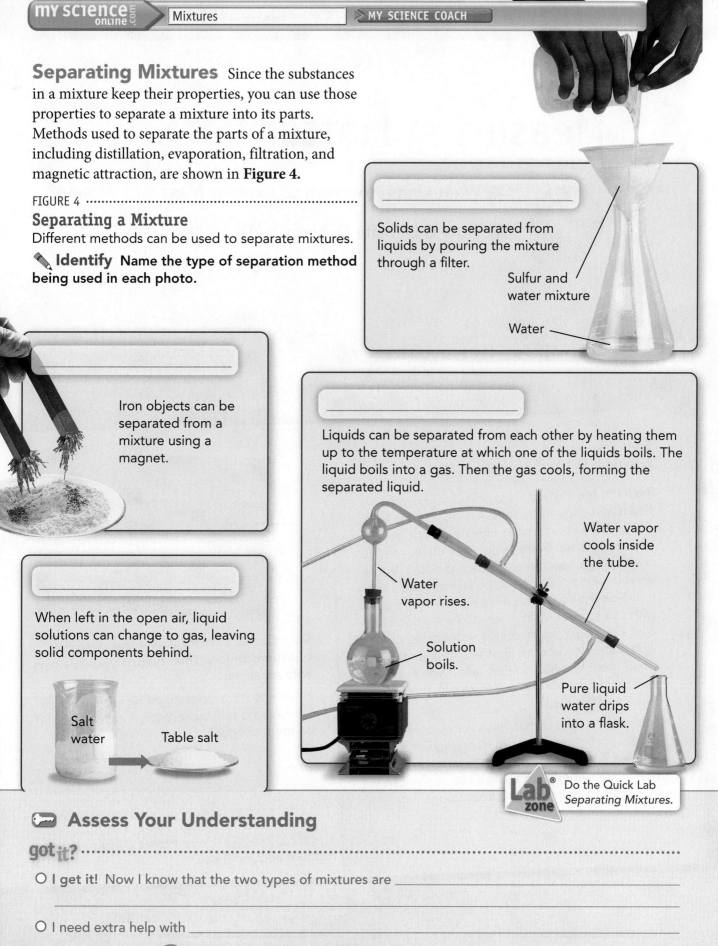

Iron objects can be separated from a mixture using a magnet.

Solids can be separated from liquids by pouring the mixture through a filter.

Sulfur and water mixture

Water

When left in the open air, liquid solutions can change to gas, leaving solid components behind.

Salt water → Table salt

Liquids can be separated from each other by heating them up to the temperature at which one of the liquids boils. The liquid boils into a gas. Then the gas cools, forming the separated liquid.

Water vapor rises.

Solution boils.

Water vapor cools inside the tube.

Pure liquid water drips into a flask.

Lab zone® Do the Quick Lab *Separating Mixtures.*

🔑 Assess Your Understanding

got it? ··

○ **I get it!** Now I know that the two types of mixtures are _____

_____

○ I need extra help with _____

Go to my science 🔵 COACH *online for help with this subject.*

Measuring Matter

UNLOCK
THE BIG
?

🔑 **What Units Are Used to Express Mass and Volume?**

🔑 **How Is Density Determined?**

my planet Diary

FIELD TRIP

Site: Lake Assal
Location: Djibouti, Republic of Djibouti

Travel to the eastern coast of Africa and you will find the country of Djibouti. There, you can visit one of the saltiest bodies of water in the world. Lake Assal is ten times saltier than the ocean. Its crystal white beaches are made up of salt. While on your visit to Lake Assal, be sure to take a dip in the clear blue waters. Take a book or magazine with you to read. Wait … what? Take a book into a lake? It might seem strange, but bodies of water with high salt contents, like Lake Assal or the Dead Sea in the Middle East, allow you to float so well that it's nearly impossible to sink below the surface of the water.

Salt water is denser than fresh water. Less-dense liquids float on top of more-dense liquids. You, too, will float on top of the salty water. In fact, it will be difficult even to swim, so what else can you do? Read a book while you float along!

Floating in the Dead Sea

Communicate Write your answers to the questions below. Then discuss your answers with a partner.

What water activities might be easier to do in Lake Assal's salty water? What activities could be more difficult?

_____

_____

_____

▶ PLANET DIARY Go to **Planet Diary** to learn more about density.

Lab zone® Do the Inquiry Warm-Up
Which Has More Mass?

Vocabulary
- weight • mass
- International System of Units
- volume • density

Skills
- ↻ Reading: Identify the Main Idea
- △ Inquiry: Calculate

What Units Are Used to Express Mass and Volume?

Here's a riddle for you: Which weighs more, a pound of feathers or a pound of sand? If you answered "a pound of sand," think again. Both weigh exactly the same—one pound.

There are all sorts of ways to measure matter, and you use these measurements every day. Scientists rely on measurements as well. In fact, scientists work hard to make sure their measurements are as accurate as possible.

Weight Your **weight** is a measure of the force of gravity on you. On another planet, the force of gravity will be more if the planet is more massive than Earth and less if the planet is less massive than Earth. On the moon, you would weigh only about one sixth of your weight on Earth. On Jupiter, you would weigh more than twice your weight on Earth.

To find the weight of an object, you could place it on a scale like the ones shown in **Figure 1.** The object's weight pulls down on the mechanisms inside the scale. These mechanisms cause beams or springs inside the scale to move. The amount of movement depends on the weight of the object. From the movement of the beams, the scale displays the weight to you.

↻ **Identify the Main Idea**
Underline the sentence(s) that describe how weight can be affected by location.

FIGURE 1 ·······················
Measuring Weight
✎ **Complete the tasks below.**

1. **Estimate** Use the weight of the first scale to estimate the weight of the fish on the other scales. Draw in the pointers.

2. **Describe** How would their weight change on a planet with less mass like Mercury? Or a planet with more mass like Neptune?

_____

_____

_____

With 10 seconds left on the clock, John makes the play at the 9.144-meter line.

9.144

If we always used the metric system

Mass How can you weigh less on the moon than on Earth when nothing about you has changed? Your weight is dependent on the gravity of the planet you are visiting. The amount of matter in an object is its **mass,** which does not change with location even if the force of gravity changes. If you travel to the moon, the amount of matter in your body—your mass—does not change. You are the same size. For this reason, scientists prefer to describe matter in terms of mass rather than weight. The mass of an object is a physical property.

To measure the properties of matter, scientists use a system called the **International System of Units** (abbreviated SI for the French name, *Système International d'Unités*). 🔑 **The SI unit of mass is the kilogram (kg).** If you weigh 90 pounds on Earth, your mass is about 40 kilograms. Often, a smaller unit is used to measure mass, the gram (g). There are 1,000 grams in a kilogram, or 0.001 kilograms in a gram. The table in **Figure 2** lists the masses of some common items.

Mass of Common Objects

Object	Mass (g)	Mass (kg)
Nickel	5	0.005
Baseball	150	
Pineapple	1,600	
Full can of soda	390	
Inflated balloon	3	

FIGURE 2 ···

Measuring Mass
The SI system uses grams and kilograms to measure mass.

✎ **Complete the following tasks about mass.**

1. **Calculate** In the table, convert the mass of each object from grams to kilograms.

2. CHALLENGE Suppose you are taking a flight to Europe. You are only allowed a 23-kg suitcase. How much is that in pounds? (*Hint:* 1 kg = 2.2 lbs.)

  ⭕ 50.6 lbs   ⭕ 46.2 lbs   ⭕ 10.5 lbs

Volume

All matter has mass and takes up space. The amount of space that matter occupies is called its **volume.** It's easy to see that solids and liquids take up space, but gases have volume, too.

🔑 **The SI unit of volume is the cubic meter (m³).** Other common SI units of volume include the cubic centimeter (cm³), the liter (L), and the milliliter (mL). Common plastic soda bottles hold 2 liters of liquid. A milliliter is 1/1,000 of a liter and is exactly the same volume as 1 cubic centimeter. A teaspoonful of water has a volume of about 5 milliliters. In a lab, volumes of liquid are often measured with a graduated cylinder.

Calculating Volume

Suppose you want to know the volume of a rectangular object, like one of the suitcases shown in **Figure 3.** First, measure the length, width, and height (or thickness) of the suitcase. Then, multiply the measurements together.

Volume = Length × Width × Height

When you multiply the three measurements, you must also multiply the units.

Units = cm × cm × cm = cm³

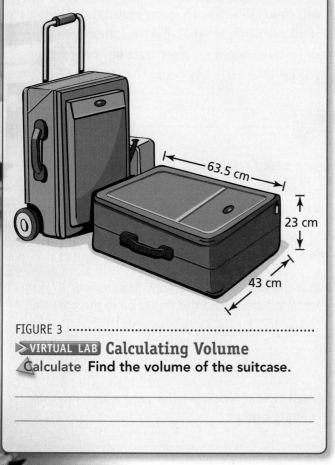

←——— 63.5 cm ———→

23 cm

43 cm

FIGURE 3 ·······················

▶ VIRTUAL LAB **Calculating Volume**
Calculate Find the volume of the suitcase.

_____

_____

Measuring Irregular Objects

How do you measure the volume of an irregular object, such as a key or a raspberry? One way is to submerge the object in a liquid in a graduated cylinder. The liquid level will rise by an amount that is equal to the volume of the object in milliliters.

Lab zone Do the Quick Lab *Calculating Volume.*

🔑 **Assess Your Understanding**

1. **Explain** Why is mass more useful than weight for measuring matter?

_____

_____

_____

_____

_____

got it? ·······························

○ **I get it!** Now I know that the SI unit for

mass is _____

and the SI unit for volume is _____

_____

○ **I need extra help with** _____

Go to MY SCIENCE ⓢ COACH *online for help with this subject.*

How Is Density Determined?

Remember the riddle about the sand and the feathers? Although they weigh the same, a kilogram of sand takes up much less space than a kilogram of feathers. The volumes differ because sand and feathers have different densities—an important property of matter.

Calculating Density Density is a measure of the mass of a material in a given volume. Density can be expressed as the number of grams in one cubic centimeter (g/cm^3). For example, the density of water at room temperature is stated as "one gram per cubic centimeter" ($1 \ g/cm^3$). Recall that volume can also be measured in milliliters. So the density of water can also be expressed as $1 \ g/mL$. **You can determine the density of a sample of matter by dividing its mass by its volume.**

$$Density = \frac{Mass}{Volume}$$

Sinking or Floating? Suppose you have a block of wood and a block of iron of equal mass. When you drop both blocks into a tub of water, you see that the wood floats and the iron sinks. You know the density of water is $1 \ g/cm^3$. Objects with densities greater than that of water will sink. Objects with lesser densities will float.

Watch a bottle of oil and vinegar salad dressing after it has been shaken. You will see the oil slowly form a separate layer above the vinegar. This happens because oil is less dense than vinegar.

Liquids can form layers based on density.

1 **Apply Concepts** Label the layers of colored liquid in the column according to their densities.

Water: 1.00 g/mL   Honey: 1.36 g/mL   Dish soap: 1.03 g/mL
Corn syrup: 1.33 g/mL   Vegetable oil: 0.91 g/mL

2 **Calculate** What is the density of a liquid with a mass of 17.4 g and a volume of 20 mL? Where would this liquid be in the column?

_____

_____

3 CHALLENGE In which layer(s) would a solid cube with 6-cm sides and a mass of 270 g float? Explain.

_____

_____

Using Density

Suppose you are a gold miner in the 1800s, like the men in **Figure 4.** One day, while panning through the sediment in a stream, you come across a shiny golden rock. How do you know if the rock is real gold? Since density is a physical property of a substance, it can be used to identify an unknown substance. You can measure the mass and volume of the rock and find its density. If it matches 19.3 g/cm³, the density of gold, then you have struck it rich!

FIGURE 4 ....

> VIRTUAL LAB **Using Density**

Density can be used to identify substances.

✎ **Estimate** Hypothesize which rock sample is gold. Then, calculate the density of each sample. Circle the rock that is real gold.

My hypothesis is that the gold rock is:

○ A   ○ B   ○ C

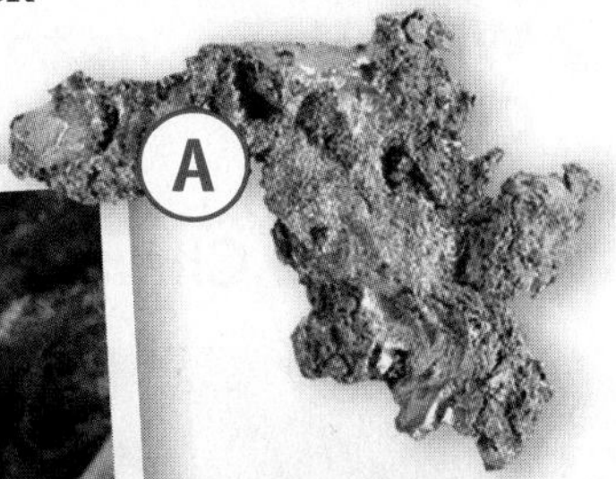

A
Mass = 108 g
Volume = 12 cm³

Density = _____

B
Mass = 126 g
Volume = 15 cm³

Density = _____

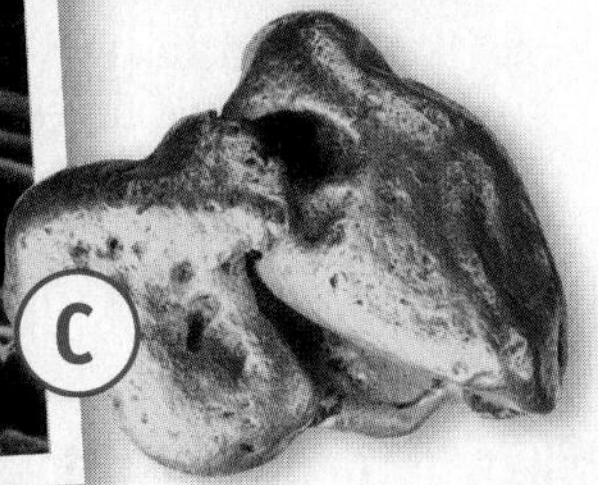

C
Mass = 386 g
Volume = 20 cm³

Density = _____

Lab zone® Do the Lab Investigation *Making Sense of Density.*

🔑 Assess Your Understanding

2a. Identify Maple syrup will (float/sink) in water because its density is greater than 1 g/cm³.

b. Calculate What is the mass of a sample of a substance with a volume of 120 mL and a density of 0.75 g/mL?

_____

c. CHALLENGE Liquid water and ice are the same substance, H_2O. How would you explain why ice floats in water?

_____
_____
_____

got it? ....

○ I get it! Now I know density is calculated by _____
_____

○ I need extra help with _____

Go to MY SCIENCE ⁵ COACH online for help with this subject.

19

Changes in Matter

UNLOCK THE BIG ?

- 🔑 **What Happens to a Substance in a Physical Change?**

- 🔑 **What Happens to a Substance in a Chemical Change?**

- 🔑 **How Are Changes in Energy and Matter Related?**

MY PLANET DIARY

BLOG

Posted by: Dylan
Location: Fountain Valley, California

Whenever I go to the beach, I spend a majority of my time building a sand castle. I try to build it after a high tide comes. That way I have a lot of time to build up the walls and they will not be destroyed as quickly by the water.

Even though the waves will eventually destroy the castle and take the sand with them back to the ocean, the sand could be easily separated from the ocean. At the end of the day when I leave and kick and stomp on my sand castle, it is still sand. Only its appearance changes.

Write your answers to the questions below.

1. Describe the differences in the ways the sand castle is changed by an ocean wave and by Dylan stomping on it.

_____

_____

_____

2. Dylan changed a formless pile of sand into a sand castle. What other natural materials can be changed into art?

_____

_____

> PLANET DIARY Go to **Planet Diary** to learn more about changes in matter.

Lab zone® Do the Inquiry Warm-Up *Is a New Substance Formed?*

Vocabulary
- physical change • chemical change
- law of conservation of mass • temperature
- thermal energy • endothermic change
- exothermic change • chemical energy

Skills
↪ Reading: Relate Cause and Effect
△ Inquiry: Draw Conclusions

What Happens to a Substance in a Physical Change?

How can matter change? A **physical change** alters the form or appearance of matter but does not turn any substance in the matter into a different substance. In **Figure 1,** a butter artist has changed a formless block of butter into artwork. Although it looks different, the sculpture is still butter. 🗝 **A substance that undergoes a physical change is still the same substance after the change.** Many physical changes, such as snow melting into water, occur in nature.

Changes of State As you may know, matter occurs in three familiar states—solid, liquid, and gas. Suppose you leave a small puddle of liquid water on the kitchen counter. When you come back two hours later, the puddle is gone. Has the liquid water disappeared? No, a physical change happened. The liquid water changed into water vapor (a gas) and mixed with the air. A change in state, such as from a solid to a liquid or from a liquid to a gas, is an example of a physical change.

FIGURE 1 ·······
Change of State
Changes between solids, liquids, and gases are physical changes.

✎ **Predict** Describe the changes the butter sculpture will undergo in a few hours if it is left out in the sun.

_____
_____
_____
_____

21

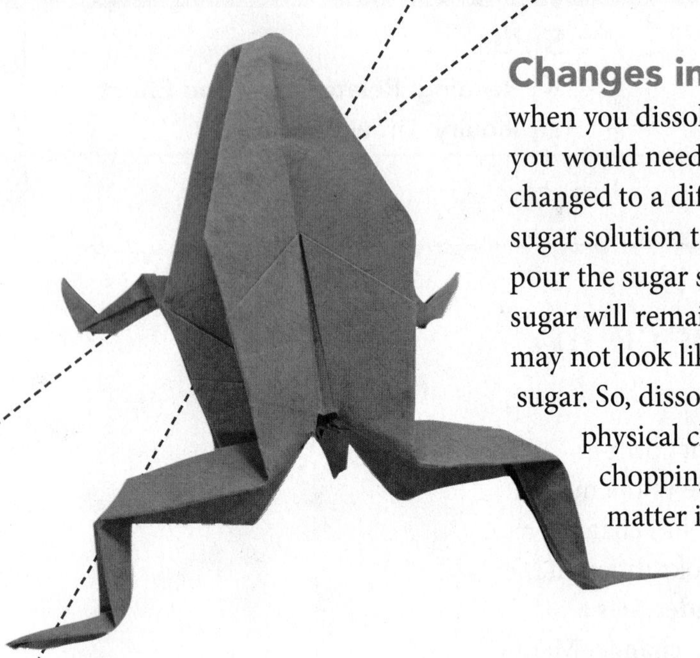

Changes in Shape or Form

Is there a physical change when you dissolve a teaspoon of table sugar in water? To be sure, you would need to know whether or not the sugar has been changed to a different substance. For example, you know that a sugar solution tastes sweet, just like the undissolved sugar. If you pour the sugar solution into a pan and let the water dry out, the sugar will remain as a crust at the bottom of the pan. The crust may not look like the sugar before you dissolved it, but it's still sugar. So, dissolving is also a physical change. Other examples of physical changes are bending, crushing, breaking, and chopping. Any change that alters only the shape or form of matter is a physical change. The methods of separating mixtures, such as filtration and distillation, also involve physical changes.

FIGURE 2 ···

Changes in Appearance

The Japanese art of origami paper folding involves physical changes.

✏️ **Complete the following tasks.**

1. **Make Models** Using the corner of this page or a separate sheet, make two physical changes to the paper.

2. **Communicate** Ask a classmate to identify and list below the changes you made.

_____

_____

3. CHALLENGE Is it correct to say that dissolving a packet of juice powder in water makes a new substance, fruit punch, so it must not be a physical change?

_____

_____

_____

_____

_____

 Do the Quick Lab *What Is a Physical Change?*

🔑 Assess Your Understanding

1a. Classify Mark all the processes that are physical changes.

◯ drying wet clothes

◯ lighting a match from a matchbook

◯ cutting snowflakes out of paper

◯ melting butter for popcorn

b. Apply Concepts Describe three physical changes that occur in nature.

_____

_____

_____

_____

got it? ···

◯ **I get it!** Now I know that a substance that undergoes a physical change is _____

_____

◯ **I need extra help with** _____

Go to MY SCIENCE 🄢 COACH *online for help with this subject.*

What Happens to a Substance in a Chemical Change?

Another kind of change occurs when a substance transforms into another substance. A change in matter that produces one or more new substances is a chemical change, or chemical reaction. In some chemical changes, a single substance breaks down into two or more other substances. For example, hydrogen peroxide breaks down into water and oxygen gas when it's poured on a cut on your skin. In other chemical changes, two or more substances combine to form different substances. Photosynthesis is a natural chemical change. Several compounds combine with energy from the sun to produce new substances.

Figure 3 shows chemical changes that are used in forensics to collect evidence. To make fingerprints more visible, a chemical found in super-strong glues is heated. Vapors from the glue react with sweat or other body chemicals in a fingerprint to form a white powder making the print visible. Luminol is a chemical that reacts with blood. It combines with traces of blood that are too small to see with the naked eye to form a new substance that glows in the dark. The footprint in Figure 3 has been treated with luminol. ⊙⊸ Unlike a physical change, a chemical change produces new substances with new and different properties.

FIGURE 3 ·······························
Chemical Changes
The prints are visible because of chemical change.

apply it!

You are a detective investigating a robbery. When you arrive at the scene, there are not many clues that you can see to help solve the crime. You're able to write down a few observations.

Solve Problems
Determine how you would use chemical changes to gather evidence at the crime scene.

An empty jewelry box is knocked over on a table.

Chemical treatment: _____
_____
_____

An open box of bandages is on the floor. Bandage wrappers are found nearby.

Chemical treatment: _____
_____
_____

Shattered glass from a window is scattered across the floor.

Chemical treatment: _____
_____
_____

Copper: before

Copper: after

Examples of Chemical Change

One common chemical change is the burning of natural gas on a gas stove. Natural gas is mostly made up of the compound methane (CH_4). When it burns, methane combines with oxygen in the air and forms new substances. These new substances include carbon dioxide gas (CO_2) and water vapor (H_2O). Both of these substances can be identified by their properties, which are different from those of methane. The chemical change that occurs when fuels, such as natural gas, candle wax, or wood, burn in air is called combustion. Other processes resulting in chemical change include electrolysis, oxidation, and tarnishing. The table in **Figure 4** describes each of these types of chemical change.

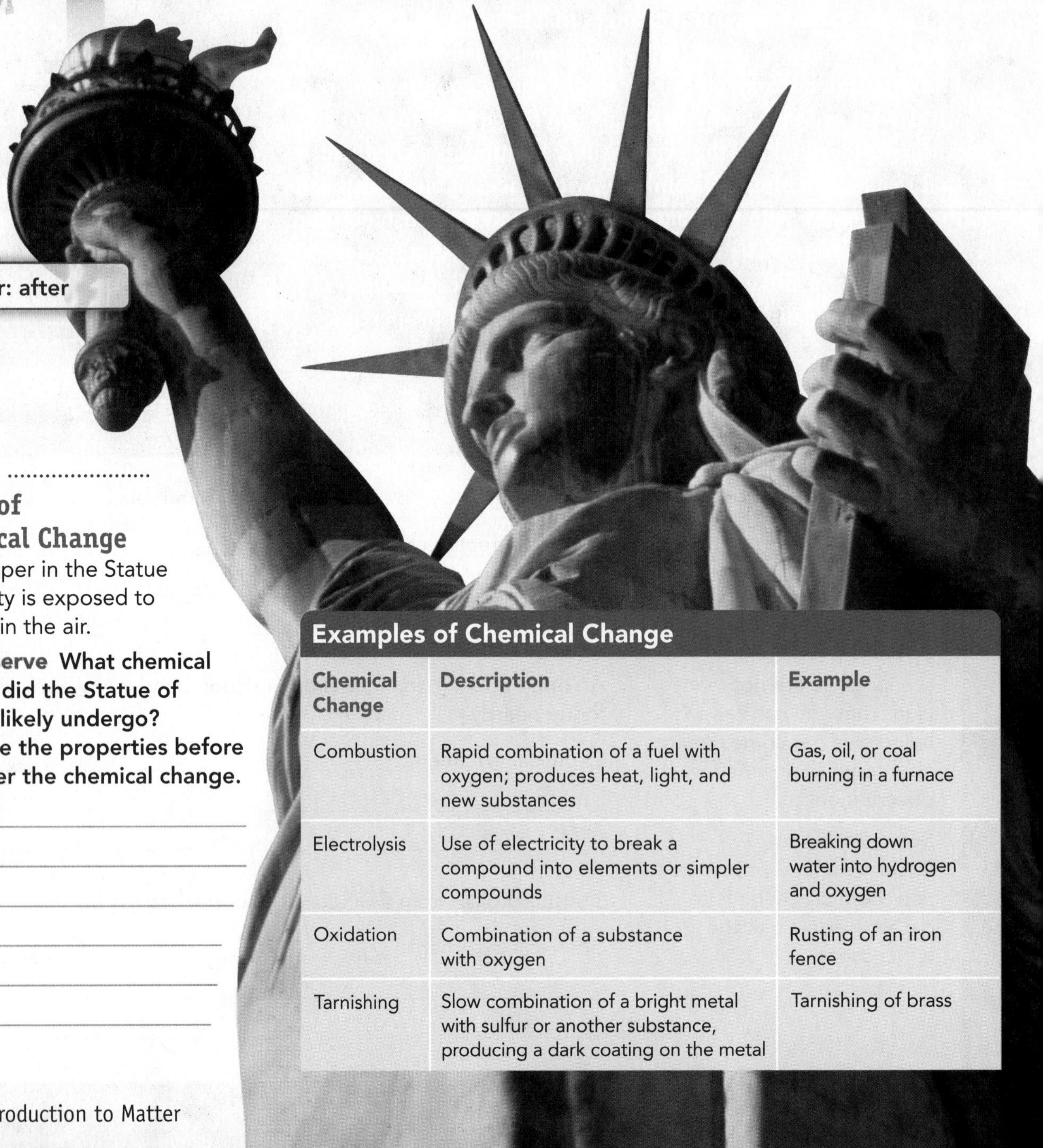

FIGURE 4 ·····················

Types of Chemical Change

The copper in the Statue of Liberty is exposed to oxygen in the air.

✎ **Observe** What chemical change did the Statue of Liberty likely undergo? Describe the properties before and after the chemical change.

_____

_____

_____

_____

_____

_____

Examples of Chemical Change		
Chemical Change	**Description**	**Example**
Combustion	Rapid combination of a fuel with oxygen; produces heat, light, and new substances	Gas, oil, or coal burning in a furnace
Electrolysis	Use of electricity to break a compound into elements or simpler compounds	Breaking down water into hydrogen and oxygen
Oxidation	Combination of a substance with oxygen	Rusting of an iron fence
Tarnishing	Slow combination of a bright metal with sulfur or another substance, producing a dark coating on the metal	Tarnishing of brass

Conservation of Mass Water may seem to "disappear" when it evaporates, but scientists long ago proved otherwise. In the 1770s, a French chemist, Antoine Lavoisier, measured mass both before and after a chemical change. His data showed that no mass was lost or gained during the change. The fact that matter is not created or destroyed in any chemical or physical change is called the **law of conservation of mass.** This law is also called the law of conservation of matter since mass is a measurement of matter.

Suppose you could measure all of the carbon dioxide and water produced when methane burns. You would find that it equals the mass of the original methane plus the mass of the oxygen from the air that was used in the burning. **Figure 5** demonstrates that during a chemical change, atoms are not lost or gained, only rearranged.

FIGURE 5 ·····························

> INTERACTIVE ART

Conservation of Mass
✎ **Interpret Diagrams** Count the atoms of each element before and after the chemical change. Is mass conserved in this reaction? Explain.

_____

_____

_____

_____

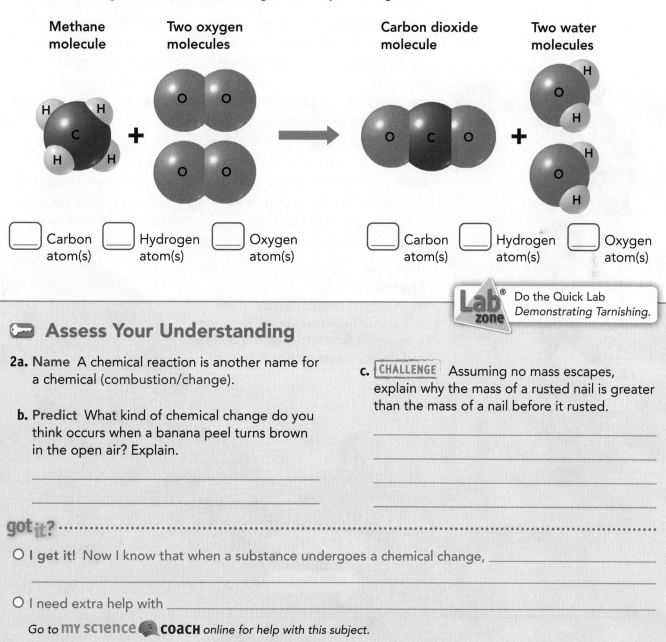

Methane molecule Two oxygen molecules   Carbon dioxide molecule Two water molecules

☐ Carbon atom(s) ☐ Hydrogen atom(s) ☐ Oxygen atom(s)   ☐ Carbon atom(s) ☐ Hydrogen atom(s) ☐ Oxygen atom(s)

Lab zone ® Do the Quick Lab
Demonstrating Tarnishing.

🔑 Assess Your Understanding

2a. Name A chemical reaction is another name for a chemical (combustion/change).

b. Predict What kind of chemical change do you think occurs when a banana peel turns brown in the open air? Explain.

_____

_____

c. CHALLENGE Assuming no mass escapes, explain why the mass of a rusted nail is greater than the mass of a nail before it rusted.

_____

_____

_____

_____

got it? ··

○ **I get it!** Now I know that when a substance undergoes a chemical change, _____

_____

○ I need extra help with _____

Go to MY SCIENCE 🅢 COACH online for help with this subject.

How Are Changes in Energy and Matter Related?

Do you feel as if you are full of energy today? Energy is the ability to do work or cause change. 🔑 **Every chemical and physical change in matter includes a change in energy.** A change as simple as bending a paper clip takes energy. When ice changes to liquid water, it absorbs energy from the surrounding matter. When candle wax burns, it gives off energy as light and heat.

Like matter, energy is conserved in a chemical change. Energy is never created or destroyed. It can only be transformed from one form to another.

Temperature and Thermal Energy

Think of how it feels when you walk inside an air-conditioned building from the outdoors on a hot day. Whew, what a difference in temperature! **Temperature** is a measure of how hot or cold something is. It is related to the energy of motion of the particles of matter. The particles of gas in the warm outside air have greater average energy of motion than the particles of air inside the cool building.

Thermal energy is the total energy of the motion of all of the particles in an object. Usually, you experience thermal energy when you describe matter as feeling hot or cold. Temperature and thermal energy are not the same thing, but the amount of thermal energy an object has is related to its temperature. Thermal energy naturally flows from warmer matter to cooler matter.

FIGURE 6 ···

Thermal Energy

✏️ **Apply Concepts** Shade in the arrow that indicates which direction energy will flow between the people and the icy water or warm mud pit.

Energy

Energy

Energy

Energy

Thermal Energy and Changes in Matter

Thermal energy is a form of energy that is often released or absorbed when matter changes. For example, ice absorbs thermal energy from its surroundings when it melts, leaving the surroundings feeling cold. That's why you can pack food and drinks in an ice-filled picnic cooler. The melting of ice is an **endothermic change,** a change in which energy is absorbed. Changes in matter can also occur when energy is given off. An **exothermic change** releases energy. Combustion is a chemical change that releases thermal energy and light.

Transforming Chemical Energy The energy stored in the chemical bonds between atoms is a form of energy called **chemical energy.** Chemical energy is stored in foods, fuels, and even the cells of your body. Animals, like the bear in **Figure 7,** gain chemical energy from food.

Burning fuels transforms chemical energy and releases some of it as thermal energy. When you ride a bike up a hill, chemical energy from foods you ate changes into energy of motion. Chemical energy can change into other forms of energy, and other forms of energy can change into chemical energy.

FIGURE 7 ⋯⋯⋯⋯⋯⋯⋯⋯⋯⋯⋯⋯⋯⋯⋯⋯⋯⋯⋯⋯⋯⋯⋯⋯

Transforming Chemical Energy
Chemical energy from food can be transformed into other types of energy needed for activity.

Relate Cause and Effect
Underline the sentence that describes how your hand would be affected if you made a snowball or held a frozen treat.

do the math! Analyzing Data

A student records the temperature of two reactions once per minute. Her data are plotted on the graph.

1 Calculate What was the change in temperature for each reaction after 10 minutes?

_____

_____

2 Draw Conclusions On the graph, label each reaction as exothermic or endothermic. How can you tell?

_____

_____

_____

_____

Temperature of Two Reactions

Temperature (°C): 0, 10, 20, 30, 40, 50, 60

Reaction A
Reaction B

Time (minutes): 0 1 2 3 4 5 6 7 8 9 10

INDIANA JANE

and the
INVESTIGATION OF MATTER

How is matter described?

FIGURE 8 ·······································

> INTERACTIVE ART Indiana Jane is hunting for lost treasures of matter. Join her in following clues to describe different types of matter.

Review Answer questions about Indiana's findings along the way. Then, complete the logbook with information you've gathered about the properties of matter.

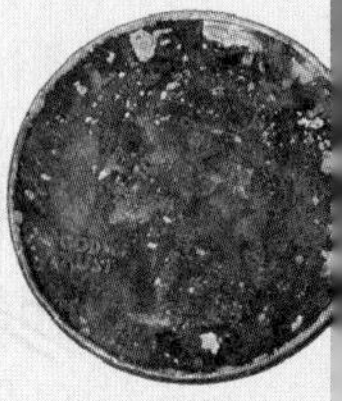

Arrowhead This arrowhead, most likely carved by an ancient hunter, was discovered in a pile of rocks. **Describe the type of mixture the arrowhead was found in.**

_____
_____
_____
_____
_____

Yellowed, torn map
Field notes: The paper of this ancient map has suffered from changes over the years making it nearly impossible to read.—IJ

Tarnished coins I found these coins near the opening of a foul-smelling cave. I believe they were a shiny metal at one point, perhaps silver, platinum, or aluminum. I've determined the mass of each coin to be 315 g and the volume to be 30 cm^3.
What element are the coins made of?
○ Aluminum (density = 2.7 g/cm^3)
○ Silver (density = 10.5 g/cm^3)
○ Platinum (density = 21.5 g/cm^3)

Mummy The mummy we found today is badly decayed, probably because its sarcophagus is not sealed airtight. I translated a scroll found nearby that says the mummy and case originally had a mass of 200 kg. The mass is now 170 kg. **Explain how the mummy and its sarcophagus decreased in mass if the law of conservation of mass must be obeyed.**

_____
_____
_____
_____
_____
_____
_____
_____

Indiana Jane has to bring all the artifacts back to the museum. Describe each object's properties and the physical or chemical changes it underwent.

Object	Properties	Changes Undergone
1. Clay pot		
2. Coins		
3. Map		

Broken clay pot Field notes: I've come across some clay pots. Many have been broken or cracked over time.—IJ

Wax statue I believe we have found the remains of the famous Carved Dove wax statue. It would have been a valuable artifact, but all that's left is a puddle of liquid.

Describe at least two changes the wax has undergone over time.

_____

_____

_____

Lab zone ® Do the Quick Lab *Where Was the Energy?*

🔑 **Assess Your Understanding**

3a. Identify What energy transformation takes place when you exercise?

_____

_____

b. ANSWER THE BIG ? How is matter described?

_____

_____

_____

_____

_____

_____

_____

_____

got it? ....

○ **I get it!** Now I know that every chemical and physical change includes _____

_____

○ **I need extra help with** _____

Go to MY SCIENCE COACH *online for help with this subject.*

1 Study Guide

Water is a _____ . A _____ property of water is that it boils at 100°C. The _____ of water is 1 g/cm³.

LESSON 1 Describing Matter

🔑 Every form of matter has two kinds of properties—physical properties and chemical properties.

Vocabulary
- matter
- chemistry
- substance
- physical property
- chemical property

LESSON 2 Classifying Matter

🔑 Scientists know that all matter in the universe is made of more than 100 different substances, called elements.

🔑 A mixture can be heterogeneous or homogeneous.

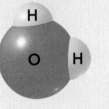

Vocabulary
- element • atom
- chemical bond • molecule • compound
- chemical formula • mixture

LESSON 3 Measuring Matter

🔑 The SI unit of mass is the kilogram (kg).

🔑 The SI unit of volume is the cubic meter (m³).

🔑 You can determine the density of a sample of matter by dividing its mass by its volume.

Vocabulary
- weight • mass • International System of Units
- volume • density

LESSON 4 Changes in Matter

🔑 A substance that undergoes a physical change is still the same substance after the change.

🔑 Unlike a physical change, a chemical change produces new substances with new and different properties.

🔑 Every chemical and physical change in matter includes a change in energy.

Vocabulary
- physical change • chemical change • law of conservation of mass
- temperature • thermal energy • endothermic change
- exothermic change • chemical energy

Review and Assessment

LESSON 1 Describing Matter

1. Which of the following is an example of a chemical property?

  a. density   **b.** flammability

  c. hardness   **d.** luster

2. A substance can be classified by its physical properties, which are properties that

_____

_____

_____

_____

_____

3. Classify Which of the following is a substance: table salt, seawater, or sand? Explain how you know.

_____

_____

_____

_____

4. Interpret Tables Write a title that describes the table below.

Helium	Colorless; less dense than air
Iron	Attracted to magnets; melting point of 1,535°C
Oxygen	Odorless; gas at room temperature

5. [Write About It] Write an e-mail to a friend explaining why the melting point of a substance is a physical property but flammability is a chemical property. Use examples to explain.

LESSON 2 Classifying Matter

6. Which of the following is an element?

  a. water   **b.** carbon dioxide

  c. oxygen   **d.** ammonia

7. Four methods that can be used to separate mixtures are _____

_____

_____

Use the diagrams to answer Questions 8–10. Each diagram represents a different kind of matter. Each ball represents an atom. Balls of the same color are the same kind of atom.

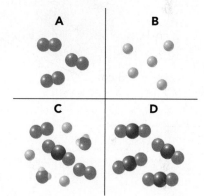

8. Interpret Diagrams Which diagram or diagrams represent a single element? Explain.

_____

_____

9. Compare and Contrast How do the atoms in Diagram A differ from those in Diagram D?

_____

_____

_____

10. Apply Concepts Which diagram or diagrams represent a mixture? Explain.

_____

_____

_____

31

1 Review and Assessment

LESSON 3 Measuring Matter

11. What is the SI unit of mass?

    a. milliliter   **b.** kilogram

    c. pound   **d.** cubic centimeter

12. The density of a substance is calculated by

_____

_____

13. Make Judgments Which measurement shown in the diagram is not needed to find the volume of the box? Explain.

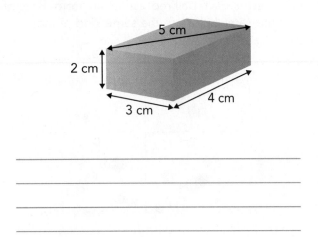

_____

_____

_____

_____

14. math! A piece of metal has a volume of 38 cm³ and a mass of 277 g. Calculate the density of the metal and identify it based on the information in the table below.

Density of Common Metals	
Iron	7.9 g/cm³
Lead	11.3 g/cm³
Tin	7.3 g/cm³
Zinc	7.1 g/cm³

LESSON 4 Changes in Matter

15. Which of the following is a physical change?

    a. burning   **b.** rusting

    c. freezing   **d.** oxidation

16. The law of conservation of mass states that

_____

_____

_____

17. Solve Problems How could you prove that dissolving table salt in water is a physical change, not a chemical change?

_____

_____

_____

_____

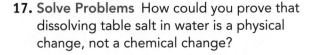

How is matter described?

18. Choose a substance you're familiar with. What are its physical and chemical properties? How would you measure its density? What are some physical and chemical changes it can undergo?

_____

_____

_____

_____

_____

_____

_____

_____

_____

_____

_____

_____

Standardized Test Prep

Multiple Choice

Circle the letter of the best answer.

1. Each diagram below represents a different kind of matter. Each ball represents an atom. Balls of the same size and shade are the same atom.

   Which diagram **best** represents a mixture of two kinds of molecules?

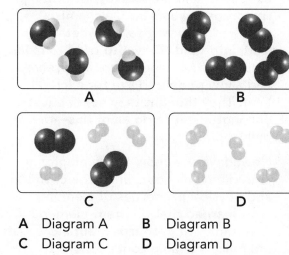

   A   Diagram A   **B**   Diagram B
   C   Diagram C   **D**   Diagram D

2. The fact that matter is neither created nor destroyed in any chemical or physical change is called the

   A   law of exothermic change.
   B   law of endothermic change.
   C   law of thermal matter.
   D   law of conservation of mass.

3. The density of a substance equals its mass divided by its volume. The density of sulfur is 2.0 g/cm^3. What is the mass of a sample of sulfur with a volume of 6.0 cm^3?

   A   3.0 g   **B**   4.0 g
   C   8.0 g   **D**   12 g

4. The abilities to dissolve in water and to conduct electric current are examples of

   A   physical properties.
   B   chemical properties.
   C   physical changes.
   D   chemical bonding.

5. Which two pieces of laboratory equipment would be the **most** useful for measuring the mass and volume of a rectangular block?

   A   a metric ruler and a stopwatch
   B   a balance and a metric ruler
   C   a graduated cylinder and a metric ruler
   D   a balance and a stop watch

Constructed Response

Use the graph below and your knowledge of science to help you answer Question 6. Write your answer on a separate sheet of paper.

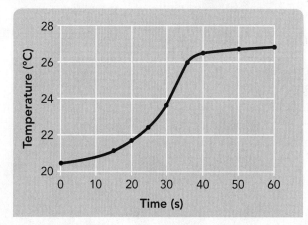

6. A student mixes two liquids of the same temperature together. The graph above shows the change in temperature after the liquids mix. Did the reaction absorb thermal energy or release it? Explain your answer.

Long Ago in a Faraway Land...

In an old German tale, a strange little man named Rumpelstiltskin spins straw into gold. Sounds far-fetched, right? It wouldn't have sounded that strange to someone in the fourteenth century. Hundreds of years ago, alchemists searched for a way to turn metals, like lead, into gold. They also tried to make medicines that would cure all diseases and allow people to live for a long time. They thought they needed just one ingredient to do all of this—the philosopher's stone.

Nowadays, we know that a magic ingredient will not change the chemical and physical properties of elements. We have learned that different elements have different properties. But alchemists did make valuable contributions to people's understanding of the physical world. Alchemists discovered alcohol and mineral acids, and recorded their observations of how these acids reacted with other substances. They worked in laboratories heating base metals and observing interactions and changes in color. They recorded their conclusions about these experiments. Their goal may have been impossible, but their research helped build the foundation of chemistry today.

Research It Throughout history, scientists have increased our understanding of the natural world by learning from those before them. Research how the fields of chemistry and medicine have developed from the experiments of alchemists. Write an essay describing the progression.

An Antiuniverse?

What if the entire universe had a mirror or negative image? Would everything happen backward? Or, would there be an opposite you? Scientists working in the field of particle physics think there just might be a mirror universe, but they don't really expect it to be the stuff of science fiction movies.

A little over a hundred years ago, scientists thought that the smallest part of matter—a part not made up of anything else—was the atom. That wasn't true. An atom is made up of a nucleus that contains protons and neutrons, surrounded by electrons. A physicist named Paul Dirac added an interesting twist to this knowledge. He correctly predicted that the electron might have a reverse twin, which he called a positron. (He won the Nobel Prize for this leap of genius back in 1933.) The positron has the same mass as an electron but the opposite charge—it's the antielectron.

Electrons, neutrons, and protons all have these antiparticles, or at least they did when the particles formed. Scientists have been able to study them in the laboratory. Inside particle accelerators, scientists can even use positrons and electrons to form entirely new atoms. But outside of the controlled laboratory environment, where are these antiparticles? Are they now part of an antiuniverse somewhere? Physicists are hoping to find the answers in the twenty-first century—your century!

Research It Write down three questions you have about particle physics and antimatter. Research to find out the answers. Articles about the CERN laboratory in Switzerland would be a good place to start. Answer your questions in one or two paragraphs.

Paul Dirac predicted that positrons might exist as the opposites of electrons. ▼

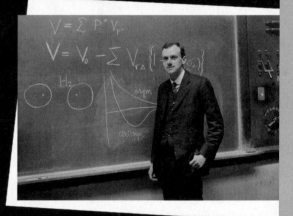

◄ Inside a special chamber, two invisible photons enter and produce a pair of electrons (colored green) and antielectrons (colored red).

HOW DID THIS BUILDING TURN TO ICE?

THE BIG
?

Why does a substance change states?

Firefighters sprayed water on a blaze in this historic building in Maine. The air temperature was −14°F, which was uncomfortably cold. This made it difficult for firefighters to battle the flames. The building was in danger of falling down because it was covered in ice 6 to 10 inches thick. **Infer How did this building get covered in ice?**

> UNTAMED SCIENCE Watch the **Untamed Science** video to learn more about changing states.

_____

_____

_____

_____

_____

Solids, Liquids, and Gases

Check Your Understanding

1. Background Read the paragraph below and then answer the question.

> The air **temperature** outside has been below freezing all week. The local pond has frozen over and is ready for ice skating. Ronnesia is excited just thinking about all the things she can do on the **ice**. She eats a good breakfast to get the **energy** she needs for ice skating.

> **Temperature** is a measure of the average energy of random motion of particles of matter.
>
> **Ice** is water in the solid form.
>
> **Energy** is the ability to do work or cause change.

- Why is the pond ready for ice skating?

_____

_____

> **MY READING WEB** If you had trouble completing the question above, visit **My Reading Web** and type in *Solids, Liquids, and Gases.*

Vocabulary Skill

Suffixes A suffix is a letter or group of letters added to the end of a word to change its meaning and often its part of speech. In this chapter, you will learn vocabulary words that end in the suffixes *-ation*, *-ine*, and *-sion*.

Suffix	Meaning	Example
-ation	State of, process of, act of	Vaporization, evaporation, condensation, sublimation
-ine	Consisting of	Crystalline solid
-sion	State of, process of, act of	Surface tension

2. Quick Check *Vapor* is another word for gas. Use the table above to predict the meaning of *vaporization*. Revise your definition as needed.

_____

_____

liquid

surface tension

melting

sublimation

Chapter Preview

LESSON 1

- solid
- crystalline solid
- amorphous solid
- liquid
- fluid
- surface tension
- viscosity
- gas
- pressure

↻ **Relate Cause and Effect**
△ **Infer**

LESSON 2

- melting
- melting point
- freezing
- vaporization
- evaporation
- boiling
- boiling point
- condensation
- sublimation

↻ **Compare and Contrast**
△ **Predict**

LESSON 3

- Charles's Law
- directly proportional
- Boyle's Law
- inversely proportional

↻ **Identify the Main Idea**
△ **Graph**

> **VOCAB FLASH CARDS** For extra help with vocabulary, visit **Vocab Flash Cards** and type in *Solids, Liquids, and Gases.*

1 States of Matter

UNLOCK THE BIG ?

🔑 **How Do You Describe a Solid?**

🔑 **How Do You Describe a Liquid?**

🔑 **How Do You Describe a Gas?**

MY PLANET DIARY

Liquid Crystals

Have you ever wondered why some television sets are referred to as LCD TVs? *LCD* stands for "liquid crystal display." An LCD is a thin, flat screen. LCDs have replaced the picture tubes in many computer monitors and television sets because they are lighter and use less power. LCDs are also found in cell phones and clock radio faces.

Liquid crystals are neither solid nor liquid—instead they fall somewhere in between. But it takes just a small amount of thermal energy to change a liquid crystal to a liquid. As a result, LCDs tend to be very sensitive to heat.

FUN FACTS

Communicate Discuss these questions with a classmate. Write your answers below.

1. List some things that contain LCDs.

_____
_____
_____

2. Why might you not want to leave a cell phone or a laptop computer outside on a hot day?

_____
_____
_____
_____

> PLANET DIARY Go to **Planet Diary** to learn more about solids, liquids, and gases.

Do the Inquiry Warm-Up *What Are Solids, Liquids, and Gases?*

LCD display with crystals cooling (background)

Vocabulary

- solid • crystalline solid • amorphous solid • liquid
- fluid • surface tension • viscosity • gas • pressure

Skills

↻ Reading: Relate Cause and Effect

△ Inquiry: Infer

How Do You Describe a Solid?

Look at the bowl in **Figure 1.** It contains the metal bismuth. Notice that the shape and size of the piece of bismuth are different from the bowl's shape and size. What would happen if you took the bismuth out of the bowl and placed it on a tabletop? Would it become flatter? What would happen if you put it in a larger bowl? Would it become larger? Of course not, because it's a solid. A **solid** has a definite shape and a definite volume. Your pencil is another example of a solid. If your pencil has a cylindrical shape and a volume of 6 cubic centimeters, it will keep this shape and volume in any position in any container.

Particles in a Solid The particles that make up a solid are packed very closely together. Also, each particle is tightly fixed in one position. 🗝 **This fixed, closely packed arrangement of particles in a solid causes it to have a definite shape and volume.** Do the particles that make up a solid move at all? Yes, but not much. The particles in a solid are closely locked in position and can only vibrate in place. This means that the particles move back and forth slightly, like a group of people running in place.

Place a check in each category that describes a solid.		
	Definite	**Indefinite**
Shape	_____	_____
Volume	_____	_____

Particles in a solid

FIGURE 1 ·······························

Solid

A solid does not take the shape or volume of its container.

✏ **Interpret Diagrams** Describe the arrangement of particles in a solid.

_____

_____

_____

FIGURE 2
Types of Solids
Solids are either crystalline or amorphous. Butter is an amorphous solid. The mineral fluorite is a crystalline solid.

✎ **Compare and Contrast** Use the Venn diagram to compare the characteristics of amorphous and crystalline solids.

Types of Solids

In many solids, the particles form a regular, repeating pattern. These patterns create crystals. Solids that are made up of crystals are called **crystalline solids** (KRIS tuh lin). Salt, sugar, and snow are examples of crystalline solids. The fluorite crystal shown in **Figure 2** is an example of a colorful crystalline solid. When a crystalline solid is heated, it melts at a distinct temperature.

In **amorphous solids** (uh MAWR fus), the particles are not arranged in a regular pattern. Unlike a crystalline solid, an amorphous solid does not melt at a distinct temperature. Instead, it may become softer and softer or change into other substances. Glass is an example of an amorphous solid. A glass blower can bend and shape glass that has been heated. Plastics and rubber are other examples of amorphous solids.

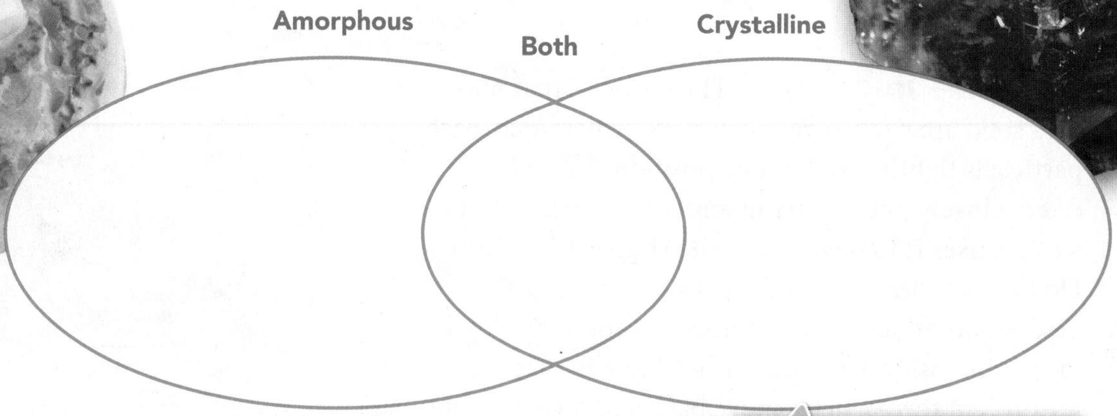

Amorphous   Both   Crystalline

Do the Quick Lab
Modeling Particles.

🔑 Assess Your Understanding

1a. Identify The two types of solids are
_____ and _____.

b. Explain Are the particles in a solid motionless? Explain your answer.
_____
_____

c. Draw Conclusions Candle wax gradually loses its shape as it is heated. What type of solid is candle wax? Explain.
_____
_____
_____
_____
_____
_____

got it? ....

○ I get it! Now I know that a solid has a definite shape and volume because_____
_____

○ I need extra help with _____

Go to MY SCIENCE 🅢 COACH *online for help with this subject.*

How Do You Describe a Liquid?

Without a container, a liquid spreads into a wide, shallow puddle. Like a solid, however, a liquid does have a constant volume. A **liquid** has a definite volume but no shape of its own. **Figure 3** shows equal volumes of iced tea in two different containers. The shape of a liquid may change with its container, but its volume remains the same.

Particles in a Liquid In general, the particles in a liquid are packed almost as closely together as those in a solid. However, the particles in a liquid move around one another freely. You can compare this movement to the way you might move a group of marbles around in your hand. Like the particles of a liquid, the marbles slide around one another but still touch. **Because its particles are free to move, a liquid has no definite shape. However, it does have a definite volume.** These freely moving particles allow a liquid to flow from place to place. For this reason, a liquid is also called a **fluid,** meaning a "substance that flows."

Relate Cause and Effect
Underline the cause and circle the effect in the boldface sentences.

Place a check in each category that describes a liquid.		
	Definite	**Indefinite**
Shape	_____	_____
Volume	_____	_____

FIGURE 3 ·······································

Liquid

Each container contains 300 cm³ of iced tea. The iced tea takes the shape of its container, but its volume does not change.

✎ **Interpret Diagrams Describe the arrangement of particles in a liquid.**

_____

_____

_____

_____

_____

Particles in a liquid

43

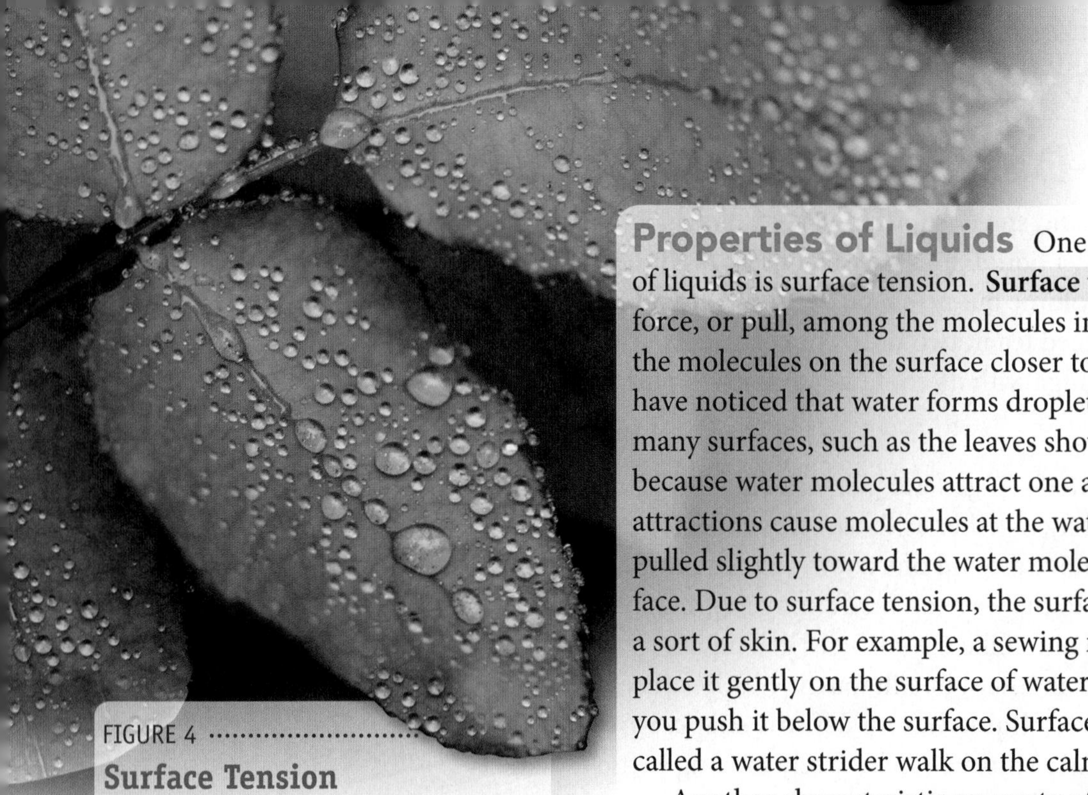

Properties of Liquids

One characteristic property of liquids is surface tension. **Surface tension** is an inward force, or pull, among the molecules in a liquid that brings the molecules on the surface closer together. You may have noticed that water forms droplets and can bead up on many surfaces, such as the leaves shown in **Figure 4.** That's because water molecules attract one another strongly. These attractions cause molecules at the water's surface to be pulled slightly toward the water molecules beneath its surface. Due to surface tension, the surface of water can act like a sort of skin. For example, a sewing needle floats when you place it gently on the surface of water, but it quickly sinks if you push it below the surface. Surface tension lets an insect called a water strider walk on the calm surface of a pond.

Another characteristic property of liquids is **viscosity** (vis KAHS uh tee), or a liquid's resistance to flowing. A liquid's viscosity depends on the size and shape of its particles and the attractions between the particles. Some liquids flow more easily than others. Liquids with high viscosity flow slowly. Honey is an example of a liquid with a very high viscosity. Liquids with low viscosity flow quickly. Water and vinegar have relatively low viscosities.

FIGURE 4 ·····················
Surface Tension
⚠ **Infer Circle the correct answer.**
Water beads up on the surface of the leaves because water molecules (attract/repel) each other strongly.

 Do the Quick Lab *As Thick as Honey.*

🔑 Assess Your Understanding

2a. Name A substance that flows is called a

_____

b. Describe Why is a liquid able to flow?

_____

_____

c. Compare and Contrast How do liquids with a high viscosity differ from liquids with a low viscosity?

_____

_____

_____

got**it?** ···

O **I get it!** Now I know that a liquid has a definite volume but not a definite shape because _____

_____

_____

O **I need extra help with** _____

Go to **MY SCIENCE COACH** online for help with this subject.

How Do You Describe a Gas?

Like a liquid, a gas is a fluid. Unlike a liquid, however, a **gas** has neither a definite shape nor a definite volume. If a gas is in a closed container such as the flask in **Figure 5,** the gas particles will move and spread apart as they fill the container.

If you could see the particles that make up a gas, you would see them moving in all directions. 🔑 **As gas particles move, they spread apart, filling all the space available. Thus, a gas has neither definite shape nor definite volume.** When working with a gas, it is important to know its volume, temperature, and pressure. So what exactly do these measurements mean?

Volume Remember that volume is the amount of space that matter fills. Volume is measured in cubic centimeters (cm^3), cubic meters (m^3), milliliters (mL), liters (L), and other units. Because gas particles move and fill all of the space available, the volume of a gas is the same as the volume of its container. For example, a large amount of helium gas can be compressed—or pressed together tightly—to fit into a metal tank. When you use the helium to fill balloons, it expands to fill many balloons that have a total volume much greater than the volume of the tank.

Place a check in each category that describes a gas.		
	Definite	**Indefinite**
Shape	_____	_____
Volume	_____	_____

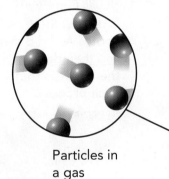

Particles in a gas

FIGURE 5 ··

> **INTERACTIVE ART** Gas

A gas takes the shape and volume of its container.

✎ **Interpret Diagrams Describe the arrangement of particles in a gas.**

_____

_____

_____

_____

_____

Calculating Pressure

When calculating pressure, force is measured in newtons (N). If the area is measured in square meters (m^2), pressure is expressed in pascals (Pa), where $1\ Pa = 1\ N/m^2$. Suppose a gas exerts a force of 252 N on a piston having an area of 0.430 m^2. What is the pressure on the piston in Pascals?

$$Pressure = \frac{Force}{Area}$$

$$= \frac{252\ N}{0.430\ m^2}$$

$$= 586\ Pa$$

Practice Problem A gas exerts a force of 5,610 N over an area of 0.342 m^2. What pressure does the gas exert in Pa?

_____

_____

_____

Pressure Gas particles constantly collide with one another and with the walls of their container. As a result, the gas pushes on the walls of the container. The **pressure** of the gas is the force of its outward push divided by the area of the walls of the container. Pressure is measured in units of pascals (Pa) or kilopascals (kPa) (1 kPa = 1,000 Pa).

$$Pressure = \frac{Force}{Area}$$

The firmness of a gas-filled object comes from the pressure of the gas. For example, the air inside an inflated ball has a higher pressure than the air outside. This higher pressure is due to the greater concentration of gas particles inside the ball than in the surrounding air. Concentration is the number of gas particles in a given unit of volume.

Why does a ball leak even when it has only a tiny hole? The higher pressure inside the ball results in gas particles hitting the inner surface of the ball more often. Therefore, gas particles inside the ball reach the hole and escape more often than gas particles outside the ball reach the hole and enter. Thus, many more particles go out than in. The pressure inside drops until it is equal to the pressure outside.

FIGURE 6 ··

Gas Pressure

Photos A and B show a beach ball being inflated and then deflated. ✎ **Interpret Photos** Circle the answers that complete the description of each process.

A
The concentration of gas particles inside the beach ball (increases/decreases). The gas pressure inside the beach ball (increases/decreases).

B
The concentration of gas particles inside the beach ball (increases/decreases). The gas pressure inside the beach ball (increases/decreases).

Faster-moving, hot gas particles

Slower-moving, cool gas particles

Temperature The balloonists in **Figure 7** are preparing the balloon for flight. To do this, they use a propane burner to heat the air inside the balloon. Once the temperature of the air is hot enough, the balloon will start to rise. But what does the temperature tell you? Recall that all particles of matter are constantly moving. Temperature is a measure of the average energy of random motion of the particles of matter. The faster the particles are moving, the greater their energy and the higher the temperature. You might think of a thermometer as a speedometer for particles.

Even at room temperature, the average speed of particles in a gas is very fast. At about 20°C, the particles in a typical gas travel about 500 meters per second—more than twice the cruising speed of a jet plane!

FIGURE 7 ·······················

Temperature of a Gas

✎ **Explain** Why are the hot gas particles moving faster than the cool gas particles?

_____

_____

_____

 Do the Quick Lab *How Do the Particles in a Gas Move?*

🔑 **Assess Your Understanding**

3a. Describe Describe how the motions of gas particles are related to the pressure exerted by the gas.

_____

_____

_____

_____

_____

b. Relate Cause and Effect Why does pumping more air into a basketball increase the pressure inside the ball?

_____

_____

_____

_____

_____

got it? ···

○ **I get it!** Now I know that a gas has neither a definite shape nor definite volume because_____

_____

○ I need extra help with _____

Go to **MY SCIENCE COACH** online for help with this subject

Changes of State

🔑 **What Happens to the Particles of a Solid as It Melts?**

🔑 **What Happens to the Particles of a Liquid as It Vaporizes?**

🔑 **What Happens to the Particles of a Solid as It Sublimes?**

my planet Diary

On the Boil

You might have noticed that as an uncovered pot of water boils, the water level slowly decreases. The water level changes because the liquid is changing to a gas. As you heat the water, the thermal energy of its molecules increases. The longer you leave the pot on the hot stove, the more energy is absorbed by the water molecules. When the water molecules gain enough energy, they change state from a liquid to a gas.

The graph shows the temperature of a small pot of water on a stove set to high heat. The starting temperature of the water is 20°C.

SCIENCE STATS

Liquid to a Gas

Graph: Temperature (°C) vs. Time (minutes). Curve labeled Liquid rising, then flat at 100°C labeled Boiling, then rising labeled Gas.

Answer the following questions.

1. How long does it take for the water to start boiling? At what temperature does the water boil?

_____

_____

_____

2. Does it take more energy to heat the water to 100°C or to boil it?

_____

_____

_____

> PLANET DIARY Go to **Planet Diary** to learn more about changes of state.

 Do the Inquiry Warm-Up *What Happens When You Breathe on a Mirror?*

Vocabulary

- melting • melting point • freezing • vaporization
- evaporation • boiling • boiling point • condensation
- sublimation

Skills

↻ Reading: Compare and Contrast
△ Inquiry: Predict

What Happens to the Particles of a Solid as It Melts?

Particles of a liquid have more thermal energy than particles of the same substance in solid form. As a gas, the particles have even more thermal energy. A change from a solid to a liquid involves an increase in thermal energy. As you might guess, a change from a liquid to a solid is just the opposite: It involves a decrease in thermal energy.

Melting The change in state from a solid to a liquid is called **melting.** In pure, crystalline solids, melting occurs at a specific temperature, called the **melting point.** Because the melting point is a characteristic property of a substance, chemists often compare melting points when trying to identify an unknown material. The melting point of pure water, for example, is 0°C at sea level.

What happens to the particles of a solid as it melts? Think of an ice cube taken from the freezer. The energy needed to melt the ice comes mostly from the air in the room. At first, the added thermal energy makes the water molecules vibrate faster, raising their temperature. 🔑 **At a solid's melting point, its particles vibrate so fast that they break free from their fixed positions.** At 0°C, the temperature of the ice stops increasing. Any added energy continues to change the arrangement of the water molecules from ice crystals into liquid water. The ice melts.

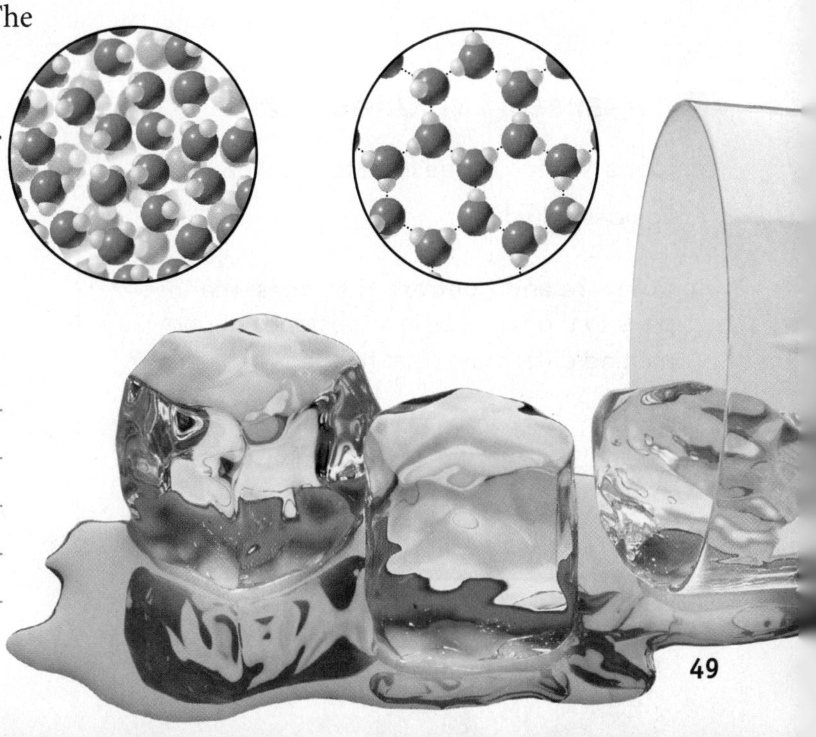

FIGURE 1 ·······························

Melting

✎ **Relate Diagrams and Photos** Draw a line matching each illustration of water molecules to either ice or liquid water. Then describe how ice and liquid water differ in the arrangement of their molecules.

_____

_____

_____

_____

_____

Freezing The change of state from a liquid to a solid is called **freezing**. It is just the reverse of melting.  **At a liquid's freezing point, its particles are moving so slowly that they begin to take on fixed positions.**

When you put liquid water into a freezer, for example, the water loses energy to the cold air in the freezer. The water molecules move more and more slowly as they lose energy. Over time, the water becomes solid ice. When water begins to freeze, its temperature stays at 0°C until freezing is complete. The freezing point of water, 0°C, is the same as its melting point.

apply it!

In metal casting, a liquid metal is poured into a container called a mold. The mold gives a shape to the metal when it cools and hardens.

1 Explain How does metal casting make use of the different characteristics of liquids and solids?

_____

_____

_____

_____

_____

_____

2 CHALLENGE The melting point of copper is 1084°C. How does the energy of the particles in a certain amount of liquid copper compare to the energy of the molecules in the same amount of liquid water? Why?

_____

_____

_____

_____

_____

_____

 Do the Lab Investigation *Melting Ice.*

Assess Your Understanding

1a. Identify The change in state from a solid to a liquid is called _____

b. Compare and Contrast How does what happens to the particles in a substance during melting differ from what happens in freezing?

_____

_____

_____

_____

_____

got it?

○ **I get it!** Now I know that melting occurs when the particles in a solid_____

_____

_____

_____

○ **I need extra help with** _____

Go to MY SCIENCE ⑤ COACH *online for help with this subject.*

What Happens to the Particles of a Liquid as It Vaporizes?

Have you ever wondered how clouds form or why puddles dry up? To answer these questions, you need to look at what happens when changes occur between the liquid and gas states.

Evaporation and Boiling The change in state from a liquid to a gas is called **vaporization** (vay puhr ih ZAY shun). ⚷ **Vaporization occurs when the particles in a liquid gain enough energy to move independently.** There are two main types of vaporization—evaporation and boiling.

Vaporization that takes place only on the surface of a liquid is called **evaporation** (ee vap uh RAY shun). A shrinking puddle is an example. Water in the puddle gains energy from the ground, the air, or the sun. The added energy enables some of the water molecules on the surface of the puddle to escape into the air, or evaporate.

Vaporization that takes place both below and at the surface of a liquid is called **boiling.** When water boils, vaporized water molecules form bubbles below the surface. The bubbles rise and eventually break the surface of the liquid. The temperature at which a liquid boils is called its **boiling point.** As with melting points, chemists use boiling points to help identify unknown substances.

✎ Compare and Contrast
Compare and contrast the two types of vaporization.

_____

_____

_____

_____

_____

_____

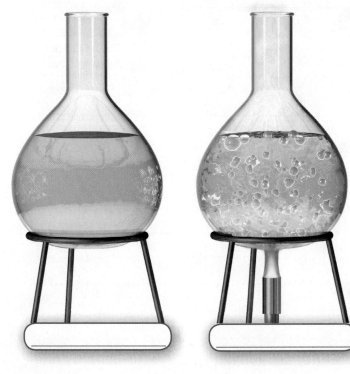

FIGURE 2 ·············

Types of Vaporization
Liquid water changes to water vapor by either evaporation or boiling.

✎ Interpret Diagrams Label the type of vaporization occurring in each flask. Then draw arrows to indicate the paths of water molecules leaving each flask.

Suppose there is the same amount of water in both of the flasks. ◁Predict Which flask does water vaporize from first? Why?

_____

_____

_____

_____

_____

Condensation Condensation is the reverse of vaporization. The change in state from a gas to a liquid is called **condensation.** You can observe condensation by breathing onto a mirror. When warm water vapor in your breath reaches the cooler surface of the mirror, the water vapor condenses into liquid droplets. 🔑 **Condensation occurs when particles in a gas lose enough thermal energy to form a liquid.**

Clouds typically form when water vapor in the atmosphere condenses into tiny liquid droplets. When the droplets get heavy enough, they fall to the ground as rain. Water vapor is a colorless gas that you cannot see. The steam you see above a kettle of boiling water is not water vapor, and neither are clouds or fog. What you see in those cases are tiny droplets of liquid water suspended in air.

Vocabulary **Suffixes** Complete the sentences using the correct forms of the word *condense*.

_____ is the change in state from a gas to a liquid. Clouds form because water vapor _____

FIGURE 3 ·······················
Foggy Mirror
✏️ **Explain** Why does a mirror fog up after a hot shower?

_____
_____
_____
_____
_____
_____

Lab® Do the Quick Lab
zone *Keeping Cool.*

🔑 **Assess Your Understanding**

2a. Identify The change in state from a liquid to a gas is called _____

b. Apply Concepts How does the thermal energy of water vapor change as the vapor condenses?

_____
_____

c. Relate Cause and Effect Why do clouds form before it rains?

_____
_____
_____
_____

got it? ·······························

○ **I get it!** Now I know that vaporization occurs when the particles in a liquid _____
_____

○ **I need extra help with** _____

Go to MY SCIENCE ⒮ COACH online for help with this subject.

What Happens to the Particles of a Solid as It Sublimes?

In places where the winters are cold, the snow may disappear even when the temperature stays well below freezing. This change is the result of sublimation. **Sublimation** occurs when the surface particles of a solid gain enough energy that they form a gas. **During sublimation, particles of a solid do not pass through the liquid state as they form a gas.**

One example of sublimation occurs with dry ice. Dry ice is the common name for solid carbon dioxide. At ordinary atmospheric pressures, carbon dioxide cannot exist as a liquid. So instead of melting, solid carbon dioxide changes directly into a gas. As it sublimes, the carbon dioxide absorbs thermal energy. This property helps keep materials near dry ice cold and dry. For this reason, using dry ice is a way to keep the temperature low when a refrigerator is not available. Some fog machines use dry ice to create fog in movies or at concerts, as shown in **Figure 4.** When dry ice becomes a gas, it cools water vapor in the nearby air. The water vapor then condenses into a liquid, forming fog near the dry ice.

did you know?

Mosquitos are attracted to the carbon dioxide gas you exhale during breathing. A mosquito trap baited with dry ice can attract up to four or five times as many mosquitos as traps baited with a light source alone.

FIGURE 4 ....

Dry Ice
A fog machine uses dry ice to create fog at this rock concert. **Explain** Why does fog form near dry ice?

_____

_____

_____

_____

_____

Dry ice subliming

The Changing States of Water

Why does a substance change states?

FIGURE 5 ··

> **VIRTUAL LAB** Four examples of how water changes states—by melting, freezing, vaporization, and condensation—are shown here.

✎ **Review** Use what you have learned about states of matter to answer the questions.

FREEZING

This lake has frozen over due to the cold weather. As liquid water freezes, its molecules (gain/lose) thermal energy. How does the motion of the water molecules change during freezing?

_____
_____
_____
_____

Freezing

Melting

Low Thermal Energy

MELTING

The air outside is so warm that this snow-man is melting. During melting, the water molecules (gain/lose) thermal energy. How does the motion of the molecules change during melting?

_____
_____
_____
_____
_____
_____

These wet footprints are disappearing due to evaporation. As water evaporates, its molecules (gain/lose) thermal energy. How does the motion of the molecules change during evaporation?

_____
_____
_____
_____
_____
_____

VAPORIZATION

High Thermal Energy

Condensation ◄

Vaporization ►

CONDENSATION

During the night, water vapor in the air condensed on this spider web. As water vapor condenses, its molecules (gain/lose) thermal energy. How does the motion of the molecules change during condensation?

_____
_____
_____
_____
_____

Lab zone® Do the Quick Lab
Observing Sublimation.

🔑 Assess Your Understanding

3a. Identify What is dry ice?

_____
_____

b. Predict If you allowed dry ice to stand in a bowl at room temperature for several hours, what would be left?

_____
_____

c. ANSWER THE BIG ? Why does a substance change states?

_____
_____
_____
_____
_____
_____

got it? ....

○ **I get it!** Now I know that sublimation occurs when the particles in a solid_____

_____
_____

○ **I need extra help with** _____

Go to **MY SCIENCE ⑤ COACH** *online for help with this subject.*

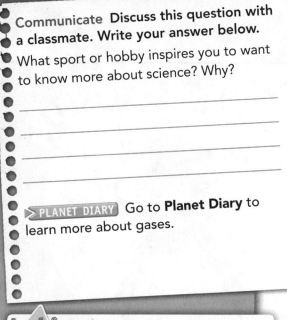

UNLOCK THE BIG Q?

🔑 **How Are Pressure and Temperature of a Gas Related?**

🔑 **How Are Volume and Temperature of a Gas Related?**

🔑 **How Are Pressure and Volume of a Gas Related?**

MY PLANET DiARY

BIOGRAPHY

Jacques Charles (1746–1823)

French scientist Jacques Charles is best known for his work on gases. But he also made contributions to the sport of ballooning. On August 27, 1783, Charles released the first hydrogen-filled balloon, which was about 4 meters in diameter. This balloon, which did not carry any people, rose to a height of 3,000 feet. Charles also improved the design of hot-air balloons. He added a valve line that allowed the pilot to release gas from the balloon. He also added a wicker basket that attached to the balloon with ropes. Charles was elected to the French Academy of Sciences in 1785.

Communicate Discuss this question with a classmate. Write your answer below.
What sport or hobby inspires you to want to know more about science? Why?

_____

_____

_____

_____

▷ PLANET DIARY Go to **Planet Diary** to learn more about gases.

Lab® zone Do the Inquiry Warm-Up *How Can Air Keep Chalk From Breaking?*

How Are Pressure and Temperature of a Gas Related?

If you dropped a few grains of sand onto your hand, you would hardly feel them. But what if you were caught in a sandstorm? Ouch! The sand grains fly around very fast, and they would sting if they hit you. Although gas particles are much smaller than sand grains, a sandstorm is a good model for gas behavior. Like grains of sand in a sandstorm, gas particles travel at high speeds. The faster the gas particles move, the greater the force with which they collide with the walls of their container.

Vocabulary
- Charles's law   • directly proportional   • Boyle's law
- inversely proportional

Skills
↻ **Reading:** Identify the Main Idea
△ **Inquiry:** Graph

Consider a gas in a closed, rigid container. If you heat the gas, its particles will move faster on average. They will collide with the walls of their container with greater force. The greater force over the same area results in greater pressure. 🔑 **When the temperature of a gas at constant volume is increased, the pressure of the gas increases. When the temperature is decreased, the pressure of the gas decreases.**

On long trips, especially in the summer, a truck's tires can become very hot. As the temperature increases, so does the pressure of the air inside the tire. If the pressure becomes greater than the tire can hold, the tire will burst. For this reason, truck drivers need to monitor and adjust tire pressure on long trips.

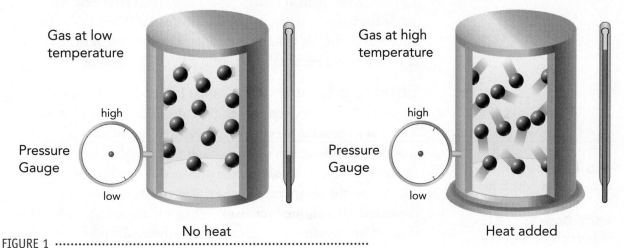

Gas at low temperature

Pressure Gauge

No heat

Gas at high temperature

Pressure Gauge

Heat added

FIGURE 1 ·······

Temperature and Gas Pressure
When a gas is heated in a closed, rigid container, the particles move faster and collide more often.

✏️ **Infer** Draw an arrow in each pressure gauge to show the change in pressure of the gas.

Do the Quick Lab
How Are Pressure and Temperature Related?

🔑 Assess Your Understanding

got it? ·······

○ **I get it!** Now I know that when the temperature of a gas at a constant volume increases, _____

_____

○ I need extra help with _____

Go to MY SCIENCE ⬤ COACH *online for help with this subject.*

57

| A gas-filled balloon is at room temperature, 20°C. | The balloon is lowered into liquid nitrogen at −196°C. | The balloon shrinks as gas volume decreases. | When the balloon is removed, the gas warms and the balloon expands. | The balloon is again at room temperature. |

FIGURE 2 ··
Cooling a Balloon
The volume of a gas-filled balloon decreases as temperature decreases and then increases as temperature increases.

How Are Volume and Temperature of a Gas Related?

Figure 2 shows what happens when a balloon is slowly lowered into liquid nitrogen at nearly −200°C and then removed. As the air inside the balloon cools, its volume decreases. When the air inside warms up again, its volume increases. The pressure remains more or less constant because the air is in a flexible container.

Charles's Law French scientist Jacques Charles examined the relationship between the temperature and volume of a gas that is kept at a constant pressure. He measured the volume of a gas at various temperatures in a container that could change volume. (A changeable volume allows the pressure to remain constant.)  **When the temperature of a gas at constant pressure is increased, its volume increases. When the temperature of a gas at constant pressure is decreased, its volume decreases.** This principle is called **Charles's law.**

FIGURE 3 ······································
Charles's Law
A gas in a cylinder with a movable piston is slowly heated.
✏ **Predict** Draw the piston and gas particles when the temperature reaches 200°C and 400°C.

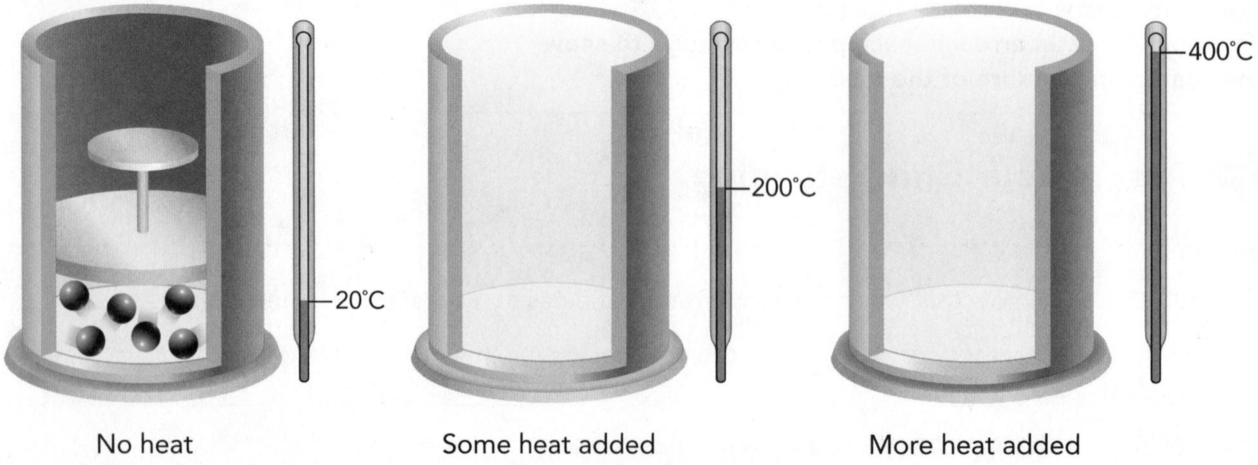

| No heat | Some heat added | More heat added |

Graphing Charles's Law
Suppose you do an experiment to test Charles's law. The experiment begins with 50 mL of gas in a cylinder with a movable piston similar to the one in **Figure 3.** The gas is slowly heated. Each time the temperature increases by 10°C, the gas volume is recorded. The data are recorded in the data table in **Figure 4.** Note that the temperatures in the data table have been converted to kelvins, the SI unit of temperature. To convert from Celsius degrees to kelvins (K), add 273.

As you can see in the graph of the data, the data points form a straight line. The dotted line represents how the graph would look if the gas could be cooled to 0 K. Notice that the line passes through the point (0, 0), called the origin. When a graph of two variables is a straight line passing through the origin, the variables are said to be **directly proportional** to each other. The graph of Charles's law shows that the volume of a gas is directly proportional to its kelvin temperature at constant pressure.

Temperature		Volume
(°C)	(K)	(mL)
0	273	50
20	293	54
40	313	58
60	333	62
80	353	66
100	373	70
120	393	74

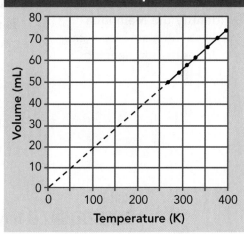

Charles's Law Graph

FIGURE 4 ....

Temperature and Gas Volume
🖊 In an experiment, a gas is heated at a constant pressure. The data shown in the table are plotted on the graph.

1. **Draw Conclusions** What happens to the volume of a gas when the temperature is increased at constant pressure?

_____

2. **CHALLENGE** Suppose the data formed a line with a steeper slope. For the same change in temperature, how would the change in volume compare?

_____

_____

 Do the Quick Lab
Hot and Cold Balloons.

🔑 Assess Your Understanding

1a. Identify The graph of Charles's law shows that the volume of a gas is

_____ to its

kelvin temperature at constant pressure.

b. Predict Suppose the gas in **Figure 4** could be cooled to 100 K (–173°C). Predict the volume of the gas at this temperature.

_____

got it? ....

○ **I get it!** Now I know that when the temperature of a gas is decreased at constant pressure _____

_____

○ **I need extra help with** _____

Go to **my science** **s** **coach** *online for help with this subject.*

How Are Pressure and Volume of a Gas Related?

Suppose you use a bicycle pump to inflate a tire. By pressing down on the plunger, you force the gas inside the pump through the rubber tube and out of the nozzle into the tire. What happens to the volume of air inside the pump cylinder as you push down on the plunger? What happens to the pressure?

Boyle's Law In the 1600s, the scientist Robert Boyle carried out experiments to try to improve air pumps. He measured the volumes of gases at different pressures. Boyle's experiments showed that gas volume and pressure were related. 🔑 **When the pressure of a gas at constant temperature is increased, the volume of the gas decreases. When the pressure is decreased, the volume increases.** This relationship between the pressure and the volume of a gas is called Boyle's law.

Boyle's law describes situations in which the volume of a gas is changed. The pressure then changes in the opposite way. For example, as you push down on the plunger of a bicycle pump, the volume of air inside the pump cylinder gets smaller, and the pressure inside the cylinder increases. The increase in pressure forces air into the tire.

🔄 **Identify the Main Idea**

Underline the main idea in the text under the red heading "Boyle's Law."

FIGURE 5 ···

> **INTERACTIVE ART** Boyle's Law

As weights are added to the top of each piston, the piston moves farther down in the cylinder. ✏ **Interpret Diagrams** First, rank the pressure in each of the cylinders. Then rank the volume. A ranking of 1 is the greatest. A ranking of 3 is the lowest.

1a. _____ pressure   **1b.** _____ pressure   **1c.** _____ pressure

2a. _____ volume   **2b.** _____ volume   **2c.** _____ volume

do the math! Analyzing Data

In an experiment, the volume of a gas was varied at a constant temperature. The pressure of the gas was recorded after each 50-mL change in volume. The data are in the table below.

1 **Graph** Use the data to make a line graph. Plot volume on the horizontal axis. Plot pressure on the vertical axis. Write a title for the graph at the top.

2 **Control Variables** The manipulated variable in this experiment is _____. The responding variable is _____.

3 **Make Generalizations** What happens to the pressure of a gas when the volume is decreased at a constant temperature?

_____

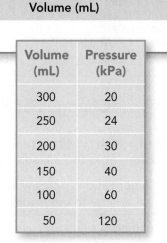

Volume (mL)	Pressure (kPa)
300	20
250	24
200	30
150	40
100	60
50	120

Graphing Boyle's Law Look at the graph that you made above. Notice that the points lie on a curve and not a straight line. The curve is steep at lower volumes, but it becomes less steep as volume increases. If you multiply the two variables at any point on the curve, you will find that the product does not change.

$$300 \text{ mL} \times 20 \text{ kPa} = 6{,}000 \text{ mL·kPa}$$
$$250 \text{ mL} \times 24 \text{ kPa} = 6{,}000 \text{ mL·kPa}$$

When the product of two variables is constant, the variables are **inversely proportional** to each other. The graph for Boyle's law shows that gas pressure is inversely proportional to volume at constant temperature.

Lab® zone Do the Quick Lab *It's a Gas.*

Assess Your Understanding

2a. Identify The graph of Boyle's law shows that the gas pressure is

_____ to volume at constant temperature.

b. Read Graphs Use the graph that you made in Analyzing Data above to find the pressure of the gas when its volume is 125 mL.

_____

got it? ....

○ **I get it!** Now I know that when the pressure of a gas at a constant temperature is increased, _____

_____

○ **I need extra help with** _____

Go to my science COACH *online for help with this subject.*

2 Study Guide

A substance (gains/loses) thermal energy when it melts or vaporizes.

A substance (gains/loses) thermal energy when it freezes or condenses.

LESSON 1 States of Matter

🔑 The fixed, closely packed arrangement of particles causes a solid to have a definite shape and volume.

🔑 Because its particles are free to move, a liquid has no definite shape. However, it does have a definite volume.

🔑 As gas particles move, they spread apart, filling all the space available. Thus, a gas has neither definite shape nor definite volume.

Vocabulary
• solid • crystalline solid • amorphous solid • liquid
• fluid • surface tension • viscosity • gas • pressure

LESSON 2 Changes of State

🔑 At a solid's melting point, its particles vibrate so fast that they break free from their fixed positions.

🔑 Vaporization occurs when the particles in a liquid gain enough thermal energy to move independently.

🔑 During sublimation, particles of a solid do not pass through the liquid state as they form a gas.

Vocabulary
• melting • melting point • freezing • vaporization • evaporation
• boiling • boiling point • condensation • sublimation

LESSON 3 The Behavior of Gases

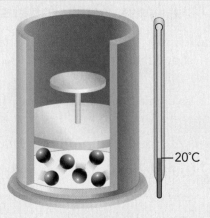

🔑 When the temperature of a gas at constant volume is increased, the pressure of the gas increases.

🔑 When the temperature of a gas at constant pressure is increased, its volume increases.

🔑 When the pressure of a gas at constant temperature is increased, the volume of the gas decreases.

Vocabulary
• Charles's law • directly proportional • Boyle's law
• inversely proportional

—20°C

No heat

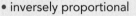

Review and Assessment

LESSON 1 States of Matter

1. A substance with a definite shape and definite volume is a

   a. solid   **b.** liquid

   c. gas   **d.** fluid

2. Rubber is considered a(n) _____ solid because it does not melt at a distinct temperature.

3. **Compare and Contrast** Why do liquids and gases take the shape of their containers while solids do not?

_____

_____

_____

_____

_____

4. **Predict** What happens to the gas particles in an inflated ball when it gets a hole? Why?

_____

_____

_____

_____

_____

_____

5. **math!** Earth's atmosphere exerts a force of 124,500 N on a kitchen table with an area of 1.5 m². What is the pressure in pascals?

_____

_____

_____

6. **Write About It** Write a short essay in which you create an analogy to describe particle motion. Compare the movements and positions of people dancing with the motions of water molecules in liquid water and in water vapor.

LESSON 2 Changes of State

7. A puddle dries up by the process of

   a. melting   **b.** freezing

   c. condensation   **d.** evaporation

8. When you see fog or clouds, you are seeing water in the _____ state.

9. **Classify** Label the correct change of state on top of the arrows in the diagram below.

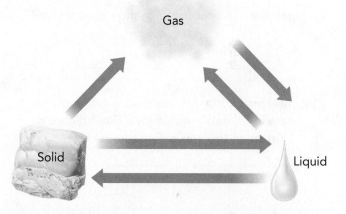

10. **Draw Conclusions** At room temperature, table salt is a solid and mercury is a liquid. What conclusion can you draw about the melting points of these substances?

_____

_____

_____

11. **Apply Concepts** When you open a solid room air freshener, the solid slowly loses mass and volume. How do you think this happens?

_____

_____

_____

_____

_____

_____

63

LESSON 3 The Behavior of Gases

12. According to Boyle's law, the volume of a gas increases when its

   a. pressure increases.   b. pressure decreases.

   c. temperature falls.   d. temperature rises.

13. According to Charles's law, when the temperature of a gas is increased at a constant pressure, its volume _____

14. **Relate Cause and Effect** How does heating a gas in a rigid container change its pressure?

   _____

   _____

15. **Interpret Data** Predict what a graph of the data in the table would look like. Volume is plotted on the x-axis. Pressure is plotted on the y-axis.

Volume (cm³)	Pressure (kPa)
15	222
21	159
31	108
50	67

   _____

   _____

   _____

   _____

16. **Relate Cause and Effect** Explain why placing a dented table-tennis ball in boiling water is one way to remove the dent in the ball. (Assume the ball has no holes.)

   _____

   _____

   _____

 APPLY THE BIG **Why does a substance change states?**

17. A fog forms over a lake. What two changes of state must occur to produce the fog? Do the water molecules absorb or release energy during these changes of state? What happens to the motion of the water molecules as a result?

   _____

   _____

   _____

   _____

   _____

   _____

   _____

   _____

   _____

   _____

   _____

   _____

   _____

   _____

Standardized Test Prep

Multiple Choice

Circle the letter of the best answer.

1. The graph below shows changes in 1 g of a solid as energy is added.

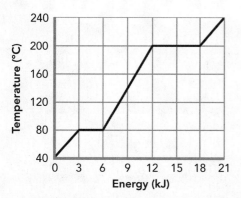

   What is the total amount of energy absorbed by the substance as it completely changes from a solid at 40°C to a gas at 200°C?

A 3 kJ	**B** 6 kJ
C 12 kJ	**D** 18 kJ

2. Which of the following correctly describes a solid?

   A The particles do not move at all.

   B The particles are closely locked in position and can only vibrate in place.

   C The particles are free to move about independently, colliding frequently.

   D The particles are closely packed but have enough energy to slide past one another.

3. A gas exerts a force of 1,000 N on a surface with an area of 5.0 m². What is the pressure on the area?

   A 200 Pa

   B 500 Pa

   C 2,000 Pa

   D 5,000 Pa

4. A gas at constant temperature is in a cylinder with a movable piston. The piston is pushed into the cylinder, decreasing the volume of the gas. The pressure increases. What are the variables in this experiment?

   A temperature and time

   B time and volume

   C volume and pressure

   D pressure and temperature

5. A wet towel is hanging on a clothesline in the sun. The towel dries by the process of

   A boiling.

   B condensation.

   C evaporation.

   D sublimation.

Constructed Response

Use the diagrams to help you answer Question 6. Write your answer on a separate sheet of paper.

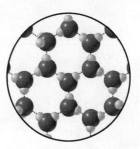
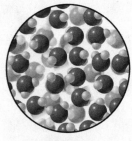

Before   After

6. The diagrams represent the molecules of water before and after a change of state. What change of state has occurred? Explain.

SCUBA DIVING

When you swim to the bottom of a pool, you can feel the pressure of the water around you. That pressure increases rapidly during a deeper dive.

To make really deep dives, people use SCUBA (self-contained underwater breathing apparatus) gear. The SCUBA tank is filled with air at very high pressure. Boyle's law states that as pressure increases under conditions of constant temperature, the volume of the gas decreases. In other words, more air will fit into the tank when the pressure is high.

Breathing air straight from the tank could damage the diver's lungs. The pressure of the air entering the diver's lungs needs to match the pressure of the gases already inside the diver's body. Valves on the tank adjust the pressure of the air as it is released to match the pressure of the water around the diver, so that when it enters the diver's body, it matches the pressure of the gases in the body.

Write About It Make an instruction card for new divers explaining that it is dangerous for divers to hold their breath during a deep dive or ascent. Use Boyle's law to explain why this is true.

◀ The regulator adjusts the pressure to match the surrounding water pressure.

A Shocking State

You touch a plasma globe, and lightning crackles. *Zap!* A plasma globe is a glass globe filled with partially ionized gas (that's the plasma!) and pumped full of high voltage power.

What's the Matter?

Plasma is different! In plasma, the electrons have been separated from the neutral atoms, so that they're no longer bound to an atom or molecule. Because positive and negative charges move independently, plasma can conduct electricity—causing the shocking light displays in a plasma globe. Plasma is its own state of matter. Like a gas, it has no shape or volume until it is captured in a container. Unlike a gas, it can form structures and layers, like the bolts in a plasma globe, or a bolt of lightning. It's shocking!

Find It Research and make a list of plasma objects. Compare your list with a partner, and discuss how plasma changes state to become a gas.

Growing Snow

You may have heard that no two snowflakes look the same. Writers use the unique structures of snowflakes as a metaphor for things that are one-of-a-kind, and impossible to reproduce. And it's probably true! A snowflake forms when water begins to freeze around small particles of dust inside a cloud. The exact shape of the crystal depends on humidity and temperature, and because there are tiny variations in both of these factors, each snowflake will differ slightly from every other snowflake.

All snowflakes share a common shape, though. The hexagonal shape of a snow crystal forms as molecules come together during the phase change from liquid to solid. The oxygen atom has a partial negative charge and the hydrogen atoms a partial positive charge, so the atoms are attracted to one another.

Graphing Research to find out how the exact shape of snow crystals change as temperature and humidity change. Draw a line graph that illustrates your findings.

The most stable arrangement of water molecules occurs when six molecules form a ring.

HOW WOULD YOU SORT OUT THIS MESS?

THE BIG

How is the periodic table organized?

Maybe you know someone with a messy room like this one. Imagine how difficult it would be to find things that you need. For example, what if you had misplaced your homework in this room? Where would you look for it? You might have to search for a long, long time! ⚐Classify **If this were your room, how would you organize the things inside it?**

_____
_____
_____
_____
_____
_____

▶ UNTAMED SCIENCE Watch the **Untamed Science** video to learn more about organizing matter.

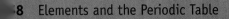

Elements and the Periodic Table

Getting Started

Check Your Understanding

1. **Background** Read the paragraph below and then answer the question.

> Katherine and her family are having a barbecue. They are burning charcoal in the grill to provide heat to cook their food. Charcoal is one form of the **element** carbon. As the charcoal burns, it reacts with oxygen **molecules** in the air. Each oxygen molecule contains two **atoms.**

> An **element** is a pure substance that cannot be broken down into any other substances by chemical or physical means.
>
> A **molecule** is a group of two or more atoms held together by chemical bonds.
>
> An **atom** is the basic particle from which all elements are made.

- How can oxygen be both an element and a molecule?

_____

_____

> MY READING WEB If you had trouble completing the question above, visit **My Reading Web** and type in *Elements and the Periodic Table.*

Vocabulary Skill

Greek Word Origins Many science words in English come from Greek. For example, the word *autograph* comes from the Greek words *auto,* meaning "self," and *graph,* meaning "written." An *autograph* is one's name written in one's own handwriting. Look at the Greek origins and their meanings below.

Greek Origin	Meaning	Key Words
atomos	Cannot be cut, indivisible	Atom, atomic number, atomic mass
di	Two, double	Diatomic molecule

2. **Quick Check** Predict the meaning of *diatomic molecule.*

_____

_____

Ga	Ge	As	Se	Br	Kr
Gallium 69.72	Germanium 72.59	Arsenic 74.922	Selenium 78.96	Bromine 79.904	Krypton 83.80

periodic table

49		52	53	54
In	Sn	Sb	Te	I	Xe
Indium 114.82	Tin 118.69	Antimony 121.75	Tellurium 127.60	Iodine 126.90	Xenon 131.30

| 81 | 82 | 83 | 84 | 85 | 86 |

corrosion

semiconductor

He Ne Ar

noble gas

Chapter Preview

LESSON 1
- atom • electron • nucleus
- proton • energy level
- neutron • atomic number
- isotope • mass number

🔁 **Compare and Contrast**
🔺 **Make Models**

LESSON 2
- atomic mass • periodic table
- chemical symbol • period
- group

🔁 **Relate Text and Visuals**
🔺 **Predict**

LESSON 3
- metal • luster • malleable
- ductile • thermal conductivity
- electrical conductivity • reactivity
- corrosion • alkali metal
- alkaline earth metal
- transition metal

🔁 **Ask Questions**
🔺 **Infer**

LESSON 4
- nonmetal • diatomic molecule
- halogen • noble gas • metalloid
- semiconductor

🔁 **Summarize**
🔺 **Classify**

LESSON 5
- radioactive decay
- nuclear reaction • radioactivity
- alpha particle • beta particle
- gamma ray • half-life
- radioactive dating • tracer

🔁 **Relate Cause and Effect**
🔺 **Calculate**

> VOCAB FLASH CARDS For extra help with vocabulary, visit **Vocab Flash Cards** and type in *Elements and the Periodic Table.*

Introduction to Atoms

🔑 How Did Atomic Theory Develop?

🔑 What Is the Modern Model of the Atom?

my planeт DiaRY

Nanowhiskers

What's more than 16,000 times thinner than a human hair, and, when added to fabric, able to repel spills, stains, and the smell of the sweatiest of socks? It's a nanowhisker!

Nanowhiskers are tiny threads that measure about 10 nanometers (nm) in length and 1.5 nanometers in diameter (1 nm equals 0.000000001 m). They are often made of carbon or silver atoms. Scientists have found a way to bond nanowhiskers to individual threads of cloth. The nanowhiskers are so small and so close together that they form a barrier that prevents substances from ever touching the fabric. Nanowhiskers made from silver can even kill bacteria on your feet and stop socks from smelling!

Communicate Write your answer to each question below. Then discuss your answers with a partner.

1. Why are nanowhiskers used to repel stains on fabrics?

_____

_____

_____

_____

_____

2. What uses for nanowhiskers can you imagine?

_____

_____

> PLANET DIARY Go to **Planet Diary** to learn more about atomic structure.

Lab zone® Do the Inquiry Warm-Up *What's in the Box?*

Vocabulary

- atom • electron • nucleus • proton • energy level
- neutron • atomic number • isotope • mass number

Skills

↻ **Reading: Compare and Contrast**
△ **Inquiry: Make Models**

How Did Atomic Theory Develop?

If you could see a single atom, what would it look like? Studying atoms is difficult because atoms are so small. The smallest visible speck of dust may contain 10 million billion atoms! Scientists have created models to describe atoms because they are so small. Models of the atom have changed many times.

Around 430 B.C., the Greek philosopher Democritus proposed that matter was formed of small pieces that could not be cut into smaller parts. He used the word *atomos,* meaning "uncuttable," for these smallest possible pieces. In modern terms, an **atom** is the smallest particle that still can be considered an element.

The idea of atoms began to develop again in the 1600s. As people did experiments, atomic theory began to take shape. ⟤ **Atomic theory grew as a series of models that developed from experimental evidence. As more evidence was collected, the theory and models were revised.**

Dalton's Atomic Theory Using evidence from many experiments, John Dalton, an English chemist, inferred that atoms had certain characteristics. Dalton thought that atoms were like smooth, hard balls that could not be broken into smaller pieces. The main ideas of Dalton's theory are summarized in **Figure 1.**

FIGURE 1 ·····························

Dalton's Model

Dalton thought that atoms were smooth, hard balls.

🖊 **Predict** Read the summary of Dalton's theory. Based on this theory, would you expect a carbon atom to have the same mass as an oxygen atom? Explain.

_____

_____

_____

_____

Dalton's Atomic Theory

- All elements consist of atoms that cannot be divided.
- All atoms of the same element are exactly alike and have the same mass. Atoms of different elements are different and have different masses.
- An atom of one element cannot be changed into an atom of a different element by a chemical reaction.
- Compounds are formed when atoms of more than one element combine in a specific ratio.

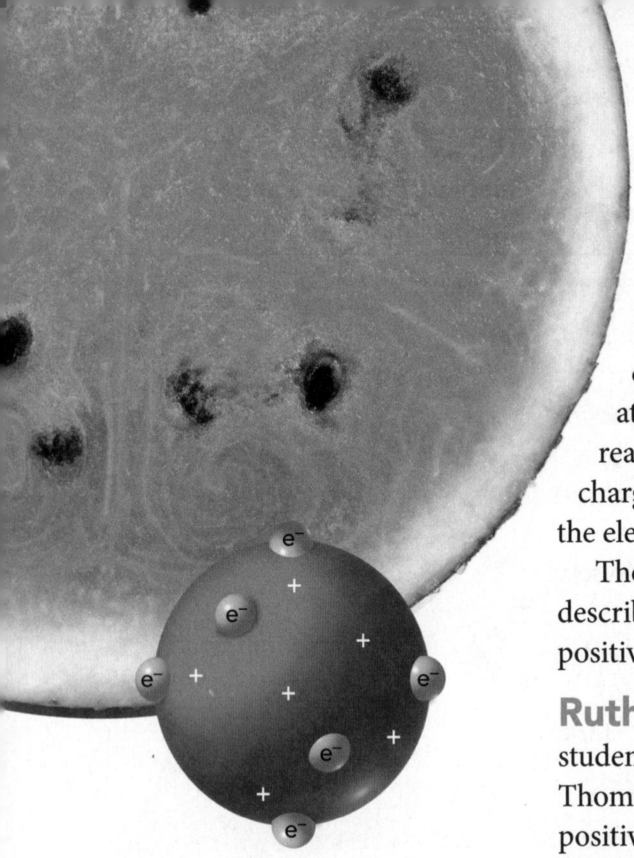

Thomson's Model

Dalton's atomic theory has some similarities to today's models, but there are many differences. One important change is that atoms are now known to be made of even smaller parts. In 1897, J.J. Thomson discovered that atoms contain negatively charged particles called **electrons.** Yet scientists knew that atoms themselves had no electrical charge. So Thomson reasoned that atoms must also contain some sort of positive charge. This positive charge must balance the negative charge of the electrons.

Thomson proposed a model like the one shown in **Figure 2.** He described an atom that had electrons scattered throughout a ball of positive charge—something like seeds in a watermelon.

Rutherford's Model

In 1911, one of Thomson's former students, Ernest Rutherford, found evidence that challenged Thomson's model. Rutherford's research team aimed a beam of positively charged particles at a thin sheet of gold foil. A diagram of the experiment is shown in **Figure 3.** Rutherford and his team predicted that, if Thomson's model were correct, the charged particles would pass straight through the foil. They also predicted that the paths of some particles would bend, or deflect, slightly. The particles would be only slightly deflected because the positive charge was thought to be spread out in the gold atoms.

Rutherford observed that most of the particles passed straight through the foil with little or no deflection. But to everyone's surprise, a few particles were deflected by the gold foil at very large angles. Based on the results of his experiment, Rutherford suggested that the atom is mostly empty space but has a positive charge at its center.

FIGURE 2 ·············
Thomson's Model
Thomson suggested that atoms had negatively charged electrons set in a positive sphere. Each electron is represented above by the symbol e⁻.

FIGURE 3 ·····························
Rutherford's Gold Foil Experiment
Rutherford was surprised that a few particles were deflected strongly. ✎ **Interpret Diagrams** Place a check (✔) to show the paths of the particles that were not predicted by Thomson's atomic model.

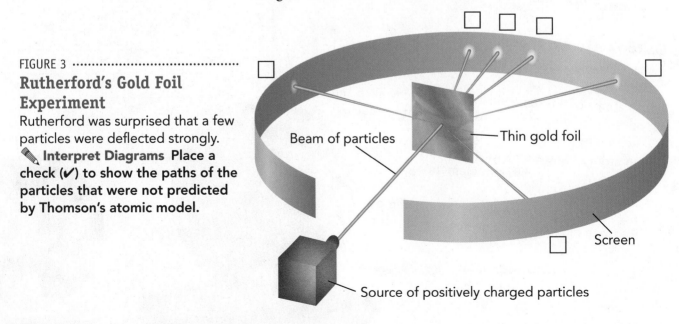

Beam of particles

Thin gold foil

Screen

Source of positively charged particles

Like charges repel each other. So Rutherford inferred that an atom's positive charge must be packed within a small region in its center, called the **nucleus** (NOO klee us). (The plural of *nucleus* is *nuclei*.) Any particle that was deflected strongly had been repelled by a gold atom's nucleus. Rutherford's new model of the atom, which is shown in **Figure 4,** is like a cherry. The pit models the nucleus of the atom. The rest of the fruit is the space taken up by the electrons. Later research suggested that the nucleus was made up of one or more positively charged particles. Rutherford called the positively charged particles in an atom's nucleus **protons.**

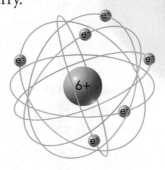

FIGURE 4 ·······························
Rutherford's Model
According to Rutherford's model, an atom was mostly open space. The "6+" in the model means that there are six protons in the nucleus.

Use the diagrams below to compare the expected and observed results of Rutherford's gold foil experiment. Part **a** shows the expected paths of the charged particles through the atoms of the gold foil. In part **b**, draw the observed paths of the charged particles. Show at least one particle that is deflected strongly.

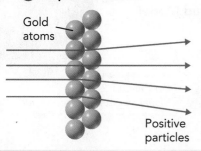

a Expected result

Gold atoms

Positive particles

b Observed result

Nucleus of gold atom

Bohr's Model One of Rutherford's students was Niels Bohr, a Danish scientist. In 1913, Bohr revised the atomic model again. Bohr suggested that electrons are found only in specific orbits around the nucleus. The orbits in Bohr's model look like planets orbiting the sun or the rings of a tree, as shown in **Figure 5.** Each possible electron orbit in Bohr's model has a fixed energy.

FIGURE 5 ·······························
Bohr's Model
Niels Bohr suggested that electrons move in specific orbits around the nucleus of an atom.

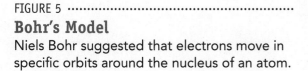

Cloud Model In the 1920s, the atomic model changed again. Scientists determined that electrons do not orbit the nucleus like planets, as Bohr suggested. Instead, electrons move rapidly within a cloudlike region around the nucleus. Look at **Figure 6.** The orange "cloud" is a visual model. It represents where electrons are likely to be found. An electron's movement is related to its **energy level,** or the specific amount of energy it has. Electrons at different energy levels are likely to be found in different places.

6+

6e⁻

FIGURE 6 ···
Cloud Model
Electrons move rapidly in different directions around the nucleus.

apply it!

Scientists have used models to help them understand atoms. You can too!

1 **Make Models** Match each object with the atomic model the object most closely represents.

2 CHALLENGE An object is missing for one of the atomic models listed. In the space provided, draw an object that represents this model.

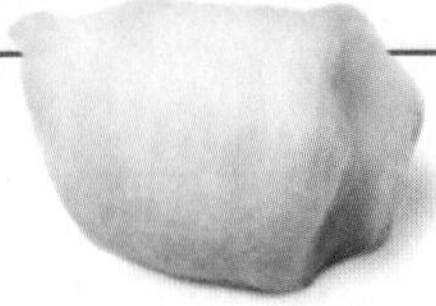

Dalton's Model

Thomson's Model

Bohr's Model

Cloud Model

Lab zone® Do the Quick Lab
Visualizing an Electron Cloud.

Assess Your Understanding

1a. Define An atom is _____
_____.

b. Describe Bohr's model of the atom consisted of a central _____ surrounded by electrons moving in specific _____.

c. Compare and Contrast How is the cloud model of the atom different from Bohr's model?
_____
_____
_____
_____
_____

got it? ···

○ **I get it!** Now I know that atomic theory changed with time because _____
_____

○ **I need extra help with** _____

Go to MY SCIENCE ⑤ COACH online for help with this subject.

What Is the Modern Model of the Atom?

In 1932, English scientist James Chadwick showed that another particle exists in the nucleus of atoms. This particle, called a **neutron,** was hard to find because it has no electric charge.

Scientists have learned more about the atom since then. One modern model of the atom is shown in **Figure 7.** 🔑 **At the center of the atom is a tiny, dense nucleus containing protons and neutrons. Surrounding the nucleus is a cloudlike region of moving electrons.**

Most of an atom's volume is the space in which the electrons move. This space is huge compared to the space taken up by the nucleus. Imagine holding a pencil while standing in the middle of a stadium. If the nucleus were the size of the pencil's eraser, the electrons would reach as far away as the top row of seats!

New research supports the modern model of the atom. However, scientists still don't know the details of the smallest scales of matter. Who will develop the next model of the atom? Maybe it will be you!

FIGURE 7 ·······················

Modern Model of an Atom

A carbon atom has a nucleus made up of positively charged protons and neutral neutrons. The nucleus is surrounded by a cloud of negatively charged electrons.

✏️ **Identify How many protons are in the carbon atom?**

_____

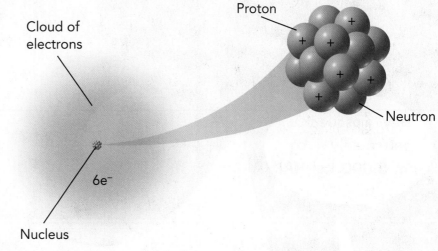

Cloud of electrons

Proton

Neutron

6e⁻

Nucleus

Particle Charges In **Figure 7,** protons are shown by a plus sign (+). Electrons are shown by the symbol e⁻. According to the scale used for measuring charge in atoms, protons have a charge of +1. Electrons have exactly the opposite charge. So electrons have a charge of −1. If you count the number of protons in **Figure 7,** you'll see there are six. The number of protons equals the number of electrons. As a result, the positive charge from the protons equals the negative charge from the electrons. The charges balance, making the atom neutral. Neutrons don't affect the charge of an atom because they have a charge of zero.

·············· ✏️ ··············

🔄 **Compare and Contrast**

A proton has a charge of _____.

An electron has a charge

of _____.

A neutron has a charge

of _____.

Comparing Particle Masses Although electrons may balance protons charge for charge, they can't compare when it comes to mass. It takes almost 1,840 electrons to equal the mass of one proton. A proton and a neutron are about equal in mass. Together, the protons and neutrons make up almost all the mass of an atom.

Figure 8 compares the charges and masses of the three atomic particles. Atoms are too small to be described by everyday units of mass, such as grams or kilograms. Sometimes scientists use units known as atomic mass units (amu). A proton or a neutron has a mass equal to about one amu.

Atomic Number Every atom of an element has the same number of protons. For example, every carbon atom has 6 protons and every iron atom has 26 protons. The number of protons in the nucleus of an atom is the **atomic number** of that atom's element. The definition of an element is based on its atomic number. Carbon's atomic number is 6 and iron's is 26.

Hey, pipsqueak... You're only 4 kg. I'm 8,000 kg! HA!

Relative to an elephant, I'm about the same mass as an electron is relative to a proton. Meow!

FIGURE 8 ⋯⋯⋯⋯⋯⋯⋯⋯⋯⋯⋯⋯⋯
> **INTERACTIVE ART** **Particles in an Atom**
An atom is made up of protons, neutrons, and electrons.
✎ **Review** Complete the table by filling in the correct charge for each atomic particle.

Particles in an Atom				
Particle	Symbol	Charge	Mass (amu)	Model
Proton	p^+	_____	1	🔵
Neutron	n	_____	1	🔵
Electron	e^-	_____	$\frac{1}{1,840}$	🔵

Isotopes All atoms of an element have the same number of protons. The number of neutrons can vary. Atoms with the same number of protons and different numbers of neutrons are called **isotopes** (EYE suh tohps). **Figure 9** shows three isotopes of carbon.

An isotope is identified by its **mass number,** which is the sum of the protons and neutrons in the atom. The most common isotope of carbon has a mass number of 12 (6 protons + 6 neutrons) and may be written as "carbon-12." About 99 percent of naturally occurring carbon is carbon-12. Two other isotopes are carbon-13 and carbon-14. Despite their different mass numbers, all three carbon isotopes react the same way chemically.

FIGURE 9 ·····················
Isotopes of Carbon
All isotopes of carbon contain 6 protons. They differ in the number of neutrons.
✎ **Relate Text and Visuals** Fill in the missing information for each isotope below.

6e⁻   6e⁻   6e⁻

Carbon-12   **Carbon-13**   **Carbon-** ☐
☐ Protons   6 Protons   6 Protons
6 Neutrons   ☐ Neutrons   8 Neutrons

Lab zone® Do the Quick Lab
How Far Away Is the Electron?

🔑 Assess Your Understanding

2a. Explain What is atomic number? How is atomic number used to distinguish one element from another?

_____
_____
_____
_____

b. Apply Concepts The atomic number of nitrogen is 7. How many protons, neutrons, and electrons make up an atom of nitrogen-15?

_____
_____
_____
_____

got it? ···

○ **I get it!** Now I know that the modern model of the atom can be described as_____
_____
_____

○ **I need extra help with** _____

Go to **MY SCIENCE** 🗨 **COACH** online for help with this subject.

Organizing the Elements

UNLOCK THE BIG ?

🔑 **What Did Mendeleev Discover?**

🔑 **What Information Does the Periodic Table Contain?**

🔑 **How Is the Periodic Table Useful?**

my PLANET DiARY   VOICES FROM HISTORY

Dmitri Mendeleev

The Russian chemist Dmitri Mendeleev (men duh LAY ef) is given credit for creating the first version of the periodic table in 1869. By arranging the elements according to their atomic masses, he predicted that new elements would be discovered:

> We must expect the discovery of many yet unknown elements—for example, elements analogous [similar] to aluminum and silicon—whose atomic weight [mass] would be between 65 and 75.

Within 17 years, chemists had discovered these missing elements.

Lab zone® Do the Inquiry Warm-Up *Which Is Easier?*

Communicate Discuss these questions with a group of classmates. Write your answers below.

1. What did Mendeleev predict?

_____

_____

_____

2. Make a prediction based on an observation or a pattern you recognize.

_____

_____

_____

> **PLANET DIARY** Go to **Planet Diary** to learn more about the periodic table.

What Did Mendeleev Discover?

By 1869, a total of 63 elements had been discovered. A few were gases. Two were liquids. Most were solid metals. Some reacted explosively as they formed compounds. Others reacted slowly. Scientists wondered if the properties of elements followed a pattern. Dmitri Mendeleev discovered a set of patterns that applied to all the elements.

Vocabulary

- atomic mass
- chemical symbol
- group
- periodic table
- period

Skills

- Reading: Relate Text and Visuals
- Inquiry: Predict

Mendeleev's Work Mendeleev knew that some elements had similar chemical and physical properties. For example, silver and copper are both shiny metals. Mendeleev thought these similarities were important clues to a hidden pattern.

To find that pattern, Mendeleev wrote each element's melting point, density, and color on an individual card. He also included the element's atomic mass. The **atomic mass** of an element is the average mass of all the isotopes of that element. Mendeleev tried arranging the cards in different ways.

🔑 **Mendeleev noticed that a pattern of properties appeared when he arranged the elements in order of increasing atomic mass. He found that the properties repeated regularly.** For example, lithium, sodium, and potassium showed several common properties. As you can see from **Figure 1,** these elements react with water in a similar way. (The letters *amu* mean "atomic mass units.") Mendeleev lined up the cards for these elements to form their own group. He did the same with other elements that shared similar properties.

FIGURE 1 ·····························

Metals That React With Water

Lithium, sodium, and potassium all react with water.

✏️ **Observe** Write down your observations of each reaction.

Lithium
Atomic mass = 7 amu

Sodium
Atomic mass = 23 amu

Potassium
Atomic mass = 39 amu

.... ✎ ....

🔵 **Relate Text and Visuals**

Using **Figure 2,** predict an element that would react with water as lithium (Li), sodium (Na), and potassium (K) did. Explain.

_____

_____

_____

_____

_____

The Periodic Table Mendeleev created the first periodic table in 1869. A **periodic table** is an arrangement of elements showing the repeating pattern of their properties. (The word *periodic* means "in a regular, repeated pattern.") The periodic table shown in **Figure 2** was an improved version published in 1871.

As scientists discovered new elements and learned more about atomic structure, the periodic table changed. It is now known that the number of protons in the nucleus, given by the atomic number, determines the chemical properties of an element. Modern periodic tables are arranged in order of increasing atomic number.

Group I	Group II	Group III	Group IV	Group V	Group VI	Group VII	Group VIII
H = 1							
Li = 7	Be = 9.4	B = 11	C = 12	N = 14	O = 16	F = 19	
Na = 23 K = 39	Mg = 24 Ca = 40	Al = 27.3 — = 44	Si = 28 Ti = 48	P = 31 V = 51	S = 32 Cr = 52	Cl = 35.5 Mn = 55	Fe = 56, Co = 59, Ni = 59, Cu = 63.
(Cu = 63) Rb = 85	Zn = 65 Sr = 87	— = 68 Yt = 88	— = 72 Zr = 90	As = 75 Nb = 94	Se = 78 Mo = 96	Br = 80 — = 100	Ru = 104, Rh = 104, Pd = 106, Ag = 108.
(Ag = 108) Cs = 133	Cd = 112 Ba = 137	In = 113 Di = 138	Sn = 118 Ce = 140	Sb = 122 —	Te = 125 —	I = 127 —	
(—) —	—	Er = 178	La = 180	Ta = 182 —	W = 184	—	Os = 195, Ir = 197, Pt = 198, Au = 199.
(Au = 199)	Hg = 200 —	Tl = 204 —	Pb = 207 Th = 231	Bi = 208 —	— U = 240	—	— — — —

FIGURE 2 ....
Mendeleev's Periodic Table
In his periodic table, Mendeleev left blank spaces. He predicted that the blank spaces would be filled by elements that had not yet been discovered. He even correctly predicted the properties of those new elements.

Do the Quick Lab
Classifying.

🔑 **Assess Your Understanding**

1a. Review In what order did Mendeleev arrange the elements in his periodic table?

_____

_____

b. Predict How could Mendeleev predict the properties of elements that had not yet been discovered?

_____

_____

_____

got it? ....

○ **I get it!** Now I know that when Mendeleev arranged the elements in order of increasing atomic mass, _____

_____

_____

○ **I need extra help with** _____

Go to **MY SCIENCE** 🔵 **COACH** *online for help with this subject.*

What Information Does the Periodic Table Contain?

The periodic table contains information about each of the known elements. 🔑 **In this book, the periodic table includes the atomic number, chemical symbol, name, and atomic mass for each element.** The information that the periodic table lists about potassium is shown below in **Figure 3.**

❶ Atomic Number The first piece of information is the number 19, the atomic number of potassium. Every potassium atom has 19 protons in its nucleus.

❷ Chemical Symbol Just below the atomic number is the letter K—the **chemical symbol** for potassium. Chemical symbols contain either one or two letters. Often, an element's symbol is an abbreviation of the element's name in English. Other elements have symbols that are abbreviations of their Latin names.

❸ Atomic Mass The last piece of information is the average atomic mass. For potassium, this value is 39.098 amu (atomic mass units). The atomic mass is an average because most elements consist of a mixture of isotopes.

The modern periodic table is shown in **Figure 4** on the next two pages. Can you find potassium?

FIGURE 3 ·····························
Potassium
Potassium has an atomic number of 19 and an atomic mass of 39.098 amu. Bananas are rich in potassium.

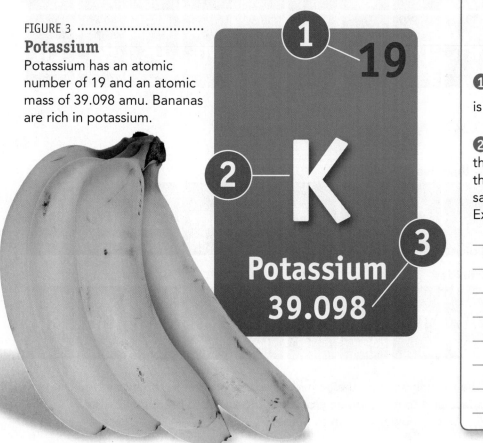

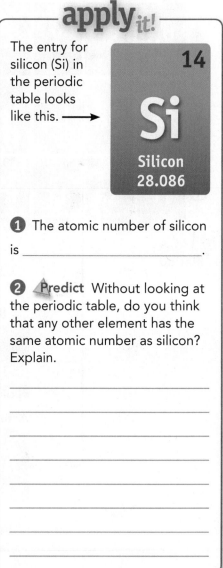

apply it!

The entry for silicon (Si) in the periodic table looks like this. ⟶

14
Si
Silicon
28.086

❶ The atomic number of silicon is _____.

❷ ⚠ **Predict** Without looking at the periodic table, do you think that any other element has the same atomic number as silicon? Explain.

_____
_____
_____
_____
_____
_____
_____
_____
_____

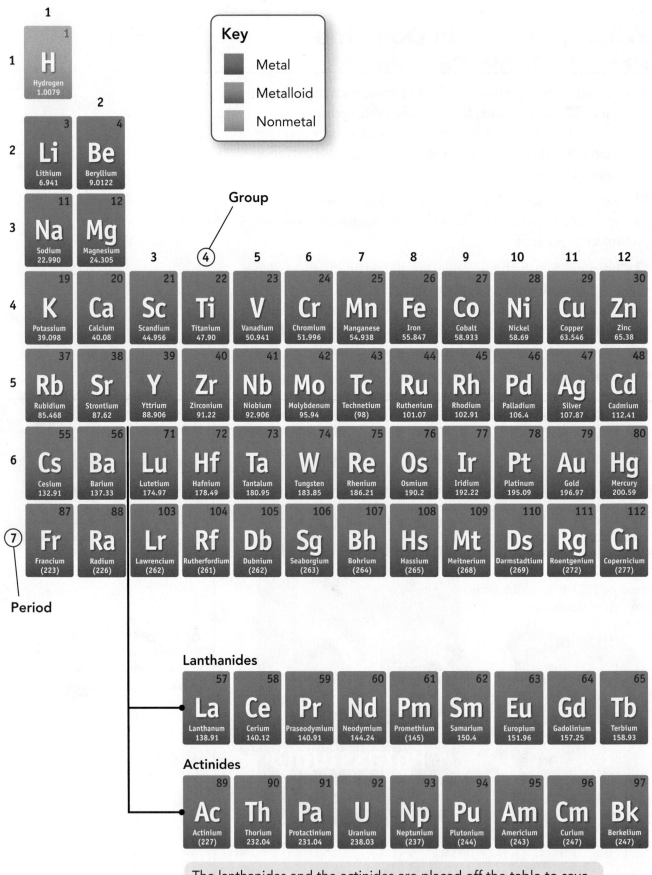

The lanthanides and the actinides are placed off the table to save space and to make the rest of the table easier to read. Follow the line to see how they fit in the table.

Many periodic tables include a zigzag line that separates the metals from the nonmetals. Metalloids, found on either side of the line, share properties of both metals and nonmetals.

18
2 **He** Helium 4.0026

13	14	15	16	17
5 **B** Boron 10.81	6 **C** Carbon 12.011	7 **N** Nitrogen 14.007	8 **O** Oxygen 15.999	9 **F** Fluorine 18.998
13 **Al** Aluminum 26.982	14 **Si** Silicon 28.086	15 **P** Phosphorus 30.974	16 **S** Sulfur 32.06	17 **Cl** Chlorine 35.453

31 **Ga** Gallium 69.72	32 **Ge** Germanium 72.59	33 **As** Arsenic 74.922	34 **Se** Selenium 78.96	35 **Br** Bromine 79.904	36 **Kr** Krypton 83.80
49 **In** Indium 114.82	50 **Sn** Tin 118.69	51 **Sb** Antimony 121.75	52 **Te** Tellurium 127.60	53 **I** Iodine 126.90	54 **Xe** Xenon 131.30
81 **Tl** Thallium 204.37	82 **Pb** Lead 207.2	83 **Bi** Bismuth 208.98	84 **Po** Polonium (209)	85 **At** Astatine (210)	86 **Rn** Radon (222)
113 ***Uut** Ununtrium (284)	114 ***Uuq** Ununquadium (289)	115 ***Uup** Ununpentium (288)	116 ***Uuh** Ununhexium (292)	117 ***Uus** Ununseptium (292)	118 ***Uuo** Ununoctium (294)

18 (above Ne): 10 **Ne** Neon 20.179
18 (above Ar): 18 **Ar** Argon 39.948

*The discoveries of elements 113 and above have not yet been officially confirmed. Atomic masses in parentheses are those of the most stable isotopes.

66 **Dy** Dysprosium 162.50	67 **Ho** Holmium 164.93	68 **Er** Erbium 167.26	69 **Tm** Thulium 168.93	70 **Yb** Ytterbium 173.04
98 **Cf** Californium (251)	99 **Es** Einsteinium (252)	100 **Fm** Fermium (257)	101 **Md** Mendelevium (258)	102 **No** Nobelium (259)

FIGURE 4 ....

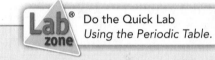 **INTERACTIVE ART** The Periodic Table

The periodic table is one of the most valuable tools to a chemist. ✎ **Interpret Tables** Find the element identified by the atomic number 25 on the periodic table. Use the information to fill in the blanks below.

Name of element: _____

Chemical symbol: _____

Atomic mass: _____

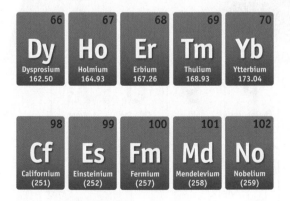 Do the Quick Lab Using the Periodic Table.

🔑 Assess Your Understanding

2a. Compare and Contrast Describe two differences between Mendeleev's periodic table and the modern periodic table.

_____
_____
_____
_____
_____
_____

b. Interpret Tables An atom of which element has 47 protons in its nucleus?

_____

got it? ....

O **I get it!** Now I know that information found in the periodic table for each element includes _____
_____
_____

O **I need extra help with** _____

Go to **MY SCIENCE COACH** online for help with this subject.

85

How Is the Periodic Table Useful?

Look at the periodic table on the previous two pages. Notice that the atomic numbers increase from left to right. Also notice that each color-coded region corresponds to a different class of elements—metals, nonmetals, and metalloids.

As you look across a row, the elements' properties change in a predictable way. 🔑 **An element's properties can be predicted from its location in the periodic table.** This predictability is the reason that the periodic table is so useful to chemists.

Periods The periodic table is arranged in rows called **periods.** A period contains a series of different elements. From left to right, the properties of the elements change in a pattern. Metals are shown on the left of the table and nonmetals are located on the right. Metalloids are found between the metals and nonmetals. This pattern is repeated in each period. **Figure 5** shows the elements of Period 3.

FIGURE 5 ···

Elements of Period 3

The properties of the Period 3 elements change as you move across the period.

✏️ **Classify** Use three different colors to fill in the key below. Then color in each element in Period 3 according to your key.

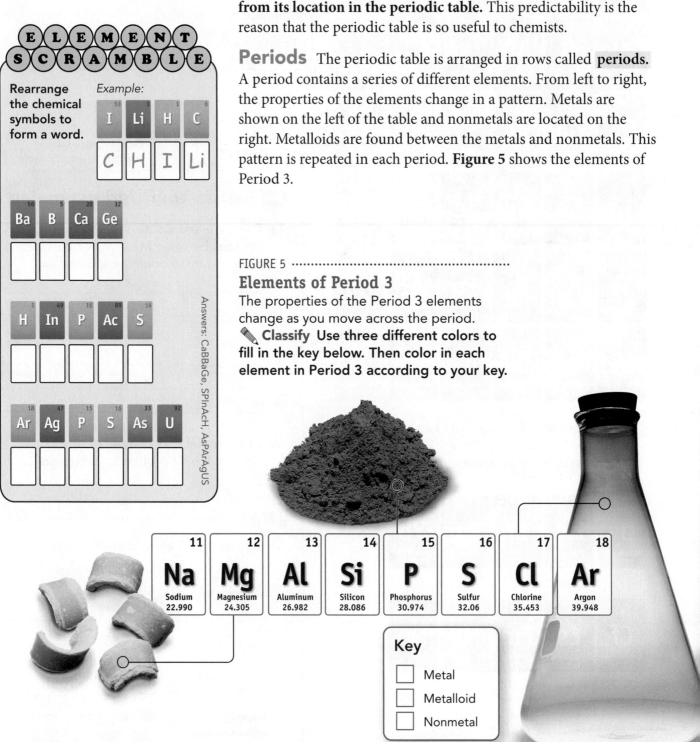

11	12	13	14	15	16	17	18
Na	**Mg**	**Al**	**Si**	**P**	**S**	**Cl**	**Ar**
Sodium	Magnesium	Aluminum	Silicon	Phosphorus	Sulfur	Chlorine	Argon
22.990	24.305	26.982	28.086	30.974	32.06	35.453	39.948

Key
☐ Metal
☐ Metalloid
☐ Nonmetal

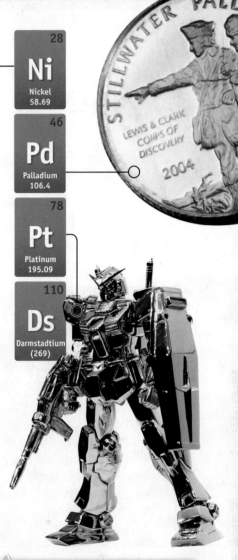

Groups

The modern periodic table has 7 periods, which form 18 columns. The elements in a column form a **group.** Groups are also known as families. The groups are numbered from Group 1 on the left of the table to Group 18 on the right.

The pattern of properties repeats in each period, so the elements in each group have similar characteristics. For example, except for hydrogen, the elements in Group 1 are all metals that react violently with water. Group 17 elements are very reactive, but Group 18 elements are generally nonreactive. The elements of Group 10 are shown in **Figure 6.**

FIGURE 6 ·····················

Elements of Group 10

The elements of Group 10 include nickel (Ni), palladium (Pd), platinum (Pt), and darmstadtium (Ds). Darmstadtium is not found in nature, but scientists believe it exhibits properties similar to the other Group 10 metals.

✎ CHALLENGE Look at the photos of nickel, palladium, and platinum. What properties would you predict for darmstadtium?

_____

_____

Lab zone® Do the Quick Lab
Expanding the Periodic Table.

🔑 Assess Your Understanding

3a. Name The rows in the periodic table are called _____. The columns in the periodic table are called _____.

b. Describe What do elements in the same group in the periodic table have in common?

_____

_____

c. Predict Use the periodic table to name two elements that you would expect to have properties very much like those of calcium (Ca).

_____

_____

_____

_____

got it? ···

○ **I get it!** Now I know that the periodic table is useful because _____

_____

○ **I need extra help with** _____

Go to **my science** ⁵ **coach** *online for help with this subject.*

UNLOCK THE BIG

🔑 **What Are the Properties of Metals?**

🔑 **How Are Metals Classified?**

my planet diary

Recycling Metals

You can find metals in many items that you use every day, including cell phones, computers, appliances, and money. In 2006, the supply of metal in the United States was more than 150 million metric tons. (One metric ton equals 1,000 kilograms.) Many of these metals can be recycled. Recycling helps conserve energy and reduces the amount of waste in landfills.

Metal	Percent of U.S. Supply That Came From Recycling
Aluminum	43
Copper	32.3
Iron and steel	48
Nickel	43
Zinc	24.5

SCIENCE STATS

Communicate Answer the question below. Then discuss your answer with a partner.

Beverage cans contain mostly aluminum. Estimate the percent of beverage cans that you recycle. What other objects that contain metal do you think can be recycled?

_____

_____

_____

_____

_____

▶ PLANET DIARY Go to **Planet Diary** to learn more about recycling.

Lab® zone Do the Inquiry Warm-Up *Why Use Aluminum?*

Vocabulary

- metal • luster • malleable • ductile • thermal conductivity
- electrical conductivity • reactivity • corrosion • alkali metal
- alkaline earth metal • transition metal

Skills

↻ Reading: Ask Questions

△ Inquiry: Infer

What Are the Properties of Metals?

It's hard to imagine modern life without metals. The cars and buses you ride in are made of steel, which is mostly iron (Fe). Airplanes are covered in aluminum (Al). Copper (Cu) wires carry electric current to lamps, stereos, and computers. Can you identify the objects that contain metals in **Figure 1** below?

Elements can be classified by their properties, including melting temperature, density, hardness, and thermal and electrical conductivity. **Metals** are elements that are good conductors of electric current and heat. They also tend to be shiny and bendable—like copper wire, for instance. The majority of elements in the periodic table are metals. The metals begin on the left side and extend across the periodic table.

FIGURE 1 ....

Metals

Many of the objects around you contain metals.

✎ **Communicate** Circle the objects that will set off the metal detector. Then, with a partner, look around your classroom and make a list of the objects you see that contain metals.

_____

_____

_____

> This stone, called magnetite, is made out of a compound of iron.
>
> _____
> _____

> Gold can be pounded into coins.
>
> _____
> _____

> Copper is often used for electrical wires.
>
> _____
> _____

FIGURE 2 ··

Physical Properties of Metals

Metals have certain physical properties.

✎ **Interpret Photos** After reading about the physical properties of metals below, identify the property or properties of metals exhibited by each of the objects above.

did you know?··········

Don't judge a coin by its coating! The U.S. penny, made of copper-plated zinc, is just 2.5 percent copper by mass. The U.S. nickel is actually 75 percent copper, and the dime and quarter contain about 92 percent copper.

Physical Properties **Figure 2** shows some common metal objects. ⌨ **The physical properties of metals include luster, malleability, ductility, and conductivity.** A material that has a high **luster** is shiny and reflective. A **malleable** (MAL ee uh bul) material is one that can be hammered or rolled into flat sheets or other shapes. A **ductile** material is one that can be pulled out, or drawn, into long wires. Copper is both malleable and ductile. It can be made into thin sheets or drawn into wires.

Thermal conductivity is the ability of an object to transfer heat. The ability of an object to carry electric current is called **electrical conductivity.** Most metals are good thermal conductors and electrical conductors. Metals also generally have low specific heats. Recall that specific heat is the amount of energy required to raise the temperature of 1 gram of a material by 1 kelvin. This means that only a small amount of thermal energy is required to raise the temperature of a metal.

Some metals are magnetic. Iron, cobalt (Co), and nickel (Ni) are attracted to magnets and can be made into magnets. Most metals are solids at room temperature. Only mercury (Hg) is a liquid at room temperature.

90 Elements and the Periodic Table

Chemical Properties The ease and speed with which an element combines, or reacts, with other substances is called its **reactivity.** Metals usually react by losing electrons to other atoms. Some metals are very reactive. For example, sodium (Na) reacts strongly with water. By comparison, gold (Au) and platinum (Pt) do not react easily with other substances.

The reactivities of other metals fall somewhere between those of sodium and gold. Iron, for example, reacts slowly with oxygen in the air, forming iron oxide, or rust. The iron chain in **Figure 3** is coated with reddish brown rust. The deterioration of a metal due to a chemical reaction in the environment is called **corrosion.**

The forks shown are made of silver (Ag).

❶ Some of the silver forks shown have lost their luster—they have become tarnished. This is an example of _____.

❷ **Infer** What properties of gold and platinum make these metals desirable for jewelry?

_____

_____

_____

FIGURE 3 ·························
Reactivity of Metals
This iron chain is coated with rust after being exposed to air and water.

Do the Lab Investigation *Copper or Carbon? That Is the Question.*

🔑 Assess Your Understanding

1a. Explain What does the term *thermal conductivity* mean?

_____

_____

_____

_____

b. Infer What property of metals led to the use of plastic or wooden handles on many metal cooking utensils? Explain.

_____

_____

_____

_____

got it? ··

○ **I get it!** Now I know that the physical properties of metals include _____

_____

○ **I need extra help with** _____

Go to MY SCIENCE COACH online for help with this subject.

How Are Metals Classified?

The metals in a group have similar properties. Properties within a group change gradually as you look across the periodic table. For example, the reactivity of metals tends to decrease from left to right across the table. 🔑 **In the periodic table, metals are classified as alkali metals, alkaline earth metals, transition metals, metals in mixed groups, lanthanides, and actinides.**

Alkali Metals The metals of Group 1, from lithium (Li) to francium (Fr), are called the **alkali metals.** These metals are the most reactive metals in the periodic table. Alkali metals are so reactive that they are never found as uncombined elements in nature. They are found only in compounds. Compounds that contain potassium (K) are used in fireworks, such as those shown in **Figure 4.**

✏️ Shade in the alkali metals on the periodic table.

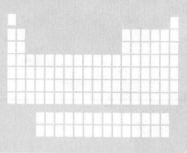

In the laboratory, chemists can isolate alkali metals from their compounds. As pure, uncombined elements, some of the alkali metals are shiny and so soft you can cut them with a plastic knife. These elements have low densities and melting points. For example, sodium melts at 98°C and has a density of 0.97 g/cm^3—less than water.

Alkaline Earth Metals

The metals of Group 2 are called the **alkaline earth metals.** These metals are harder and denser, and melt at higher temperatures than the alkali metals. For example, magnesium (Mg) is a hard metal that melts at 648.8°C.

✏️ Shade in the alkaline earth metals on the periodic table.

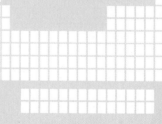

Alkaline earth metals are very reactive, though not as reactive as the alkali metals. These metals are also never found uncombined in nature. Calcium (Ca) is one of the most common alkaline earth metals. Calcium compounds are essential for bone health. **Figure 5** shows an X-ray of healthy bones.

FIGURE 4 ·····
Fireworks
Compounds containing potassium are used in fireworks.

FIGURE 5 ·····
X-Ray of Healthy Bones
Calcium compounds are an essential part of teeth and bones.

20
Ca
Calcium
40.08

do the math! Analyzing Data

Melting Points in a Group of Elements

Properties of elements in a single group in the periodic table often change according to a certain pattern. The graph shows the melting points of the Group 1 elements, or the alkali metals.

1 Read Graphs The melting points of the alkali metals (increase/decrease) from lithium to francium.

2 Interpret Data Which of the alkali metals are liquids at 50°C?

3 CHALLENGE If element 119 were discovered, it would fall below francium in Group 1. Predict the approximate melting point of element 119.

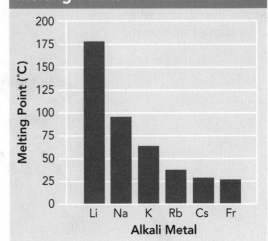

Melting Points of Alkali Metals

Transition Metals
The elements in Groups 3 through 12 are called the **transition metals.** The transition metals include iron, copper, nickel, gold, and silver. Most of these metals are hard and shiny solids. However, mercury is a liquid at room temperature. Except for mercury, the transition metals often have high melting points and high densities. They are also good conductors of heat and electric current, and are very malleable. As shown in **Figure 6**, gold is sometimes used to coat an astronaut's visor.

The transition metals are less reactive than the metals in Groups 1 and 2. When iron reacts with air, forming rust, it sometimes takes many years to react completely.

Shade in the transition metals on the periodic table.

79
Au
Gold
196.97

FIGURE 6
Astronaut Visor
The gold film in an astronaut's visor protects the eyes and face from the sun without interfering with vision.

FIGURE 7
Aluminum Bicycle Frame
Bicycle frames and wheel rims often contain aluminum.

Shade in the metals in mixed groups on the periodic table.

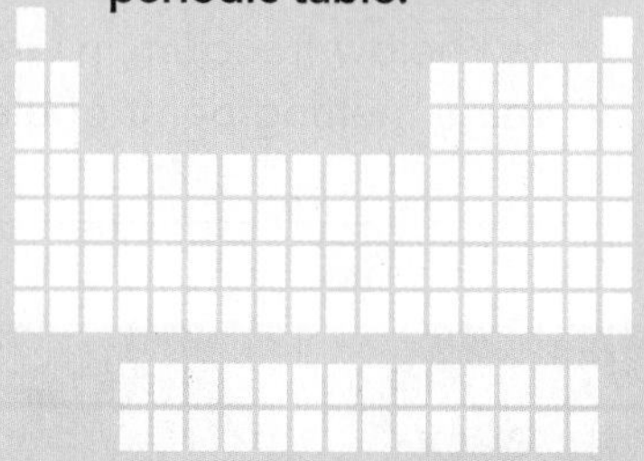

13
Al
Aluminum
26.982

Metals in Mixed Groups

Bicycle frames, such as the one in **Figure 7**, often contain aluminum because it is durable but light. Aluminum is in Group 13 of the periodic table. Only some of the elements in Groups 13 through 16 are metals. Other metals in these groups that you may be familiar with are tin (Sn) and lead (Pb). A thin coating of tin protects steel from corrosion in some cans of food. Lead was once used in paints and water pipes. Lead is no longer used for these purposes because it was found to be poisonous. Now its most common use is in automobile batteries.

Shade in the lanthanides and actinides on the periodic table.

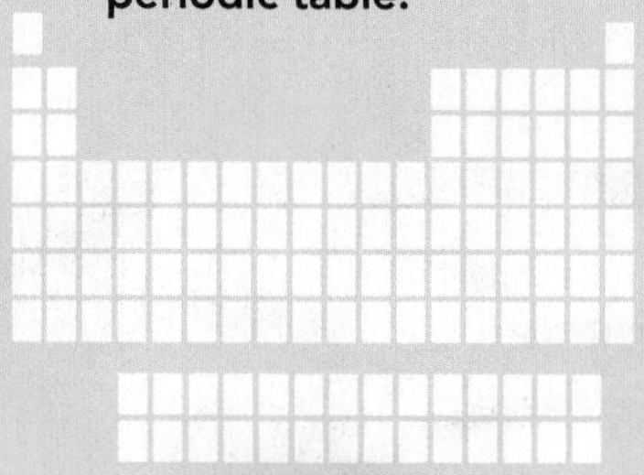

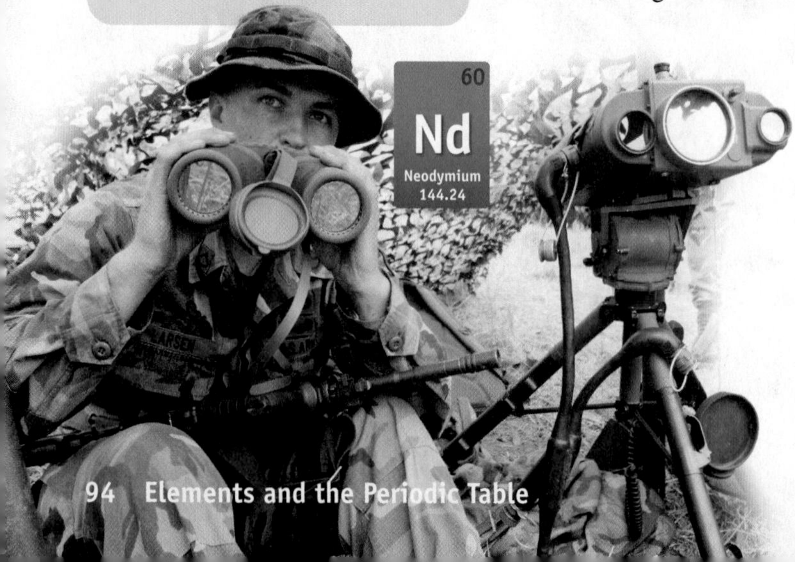

Lanthanides and Actinides
Two rows of elements are placed below the main part of the periodic table. The elements in the top row are the lanthanides (LAN thuh nydz). Compounds containing neodymium (Nd), a lanthanide, are used to make laser light. These lasers are used for surgery, for cutting metals, and in laser range finders, such as the one shown in **Figure 8.**

The elements below the lanthanides are called actinides (AK tuh nydz). Many of these elements are not found in nature but are made artificially in laboratories.

60
Nd
Neodymium
144.24

FIGURE 8
Laser Range Finder
A compound containing neodymium is used to produce the laser light in a range finder. The range finder uses a laser beam to determine the distance to an object.

Transuranium Elements Elements that follow uranium (U) in the periodic table are transuranium elements. These elements are made, or synthesized, when nuclear particles are forced to crash into one another. They are sometimes called synthetic elements. For example, plutonium (Pu) is synthesized by bombarding nuclei of uranium-238 with neutrons in a nuclear reactor.

To make elements with atomic numbers above 95, scientists use devices called particle accelerators that move atomic nuclei at extremely high speeds. If these nuclei crash into the nuclei of other elements with enough energy, the particles can combine into a single nucleus. An example of a particle accelerator is shown in **Figure 9.**

In general, the difficulty of synthesizing new elements increases with atomic number. So new elements have been synthesized only as more powerful particle accelerators have been built. Elements in the periodic table with atomic numbers greater than 111 do not yet have permanent names or symbols. In the future, scientists around the world will agree on permanent names and symbols for these elements.

✎ **Ask Questions** Before reading about transuranium elements, ask a *What* or *How* question. As you read, write the answer to your question.

_____

_____

_____

_____

_____

_____

FIGURE 9 ....
Particle Accelerator
The heaviest synthetic elements are synthesized using particle accelerators.

Lab zone® Do the Quick Lab *Finding Metals.*

🔑 Assess Your Understanding

2a. Identify Which family of elements in the periodic table contains the most reactive metals?

_____

b. Infer Period 4 of the periodic table contains the elements potassium, calcium, and copper. Which is the least reactive?

_____

c. Apply Concepts How is plutonium made?

_____

_____

_____

got it? ....

○ I get it! Now I know that metals are classified in the periodic table as _____

_____

_____

_____

_____

○ I need extra help with _____

Go to MY SCIENCE ⓢ COACH *online for help with this subject.*

95

LESSON

4 Nonmetals and Metalloids

UNLOCK THE BIG ?

🔑 What Are the Properties of Nonmetals?

🔑 What Are the Families Containing Nonmetals?

my planet Diary

MISCONCEPTION

Something in the Air

A common misconception is that the air in the atmosphere is mostly oxygen.

Fact: At sea level, air is actually only about 21 percent oxygen by volume. Nitrogen makes up about 78 percent of the atmosphere. The remaining one percent is made up of several gases, including argon and carbon dioxide.

Evidence: Oxygen is actually toxic at high concentrations. If you breathed in pure oxygen, you would eventually get very sick.

Communicate Write your answer to each question below. Then discuss your answers with a partner.

1. Why don't scuba divers fill their tanks with pure oxygen?

_____
_____
_____
_____
_____

2. Can you think of anything else that is good for you in small amounts but bad for you in large amounts?

_____
_____
_____
_____

▷ PLANET DIARY Go to **Planet Diary** to learn more about nonmetals.

 Do the Inquiry Warm-Up *What Are the Properties of Charcoal?*

Vocabulary
- nonmetal • diatomic molecule • halogen
- noble gas • metalloid • semiconductor

Skills
🔄 Reading: Summarize
△ Inquiry: Classify

What Are the Properties of Nonmetals?

Life on Earth depends on many nonmetals. For example, carbon (C), nitrogen (N), phosphorus (P), hydrogen (H), and oxygen (O) are all nonmetal elements found in your body's DNA. A model of DNA is shown in **Figure 1.** While many compounds made with nonmetals are essential to life, some nonmetals are poisonous and highly reactive. Still others are nonreactive. Compared to metals, nonmetals have a much wider variety of properties. However, non-metals do have several properties in common.

Physical Properties A **nonmetal** is an element that lacks most of the properties of a metal. Except for hydrogen, the non-metals are found on the right side of the periodic table. 🗝 **In general, most nonmetals are poor conductors of electric current and heat. Solid nonmetals tend to be dull and brittle.** If you were to hit most solid nonmetals with a hammer, they would break or crumble into a powder. Also, nonmetals usually have lower densi-ties than metals.

Many nonmetals are gases at room temperature. The air you breathe contains mostly nitrogen and oxygen. Some nonmetal elements, such as carbon, sulfur (S), and iodine (I), are solids at room temperature. Bromine (Br) is the only nonmetal that is a liquid at room temperature.

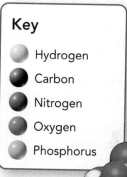

Key
- ⚪ Hydrogen
- ⚫ Carbon
- ● Nitrogen
- ● Oxygen
- ● Phosphorus

FIGURE 1 ···

DNA

DNA, which is made up of atoms of nonmetals, is essential to life.

✏️ Identify **Can you think of other substances essential to life that contain nonmetals?**

_____

_____

_____

Chemical Properties Atoms of nonmetals usually gain or share electrons when they react with other atoms. When non-metals and metals react, electrons move from the metal atoms to the nonmetal atoms. For example, when sodium and chlorine react to form table salt (NaCl), an electron moves from the sodium atom to the chlorine atom.

Many nonmetals can form compounds with other nonmetals. In these types of compounds, the atoms share their electrons to form bonds. When two or more atoms bond this way, they form a molecule. A water (H_2O) molecule consists of two hydrogen atoms and one oxygen atom.

Most properties of nonmetals are the opposite of the properties of metals.

❶ Compare and Contrast Complete the table about the properties of metals and nonmetals.

❷ Observe Sulfur, shown at the right, is a nonmetal. What properties can you observe from the photo? What additional properties can you predict?

_____
_____
_____
_____

Properties of Metals	Properties of Nonmetals
Shiny	Dull
Malleable	_____
Good conductors of electric current	_____ _____ _____
_____ _____ _____	Poor conductors of heat

Do the Quick Lab
Carbon—A Nonmetal.

Assess Your Understanding

1a. Identify What property of nonmetals is the opposite of being *malleable* and *ductile*?

_____
_____

b. Make Generalizations What happens to the atoms of most nonmetals when they react with other elements?

_____
_____
_____

got it?

○ **I get it!** Now I know that the physical properties of nonmetals are that_____

_____
_____
_____

○ **I need extra help with** _____

_____

Go to MY SCIENCE COACH *online for help with this subject.*

What Are the Families Containing Nonmetals?

Look back at the periodic table. There are nonmetals in Group 1 and in Groups 14–18. 🔑 **The families containing nonmetals include the carbon family, the nitrogen family, the oxygen family, the halogen family, the noble gases, and hydrogen.**

Before you read about the families containing nonmetals, refer to the periodic table to complete the table below.

Family	Group	Nonmetals in Family
Carbon family	14	
Nitrogen family	15	
Oxygen family	16	
Halogen family	17	
Noble gases	18	
Hydrogen	1	

The Carbon Family

In Group 14, only carbon is a nonmetal. Carbon is especially important in its role in the chemistry of life. Proteins, DNA, and fats all contain carbon.

Most of the fuels that are burned to yield energy contain carbon. Coal contains large amounts of carbon. Gasoline is made from crude oil, a mixture of carbon compounds with one carbon atom to chains of several hundred carbon atoms. A diamond, which is shown in **Figure 2**, is made of pure carbon.

6
C
Carbon
12.011

Shade in the nonmetal in Group 14 on the periodic table.

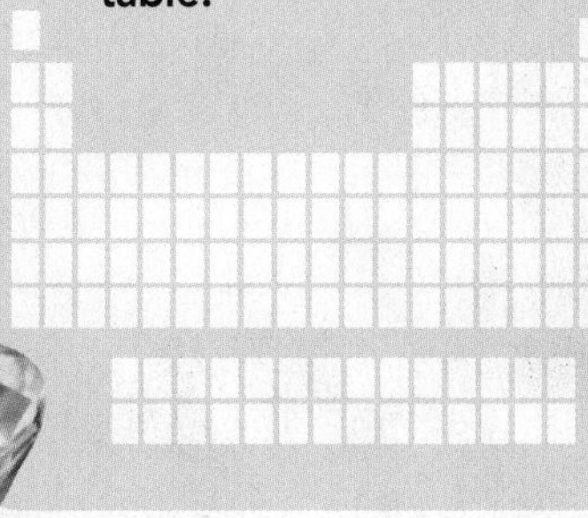

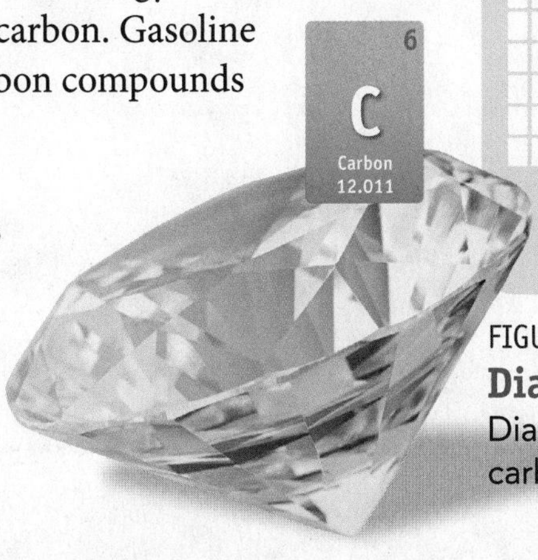

FIGURE 2 ·····················
Diamond
Diamonds are made of pure carbon.

The Nitrogen Family

Group 15, the nitrogen family, contains two nonmetals, nitrogen and phosphorus. Nitrogen makes up about 78 percent of Earth's atmosphere by volume. In nature, nitrogen exists as two nitrogen atoms bonded together to form a diatomic molecule, N_2. A **diatomic molecule** is made up of two atoms. In this form, nitrogen is not very reactive.

Although living things need nitrogen, most of them are unable to use nitrogen from the air. However, certain kinds of bacteria can use the nitrogen from the air to form compounds. This process is called nitrogen fixation. Plants can then take in these nitrogen compounds formed by the bacteria in the soil. Farmers also add nitrogen compounds to the soil in the form of fertilizers. Lightning, shown in **Figure 3,** also converts nitrogen in the atmosphere into a form that can be used by plants.

Phosphorus is the other nonmetal in the nitrogen family. Much more reactive than nitrogen, phosphorus in nature is always found in compounds.

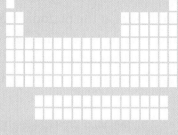

Shade in the nonmetals in Group 15 on the periodic table.

FIGURE 3 ···

Lightning

The energy released in the atmosphere in the form of lightning is able to break the bonds between nitrogen atoms, causing them to react with oxygen. Plants are able to use the nitrogen in this form.

✎ CHALLENGE **How do you get the nitrogen you need?**

_____

_____

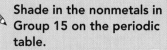

7

N

Nitrogen
14.007

The Oxygen Family
Group 16, the oxygen family, contains three nonmetals—oxygen, sulfur, and selenium (Se). Oxygen is a gas at room temperature, whereas sulfur and selenium are both solids.

You are using oxygen right now. With every breath, oxygen travels into your lungs. There, it is absorbed into your bloodstream, which distributes it all over your body. Like nitrogen, oxygen (O_2) is a diatomic molecule. Oxygen is relatively reactive, so it can combine with almost every other element.

If you have ever smelled the odor of a rotten egg, then you are already familiar with the smell of some sulfur compounds. Sulfur is used in the manufacturing of rubber for rubber bands and automobile tires, like the one shown in **Figure 4.**

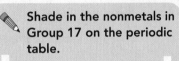
🖉 Shade in the nonmetals in Group 16 on the periodic table.

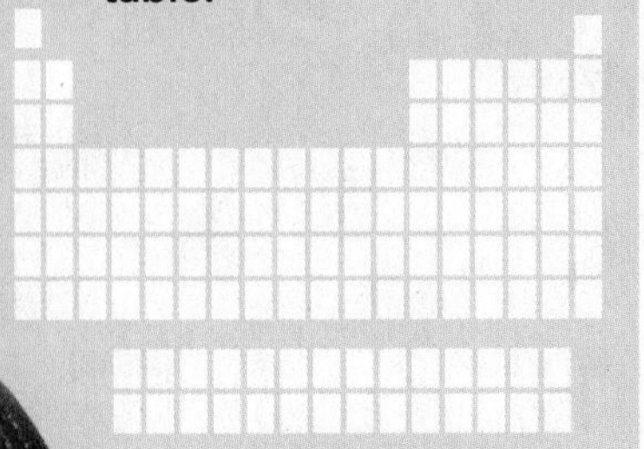

FIGURE 4 ··················
Rubber Tires
Automobile tires are made out of rubber that contains sulfur compounds.

16
S
Sulfur
32.06

The Halogen Family
Group 17 contains the nonmetals fluorine (F), chlorine (Cl), bromine, and iodine. These elements are also known as the **halogens,** which means "salt forming." The properties of astatine (At) are unknown because it is extremely rare.

All of the halogens are very reactive. Fluorine is the most reactive of all the elements. It is so reactive that it reacts with almost every known substance, including water. Chlorine gas is extremely dangerous, but it is used in small amounts to kill bacteria in water supplies.

Though the halogen elements are dangerous, many of the compounds that halogens form are quite useful. Compounds of fluorine make up the nonstick coating on cookware. Fluorine compounds are also found in toothpaste, which is shown in **Figure 5,** because they help prevent tooth decay.

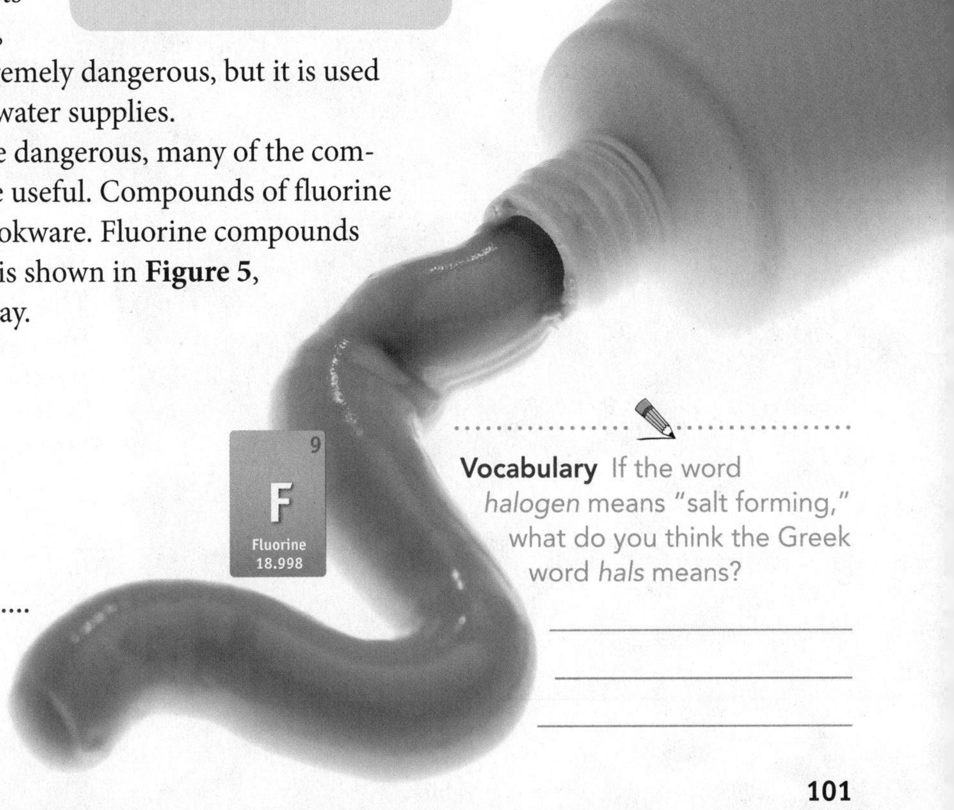

🖉 Shade in the nonmetals in Group 17 on the periodic table.

9
F
Fluorine
18.998

FIGURE 5 ··················
Toothpaste
Toothpastes often contain fluorine compounds.

🖉 **Vocabulary** If the word *halogen* means "salt forming," what do you think the Greek word *hals* means?

_____

_____

_____

101

He Ne Ar Kr Xe

FIGURE 6 ·······························
Neon Lights
Glowing electric lights are often called "neon lights" even though they are usually filled with other noble gases or mixtures of them. The lights above show the symbols for helium (He), neon (Ne), argon (Ar), krypton (Kr), and xenon (Xe).

The Noble Gases
The elements in Group 18 are known as the **noble gases.** They do not ordinarily form compounds because atoms of noble gases do not usually gain, lose, or share electrons. As a result, the noble gases are usually nonreactive. Even so, scientists have been able to synthesize some noble gas compounds in the laboratory.

You have probably seen a floating balloon filled with helium (He). Noble gases are also used in glowing electric lights, such as the ones shown in Figure 6.

Shade in the noble gases on the periodic table.

Hydrogen
Alone in the upper left corner of the periodic table is hydrogen—the element with the simplest atoms. The chemical properties of hydrogen are very different from those of the other elements, so it cannot be grouped in with a family.

Hydrogen makes up more than 90 percent of the atoms in the universe. Stars—like the sun, shown in Figure 7—contain massive amounts of hydrogen. But, hydrogen makes up only 1 percent of the mass of Earth's crust, oceans, and atmosphere. Hydrogen is rarely found on Earth as a pure element. Most hydrogen is combined with oxygen in water.

Shade in hydrogen on the periodic table.

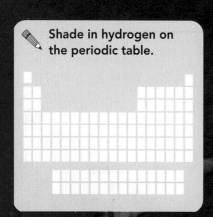

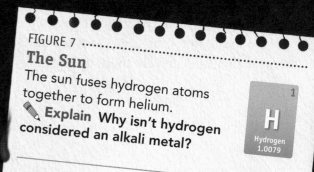

FIGURE 7 ·······························
The Sun
The sun fuses hydrogen atoms together to form helium.
Explain Why isn't hydrogen considered an alkali metal?

1

H

Hydrogen
1.0079

FIGURE 8 ··············
Solar Cells
The solar cells
on the International
Space Station transform energy
from the sun into electrical energy.
Some solar cells contain silicon,
which is a semiconductor.

Shade in the metalloids on the periodic table.

Metalloids Between the metals
and the nonmetals in the periodic table
lie the metalloids. The **metalloids** have
some properties of metals and some properties
of nonmetals. All metalloids are solids at room temperature. The
metalloids are brittle, hard, and somewhat reactive.

The most common metalloid is silicon (Si). Ordinary sand,
which is mostly silicon dioxide, (SiO_2) is the main component of
glass. A compound of boron (B) and oxygen is added during the
process of glassmaking to make heat-resistant glass.

A metalloid's most useful property is the ability to conduct
electric current. The conductivity of a metalloid can depend on
temperature, exposure to light, or the presence of impurities.
For this reason, metalloids such as silicon and germanium (Ge) are
used to make semiconductors. **Semiconductors** are substances that
can conduct electric current under some conditions but not under
other conditions. Semiconductors are used to make computer
chips, transistors, and lasers. Semiconductors are also used in solar
cells, such as the ones shown in **Figure 8**.

🔄 **Summarize** Summarize the
properties of the metalloids.

_____

_____

_____

_____

_____

_____

_____

apply it!

Use this portion of the periodic table to answer the questions.

❶ ⚠ **Classify** List the chemical symbols of the nonmetals:

_____. The remaining

elements are classified as _____

❷ Selenium has properties similar to (sulfur/bromine)
because they are in the same (period/group).

14	15	16	17
Si Silicon 28.086	**P** Phosphorus 30.974	**S** Sulfur 32.06	**Cl** Chlorine 35.453
32	33	34	35
Ge Germanium 72.59	**As** Arsenic 74.922	**Se** Selenium 78.96	**Br** Bromine 79.904

Alien Periodic Table

How is the periodic table organized?.

FIGURE 9 ....

▶ REAL-WORLD INQUIRY Imagine that inhabitants of another planet send a message to Earth that contains information about 30 elements. However, the message contains different names and symbols for these elements than those used on Earth. ✎ Infer Using the clues provided, fill in the periodic table with these "alien" names.

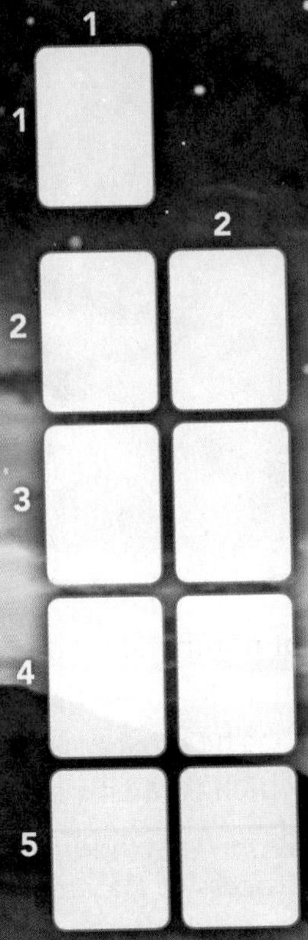

Alien Elements

The noble gases are **bombal** (Bo), **wobble** (Wo), **jeptum** (J), and **logon** (L). Among these gases, wobble has the greatest atomic mass and bombal the least. Logon is lighter than jeptum.

The most reactive group of metals are **xtalt** (X), **byyou** (By), **chow** (Ch), and **quackzil** (Q). Of these metals, chow has the lowest atomic mass. Quackzil is in the same period as wobble.

Apstrom (A), **vulcania** (Vc), and **kratt** (Kt) are non-metals in Group 17. Vulcania is in the same period as quackzil and wobble.

The metalloids are **ernst** (E), **highho** (Hi), **terriblum** (T), and **sississ** (Ss). Sississ is the metalloid with the greatest atomic mass. Ernst is the metalloid with the lowest atomic mass. Highho and terriblum are in Group 14. Terriblum has more protons than highho. **Yazzer** (Yz) touches the zigzag line, but it's a metal, not a metalloid.

The lightest element of all is called **pfsst** (Pf). The heaviest element in the group of 30 elements is **eldorado** (El). The most chemically active non-metal is apstrom. Kratt reacts with byyou to form table salt.

18

13   14   15   16   17

The element **doggone** (D) has only 4 protons in its atoms.

Floxxit (Fx) is important in the chemistry of life. It forms compounds made of long chains of atoms. **Rhaatrap** (R) and **doadeer** (Do) are metals in the fourth period, but rhaatrap is less reactive than doadeer.

Magnificon (M), **goldy** (G), and sississ are all members of Group 15. Goldy has fewer electrons than magnificon.

Urrp (Up), **oz** (Oz), and **nuutye** (Nu) are in Group 16. Nuutye is found as a diatomic molecule and has the same properties as a gas found in Earth's atmosphere. Oz has a lower atomic number than urrp.

The element **anatom** (An) has atoms with a total of 49 electrons. **Zapper** (Z) and **pie** (Pi) are both members of Group 2. Zapper has fewer protons than pie.

Do the Quick Lab
Finding Nonmetals.

Assess Your Understanding

2a. List What are the nonmetals in Group 16 of the periodic table?

_____

_____

_____

b. Compare and Contrast How do the chemical properties of the halogens compare to those of the noble gases?

_____

_____

_____

_____

c. ANSWER THE BIG ? How is the periodic table organized?

_____

_____

_____

_____

_____

_____

_____

_____

_____

_____

got it? ....

○ **I get it!** Now I know that the families containing nonmetals include _____

_____

_____

_____

○ **I need extra help with** _____

Go to MY SCIENCE COACH *online for help with this subject.*

105

Radioactive Elements

UNLOCK THE BIG ?

🗝 **What Happens to an Atom During Radioactive Decay?**

🗝 **What Does Radioactive Decay Produce?**

🗝 **How Are Radioactive Isotopes Useful?**

my planet DiARY

Running on Radioactive Isotopes

Did you know that the *Cassini* spacecraft, which is being used to explore Saturn, runs on batteries? The batteries are called radioisotope thermoelectric generators (RTGs).

The batteries you can buy in the store use chemical reactions to generate electrical energy. However, RTGs produce electrical energy by using radioactive decay. RTGs contain unstable isotopes, which are called radioactive isotopes. Heat is released as the radioactive isotopes lose particles from their atoms. The heat is then converted into electrical energy. A single RTG contains several pounds of radioactive material. This is enough fuel to provide power for up to 23 years!

FUN FACTS

Communicate Write your answer to each question below. Then discuss your answers with a partner.

1. How are RTGs different from the batteries you buy at a store?

_____

_____

_____

_____

_____

2. Imagine being on a spacecraft traveling to distant planets. What are some of the things you might see?

_____

_____

_____

_____

> **PLANET DIARY** Go to **Planet Diary** to learn more about radioactive decay.

Lab zone® Do the Inquiry Warm-Up *How Much Goes Away?*

Vocabulary

- radioactive decay • nuclear reaction • radioactivity
- alpha particle • beta particle • gamma ray
- half-life • radioactive dating • tracer

Skills

↩ Reading: Relate Cause and Effect

△ Inquiry: Calculate

What Happens to an Atom During Radioactive Decay?

Suppose you could find a way to turn dull, cheap lead into valuable gold. More than a thousand years ago, many people tried, but nothing worked. As the young scientist in **Figure 1** will soon discover, there is no chemical reaction that converts one element into another. Even so, elements do sometimes change into other elements. For example, atoms of carbon can become atoms of nitrogen. How are these changes possible?

Radioactive Decay Recall that atoms with the same number of protons and different numbers of neutrons are called isotopes. Some isotopes are unstable, so their nuclei do not hold together well. These unstable isotopes are also called radioactive isotopes. In a process called **radioactive decay,** the atomic nuclei of radioactive isotopes release fast-moving particles and energy. ⚷ **During radioactive decay, the identity of an atom changes.**

Radioactive decay is an example of a nuclear reaction. **Nuclear reactions** involve the particles in the nucleus of an atom. Nuclear fission, a process in which an atom's nuclei split apart, and nuclear fusion, the process in which atomic nuclei join together, are both nuclear reactions. These physical processes make it possible for scientists to turn one element into another.

Goldy, it won't work because

_____

_____

_____

_____

_____

_____

FIGURE 1 ·······································

Trying to Turn Lead Into Gold

Goldy is furiously trying to turn lead into gold in the chemistry lab. Meanwhile, her lab partner Lucy is trying to convince her that it can't be done with a chemical reaction.

✎ **Communicate** Use what you know about nuclear and chemical reactions to complete Lucy's argument.

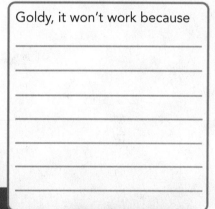

Discovery of Radioactive Decay

In 1896, the French scientist Henri Becquerel accidentally discovered the effects of radioactive decay. He observed that when a mineral containing uranium was exposed to sunlight, it gave off an energy that could fog photographic film plates. Becquerel thought that sunlight was necessary for the energy release. So, on a cloudy day, he put away the mineral in a desk drawer next to a photographic plate wrapped in paper. Later, when Becquerel opened his desk to retrieve his materials, he found an image of the mineral on the photographic plate. Sunlight wasn't necessary after all. Becquerel hypothesized that uranium gives off energy, called radiation, all the time.

Becquerel presented his findings to a young Polish researcher, Marie Curie, and her husband, French chemist Pierre Curie. The Curies showed that a reaction was taking place within the uranium nuclei. The uranium was able to spontaneously emit radiation. Marie Curie called this property **radioactivity.** The Curies, along with Becquerel, won the Nobel Prize in physics for their work on radioactivity. Marie Curie, shown in **Figure 2,** was later awarded the Nobel Prize in chemistry for her research on radioactive elements. She eventually died of cancer, a result of her years of exposure to radium.

FIGURE 2 ··

Marie Curie

Marie Curie was the first scientist to win the Nobel Prize in two different subject areas (physics and chemistry). She was also the first woman ever to receive a Nobel Prize.

Do the Quick Lab *What Happens When an Atom Decays?*

🔑 Assess Your Understanding

1a. Define The spontaneous emission of radiation by an unstable atomic nucleus is called

_____

b. Apply Concepts What caused the fogging of the photographic plates that Becquerel observed in 1896?

_____

_____

_____

_____

got it?

○ **I get it!** Now I know that during radioactive decay _____

_____

_____

○ **I need extra help with** _____

_____

_____

Go to MY SCIENCE ⓢ COACH *online for help with this subject.*

What Does Radioactive Decay Produce?

Figure 3 illustrates the three major forms of radiation produced during the decay of an unstable nucleus. 🔑 **Radioactive decay can produce alpha particles, beta particles, and gamma rays.**

FIGURE 3 ....

> **ART IN MOTION** **Radioactive Decay**

Radioactive elements give off particles and energy during radioactive decay. ✏️ **Compare and Contrast Identify the change (if any) that occurs in an unstable nucleus during each form of radioactive decay.**

Radioactive nucleus

Alpha particle

2 protons lost
2 neutrons lost

Alpha Decay

An **alpha particle** consists of two protons and two neutrons. It is positively charged. The release of an alpha particle by an atom during alpha decay decreases the atomic number by 2 and the mass number by 4. For example, a thorium-232 nucleus decays to produce an alpha particle and a radium-228 nucleus.

Beta Decay

During beta decay, a neutron in an unstable nucleus changes into a negatively charged beta particle and a proton. A **beta particle** is a fast-moving electron given off by a nucleus during radioactive decay. The new proton remains inside the nucleus. The nucleus is then left with one less neutron and one more proton. Its mass number remains the same but its atomic number increases by one. For example, a carbon-14 nucleus decays to produce a beta particle and a nitrogen-14 nucleus.

Radioactive nucleus

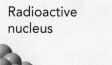

Beta particle

☐ proton(s) (lost/gained)

☐ neutron(s) (lost/gained)

Gamma Radiation

Alpha and beta decay are almost always accompanied by gamma radiation. **Gamma rays** consist of high-energy waves, similar to X-rays. Gamma rays (also called gamma radiation) have no charge and do not cause a change in either the atomic mass or the atomic number.

Radioactive nucleus

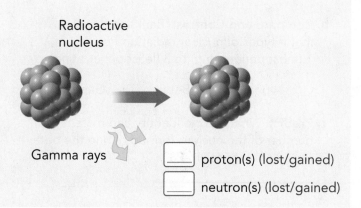

Gamma rays

☐ proton(s) (lost/gained)

☐ neutron(s) (lost/gained)

Effects of Nuclear Radiation

Effects of Nuclear Radiation **Figure 4** depicts a radioactive source that emits alpha particles, beta particles, and gamma rays. Alpha particles move very fast, they can be blocked by just a sheet of paper. Alpha radiation can cause an injury to human skin that is much like a bad burn.

Beta particles are much faster and more penetrating than alpha particles. They can pass through paper. But, they are blocked by an aluminum sheet 5 millimeters thick. Beta particles can also travel into the human body and damage its cells.

Gamma radiation is the most penetrating. You would need a piece of lead several centimeters thick or a concrete wall about a meter thick to stop gamma rays. They can pass right through a human body. Gamma rays deliver intense energy to cells and can cause severe damage.

FIGURE 4 ·······························

The Effects of Nuclear Radiation

The three main types of nuclear radiation vary in their ability to penetrate materials.

✎ **Apply Concepts** Use the key to complete the paths of the alpha particle, beta particle, and gamma ray emitted by the radioactive sample. Each path should end at the point where the radiation is blocked.

Key

—— Alpha particle

----- Beta particle

〰〰 Gamma ray

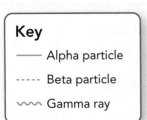

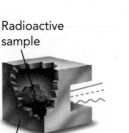

Radioactive sample

Lead box

Paper

Aluminum sheet

Concrete

Lab zone® Do the Quick Lab *Modeling Beta Decay.*

🔑 Assess Your Understanding

2a. Identify What is the name of the particle produced by radioactive decay that consists of 2 protons and 2 neutrons?

_____

b. Compare and Contrast Rank the three major types of nuclear radiation from 1 (most penetrating) to 3 (least penetrating).

____ Alpha ____ Beta ____ Gamma

c. Predict What are the identity and mass number of the nucleus formed during the beta decay of magnesium-28?

_____

got it?

○ **I get it!** Now I know that the three major forms of radiation produced during radioactive decay are _____

_____

_____

_____

○ I need extra help with _____

_____

Go to **MY SCIENCE** ⓢ **COACH** *online for help with this subject.*

How Are Radioactive Isotopes Useful?

Radioactive isotopes have many uses in science and industry. In some cases, the energy released by radioactive isotopes is itself useful. In other cases, radiation is useful because it can be easily detected. 🔑 **Uses of radioactive isotopes include determining the ages of fossils, tracing the steps of chemical reactions and industrial processes, diagnosing and treating disease, and providing sources of energy.**

Radioactive Dating Radioactive isotopes decay at different rates. The **half-life** of a radioactive isotope is the length of time needed for half of the atoms of a sample to decay. The half-life is different for each radioactive isotope. Half-lives can range from less than a second to billions of years!

Fossils are traces or remains of living things that have been preserved. For fossils millions or billions of years old, ages are found from radioactive isotopes with very long half-lives, like uranium. For much younger fossils, carbon-14 is often used. As plants grow, they use carbon dioxide (CO_2) from the air. A fraction of all carbon dioxide contains the radioactive isotope carbon-14. This becomes part of a plant's structures. After the plant dies, it stops taking in carbon dioxide. If the plant's remains are preserved, the amount of carbon-14 present can be measured. Scientists can calculate how many half-lives have passed since the plant died and estimate the age of the fossil. This process is called **radioactive dating.**

do the math!

Data from a fossil of a mammoth tooth shows that carbon-14 has been decaying in the tooth for five half-lives.

1 **Calculate** Calculate the age of the tooth.

_____ half-lives × _____ years/half-life = _____ years.

2 **CHALLENGE** What fraction of the amount of carbon-14 that was in the mammoth's tooth when it died is left after five half-lives?

$\left(\dfrac{1}{2}\right)^5 =$ —— × —— × —— × —— × —— = ——

Half-Lives of Some Radioactive Isotopes

Element	Half-Life
Polonium-216	0.16 second
Sodium-24	15 hours
Iodine-131	8.07 days
Phosphorus-32	14.3 days
Cobalt-60	5.26 years
Radium-226	1,600 years
Carbon-14	5,730 years
Chlorine-36	310,000 years
Uranium-235	710 million years
Uranium-238	4.5 billion years

Relate Cause and Effect

Why are radioactive isotopes useful for following the steps of a chemical reaction?

_____

_____

_____

_____

_____

_____

Uses in Science and Industry

A radioactive isotope, like a lighthouse flashing in the night, "signals" where it is by emitting radiation that can be detected. **Tracers** are radioactive isotopes that can be followed through the steps of a chemical reaction or an industrial process. Tracers behave chemically like nonradioactive forms of an element. For example, phosphorus is used by plants in small amounts for healthy growth. The plant in **Figure 5** will absorb radioactive phosphorus-32 just as it does the nonradioactive form. Radiation will be present in any part of the plant that contains the isotope. In this way, biologists can learn where and how plants use phosphorus.

Tracers are used to find weak spots in metal pipes, especially in oil pipelines. When added to a liquid, tracers can be easily detected if they leak out of the pipes. Gamma rays can pass through metal and be detected by photographic film. The gamma ray images allow structural engineers to detect small cracks in the metal of bridges and building frames before a disaster occurs.

FIGURE 5 ···

Radioactive Tracers

Phosphorus-32 added to soil is absorbed through a plant's roots. The tracer can be detected in any plant structures in which phosphorus is used. ✎ **Explain Write a short caption under each figure to explain what is happening.**

Gamma radiation

Uses in Medicine Doctors use radioactive isotopes to detect medical problems and to treat some diseases. Tracers are injected into the body and travel to organs and other structures in which that chemical is normally used. Technicians make images of the bone, blood, vessel, or organ affected using equipment that detects radiation.

Cancer tumors are sometimes treated from outside the body with high-energy gamma rays. Gamma radiation directed toward a cancer tumor damages the cancer cells so that they can no longer function.

Nuclear Energy Many power plants, like the one shown in **Figure 6,** use radioactive isotopes as fuel. Both nuclear fission and nuclear fusion release huge amounts of energy when they react. In a nuclear reactor, atoms of uranium-235 are split under controlled conditions. The energy produced heats water to produce steam. The steam turns a turbine. This generates electricity. Nuclear power plants provide electrical energy in many parts of the world. Nuclear reactions also provide the energy for large submarines and other types of ocean vessels.

FIGURE 6 ·····························

Nuclear Power Plant
The cooling tower of a nuclear power plant helps control the temperature inside the reactor. The power plant converts thermal energy to electrical energy.

 Do the Quick Lab *Designing Experiments Using Radioactive Tracers.*

🔑 Assess Your Understanding

3a. Explain Why is half-life useful to an archaeologist?

_____

_____

_____

_____

b. 🔁 **Relate Cause and Effect** Why are radioactive isotopes that emit gamma rays useful for treating some forms of cancer?

_____

_____

_____

got it? ··

○ **I get it!** Now I know that four uses of radioactive isotopes are _____

_____

_____

_____

○ I need extra help with _____

Go to MY SCIENCE COACH online for help with this subject.

CHAPTER 3 Study Guide

In the periodic table, the elements are organized in order of _____ atomic number. The properties of the elements repeat in each _____.

LESSON 1 Introduction to Atoms

🔑 Atomic theory grew as a series of models that developed from experimental evidence.

🔑 At the center of the atom is a tiny, dense nucleus containing protons and neutrons. Surrounding the nucleus is a cloudlike region of moving electrons.

Vocabulary
- atom • electron • nucleus • proton
- energy level • neutron • atomic number
- isotope • mass number

LESSON 2 Organizing the Elements

🔑 Mendeleev noticed a pattern of properties in elements arranged by increasing atomic mass.

🔑 The periodic table includes each element's atomic number, symbol, name, and atomic mass.

🔑 The properties of an element can be predicted from its location in the periodic table.

Vocabulary
- atomic mass • periodic table
- chemical symbol • period • group

LESSON 3 Metals

🔑 The physical properties of metals include luster, malleability, ductility, and conductivity.

🔑 Metals are classified as alkali metals, alkaline earth metals, transition metals, metals in mixed groups, lanthanides, and actinides.

Vocabulary
- metal • luster • malleable • ductile
- thermal conductivity • electrical conductivity
- reactivity • corrosion • alkali metal
- alkaline earth metal • transition metal

LESSON 4 Nonmetals and Metalloids

🔑 In general, most nonmetals are poor conductors. Solid nonmetals tend to be dull and brittle.

🔑 The families containing nonmetals include the carbon family, the nitrogen family, the oxygen family, the halogen family, the noble gases, and hydrogen.

Vocabulary
- nonmetal • diatomic molecule • halogen
- noble gas • metalloid • semiconductor

LESSON 5 Radioactive Elements

🔑 During radioactive decay, the identity of an atom changes.

🔑 Radioactive decay can produce alpha particles, beta particles, and gamma rays.

🔑 Uses of radioactive isotopes include determining the ages of fossils, tracing the steps of chemical and industrial processes, and providing sources of energy.

Vocabulary
- radioactive decay • nuclear reaction • radioactivity • alpha particle
- beta particle • gamma ray • half-life • radioactive dating • tracer

Review and Assessment

Introduction to Atoms

1. The atomic number of an element is determined by the number of
   a. protons.
   b. electrons.
   c. neutrons.
   d. isotopes.

2. Two isotopes of an element have the same number of _____ but different numbers of _____.

3. **Relate Cause and Effect** How can an atom be electrically neutral when it contains particles that are charged?

   _____

   _____

   _____

   _____

4. **Relate Evidence and Explanation** How did Rutherford's experimental evidence lead to the development of a new atomic model?

   _____

   _____

   _____

   _____

   _____

   _____

   _____

   _____

5. **Write About It** Write a letter that Thomson might have sent to another scientist explaining why an atom must contain positive charges as well as negative charges. The letter should also explain why Thomson proposed the atomic model that he did.

Organizing the Elements

6. The rows in the periodic table are called
   a. groups.
   b. periods.
   c. nonmetals.
   d. metals.

7. Dmitri Mendeleev constructed the first periodic table, which is _____

   _____

   _____

   _____

8. **Apply Concepts** Below is an entry taken from the periodic table. Identify the type of information given by each labeled item.

   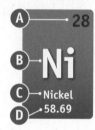

   A — 28
   B — Ni
   C — Nickel
   D — 58.69

   _____

   _____

   _____

   _____

9. **Make Generalizations** Why aren't the atomic masses of most elements whole numbers?

   _____

   _____

   _____

   _____

10. **Write About It** Write an advertisement that you could use to sell copies of Mendeleev's periodic table to chemists in 1869. Be sure to emphasize the benefits of the table to the chemical profession. Remember, the chemists have never seen such a table.

LESSON 3 Metals

11. Of the following, the group that contains elements that are the most reactive is the

a. alkali metals.　　b. alkaline earth metals.

c. carbon family.　　d. noble gases.

12. A property of metals is high thermal conductivity, which is _____

_____ .

13. Predict Using the periodic table, predict which element—potassium, aluminum, or iron—is most reactive. Explain your answer.

_____

_____

_____

_____

LESSON 4 Nonmetals and Metalloids

14. Unlike metals, solid nonmetals are

a. good conductors of heat and electric current.

b. malleable.

c. dull and brittle.

d. ductile.

15. Two elements that have properties similar to those of chlorine are _____

_____ .

16. Infer What property of the materials used in computer chips makes them useful as switches that turn electricity on and off?

_____

_____

_____

_____

LESSON 5 Radioactive Elements

17. Unstable atomic nuclei that release fast-moving particles and energy are

a. radioactive.　　b. alloys.

c. isotopes.　　　 d. alpha particles.

18. A radioactive isotope that can be followed through a chemical reaction or industrial process is called a(n) _____ .

19. Classify What type of radioactive decay results in uranium-238 becoming thorium-234?

_____

20. Write About It Suppose you could go back in time to interview Henri Becquerel on the day he discovered radioactivity. From his perspective, write an account of the discovery.

APPLY THE BIG ? How is the periodic table organized?

21. A portion of the periodic table is shown above. Which element on the periodic table has properties that are most similar to those of nitrogen (N)? Explain.

_____

_____

_____

_____

_____

Standardized Test Prep

Multiple Choice

Circle the letter of the best answer.

1. A portion of the periodic table is shown below.

Which elements are noble gases?

A oxygen, fluorine, and neon
B sulfur, chlorine, and argon
C fluorine and chlorine
D neon and argon

2. Why is the mass of a carbon atom greater than the total mass of its protons and electrons?

A The mass of a proton is greater than the mass of an electron.
B A proton is positively charged and an electron is negatively charged.
C Most of the atom's volume is the sphere-shaped cloud of electrons.
D The neutrons in the nucleus add mass to the atom.

3. Elements that are gases at room temperature are likely to be classified as which of the following?

A metals
B nonmetals
C metalloids
D semiconductors

4. Which property of aluminum makes it a suitable metal for soft-drink cans?

A It has good electrical conductivity.
B It can be hammered into a thin sheet (malleability).
C It can be drawn into long wires (ductility).
D It can reflect light (luster).

5. Radioactive isotopes give off radiation that can be detected. This property makes them useful in which of the following ways?

A as tracers in chemical reactions
B in detecting leaks in oil pipelines
C in diagnosing certain medical problems
D all of the above

Constructed Response

Use the table below to help you answer Question 6. Write your answer on a separate sheet of paper.

Element	Appearance	Reactivity	Conducts Electricity
A	Greenish-yellow gas	High	No
B	Shiny red solid	Moderate	Yes
C	Colorless gas	None	No
D	Silver-white solid	High	Yes

6. Identify each element as an alkali metal, transition metal, halogen, or noble gas. Explain your answers.

Discovery of the Elements

More than 100 chemical elements have been discovered or created on Earth. The following stories describe some of the spectacular ways in which elements have been discovered:

1669 Phosphorus

In 1669, alchemist Hennig Brand was searching for a way to turn lead into gold. He hypothesized that animal urine might contain a substance that could cause the transformation. In the process of heating the urine to obtain a pure substance, he discovered a material that glowed in the dark. That material is phosphorus, which is important in maintaining a healthy body.

1811 Iodine

As French chemist Barnard Courtois isolated sodium and potassium compounds from seaweed ashes, he accidentally added too much sulfuric acid. The mess he created sent out a cloud of violet-colored gas that condensed on metal surfaces in the room. That gas was iodine. Even today, some iodine is isolated from seaweed. Having enough iodine in your diet can prevent illness and allow for healthy development.

1936 Technetium

Italian chemists Emilio Segrè and Carlo Perrier made technetium in a cyclotron in 1936. This was the first element to be produced artificially. Technetium is similar in appearance to platinum, but is very radioactive. Because it breaks down quickly, technetium is not found in nature.

Flame tests historically helped chemists to identify elements. ▶

Research It Find out more about the discovery of the following elements: helium, copper, Americium, aluminum, and silicon. Then, create a timeline that shows when each element was discovered and how that discovery affected human life.

Elements
of the Human Body

It's elemental! Atoms of only five different elements make up 98 percent of the mass of the human body.

Oxygen and Hydrogen About two thirds of the body consists of water. So, in terms of mass, more than half of the body is oxygen atoms, and another 10 percent is hydrogen atoms. Both oxygen and hydrogen are also present in other body parts.

Carbon The key element in organic molecules is carbon. Organic molecules make up all body tissues, including muscles.

Calcium and Phosphorus The hard, strong parts of bones are built mostly of calcium phosphate crystals, which contain calcium, phosphorus, and oxygen.

Trace Elements Some elements exist in the body in small amounts, but play important roles. For example, chemical reactions inside body organs require enzymes that contain magnesium. The thyroid gland needs iodine to control growth. The element iron makes up less than one twentieth of 1 percent of the body, yet is an extremely important part of the hemoglobin molecule. Red blood cells use hemoglobin to carry oxygen throughout the body.

Graph It Research how the human body acquires these elements. Then use the data from the table of Elements in the Human Body to create a circle graph that shows the relative percentages of each element in the body.

Elements in the Human Body	
Element	Approximate mass (%)
Oxygen	65
Carbon	18
Hydrogen	10
Nitrogen	3
Calcium	1
Phosphorus	1
Potassium, Sulfur, Sodium, Chlorine	0.1–0.3 percent each
Copper, Magnesium, Zinc, Iron, Selenium, Molybdenum, Fluorine, Iodine, Manganese, Cobalt	less than 0.1 percent each

WHAT IS GROWING IN THIS CAVE?

THE BIG ?

How can bonding determine the properties of a substance?

Mexico's Cave of Crystals contains the world's largest natural crystals. These rocks are made of the mineral gypsum. They grew under water for as many as 500,000 years. The water was pumped out to reveal thousands of giant crystals up to 11 meters in length and 50,000 kilograms in mass. The cave might appear to be a fun place to climb around, but temperatures inside can reach 65°C (hotter than a desert afternoon). This makes it deadly for human exploration without specialized equipment.

Form Operational Definitions Based on the photograph of the Cave of Crystals, how would you define a crystal?

_____

_____

_____

UNTAMED SCIENCE Watch the **Untamed Science** video to learn more about chemical bonding.

Atoms and Bonding

Check Your Understanding

1. Background Read the paragraph below and then answer the question.

Marcy fills an ice cube tray with water and places it in a freezer. The temperature in the freezer is −18°C, which is lower than the **melting point** of water (0°C). When Marcy opens the freezer a few hours later, she finds that the water has frozen into **solid** ice cubes.

The **melting point** of a substance is the temperature at which the substance changes from a solid to a liquid.

A **solid** has a definite shape and a definite volume.

• What will happen to an ice cube if it is left outside on a warm, sunny day? Explain.

_____

_____

_____

> **MY READING WEB** If you had trouble answering the question above, visit **My Reading Web** and type in *Atoms and Bonding.*

Vocabulary Skill

High-Use Academic Words High-use academic words are words you are likely to encounter while reading textbooks. Look for the following words in context as you read this chapter.

Word	Definition	Example Sentence
stable	*adj.* not easily or quickly changed from one state to another	Gold is a *stable* metal that does not rust or tarnish.
symbol	*n.* a written sign that stands for something else	The *symbol* for the element oxygen is O.

2. Quick Check Choose the word that best completes the sentence.

• The letter H is the _____ for hydrogen.

• Platinum jewelry lasts a long time because the metal is very

_____

electron dot diagram

Li·   Be·   ·B·

Lithium   Beryllium   Boron

ionic compound

CaCO₃

crystal

I want it!   I want it more!

polar bond

Chapter Preview

▷ VOCAB FLASH CARDS For extra help with vocabulary, visit **Vocab Flash Cards** and type in *Atoms and Bonding.*

Atoms, Bonding, and the Periodic Table

🔑 **What Determines an Element's Chemistry?**

UNLOCK
THE BIG
?

my planet diary

Elemental Effects

Many people enjoy fireworks displays. Did you know that chemistry plays a big part in the beauty and the noise? The different colors and effects produced depend on the properties of the elements in the chemical compounds used in each firework rocket. These compounds produce smoke, color bursts, loud noises, or a combination of these effects when they are detonated.

The table below lists some elements found in the compounds used in rockets. It shows the effects these elements produce.

Using what you know about the periodic table, answer the questions below. After you finish the lesson, check your answers.

What elements do you think were used to produce the fireworks display in the photo? What groups of the periodic table do these elements belong to?

_____

_____

_____

Element	Effect
Strontium	Red color
Barium	Green color
Copper	Blue color
Sodium	Yellow color
Magnesium or aluminum	White color
Potassium or sodium	Whistling sound
Potassium and sulfur	White smoke

▶ PLANET DIARY Go to **Planet Diary** to learn more about elements.

Lab® Do the Inquiry Warm-Up *What Are zone the Trends in the Periodic Table?*

Vocabulary
- valence electron
- electron dot diagram
- chemical bond

Skills
- Reading: Relate Cause and Effect
- Inquiry: Predict

What Determines an Element's Chemistry?

How do atoms combine to form compounds? The answer has to do with electrons and their energy levels.

Valence Electrons The number of protons in a neutral atom equals the number of electrons. The electrons of an atom are found in different energy levels. Electrons at higher energy levels have higher amounts of energy. The **valence electrons** (VAY luns) of an atom are those electrons that have the highest energy. Valence electrons are involved in chemical bonding. 🔑 **The number of valence electrons in each atom helps determine the chemical properties of that element.**

Electron Dot Diagrams Each atom of an element has a certain number of valence electrons. The number of valence electrons is specific to that element. Different elements can have from 1 to 8 valence electrons. **Figure 1** demonstrates one way to show the number of valence electrons in an element. An **electron dot diagram** includes the symbol for the element surrounded by dots. Each dot stands for one valence electron.

Bonding Atoms tend to be more stable if they have 8 valence electrons. Atoms of neon (Ne), argon (Ar), krypton (Kr), and xenon (Xe) have 8 valence electrons. These elements are nonreactive, or stable. Helium (He) is stable with 2 electrons.

Atoms tend to form bonds so that they have 8 valence electrons and become more stable. Hydrogen needs only 2 to be stable. When atoms bond, valence electrons may be transferred from one atom to another. Or they may be shared between the atoms. A **chemical bond** is the force of attraction that holds atoms together as a result of the rearrangement of electrons between them.

H· · Ċ · · Ö :

Hydrogen   Carbon   Oxygen

Neon

FIGURE 1 ....
Electron Dot Diagrams
The valence electrons of an atom are shown as dots around the symbol of the element.

✏️ **Interpret Diagrams Complete the electron dot diagram for neon by drawing the correct number of dots.**

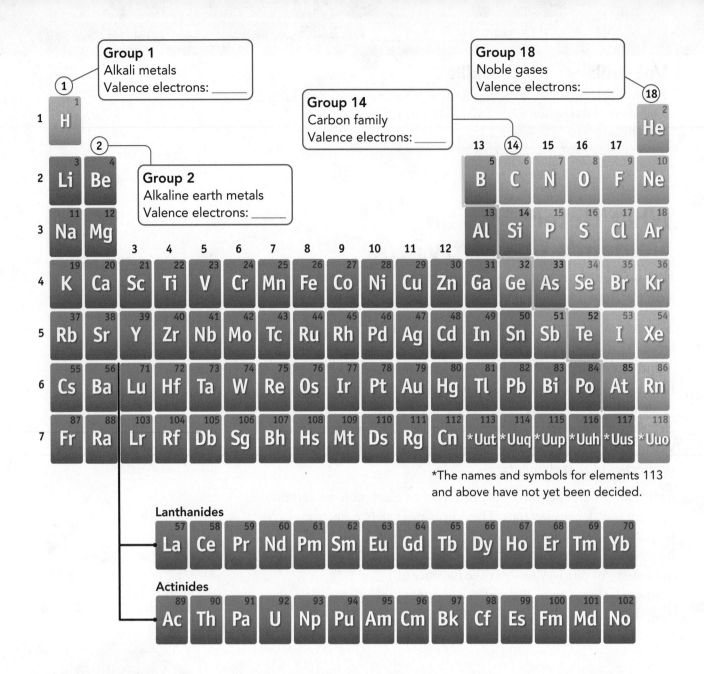

Group 1
Alkali metals
Valence electrons: _____

Group 2
Alkaline earth metals
Valence electrons: _____

Group 14
Carbon family
Valence electrons: _____

Group 18
Noble gases
Valence electrons: _____

*The names and symbols for elements 113 and above have not yet been decided.

Lanthanides

Actinides

FIGURE 2 ·······························
> INTERACTIVE ART Periodic Table of the Elements
The periodic table is arranged in order of increasing atomic number. The number of valence electrons also increases from left to right across a period.

✎ Interpret Tables As you read the lesson, fill in the number of valence electrons for each group circled above.

Applying the Periodic Table The periodic table is shown in **Figure 2.** It gives you information about the valence electrons in atoms. The table is organized into rows, called periods, and columns, called groups. The atomic number of an element is the number of protons in each atom of that element.

The elements in the periodic table are in order by increasing atomic number. The number of valence electrons increases from left to right across each period. Each period begins with an element that has 1 valence electron. Except for Period 1, a given period ends with an element that has 8 valence electrons. This repeating pattern means that the elements within a group (except for Period 1) always have the same number of valence electrons. As a result, the elements in each group have similar properties.

Each element in Periods 2 and 3 has one more valence electron than the element to its left. Group 1 elements have 1. Group 2 elements have 2. Group 13 elements have 3 valence electrons. Group 14 elements have 4, and so on. (Elements in Groups 3 to 12 follow a slightly different pattern.)

apply it!

The symbols for the elements in Periods 2 and 3 are shown below. The correct electron dot diagrams are shown for only half of the elements.

① Complete the electron dot diagrams for nitrogen, oxygen, fluorine, sodium, magnesium, aluminum, silicon, and argon.

② Fluorine (F) and Chlorine (Cl) are in Group ____.
A fluorine atom has _____ valence electrons.
A chlorine atom has _____ valence electrons.

③ Predict How many valence electrons does a bromine (Br) atom have? _____

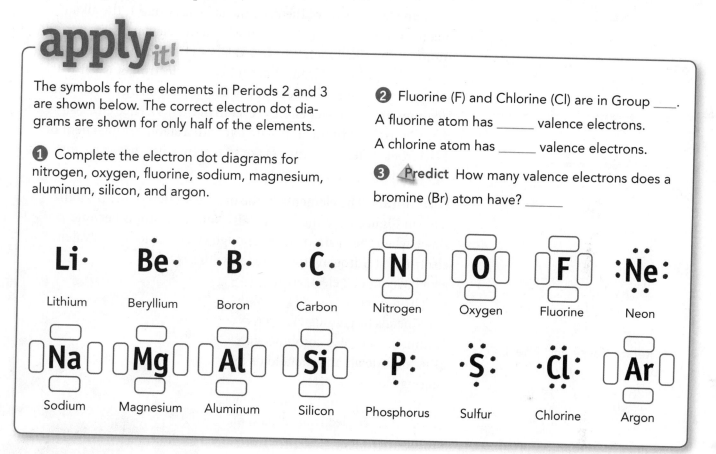

Lithium — Li·
Beryllium — Be·
Boron — ·B·
Carbon — ·C·
Nitrogen — N
Oxygen — O
Fluorine — F
Neon — :Ne:
Sodium — Na
Magnesium — Mg
Aluminum — Al
Silicon — Si
Phosphorus — ·P·
Sulfur — ·S·
Chlorine — ·Cl:
Argon — Ar

Noble Gases The Group 18 elements are the noble gases. Atoms of the noble gases have 8 valence electrons, except for helium, which has 2. Atoms with 8 valence electrons (or 2, in the case of helium) are stable. They are unlikely to gain or lose electrons or to share electrons with other atoms. Noble gases do not react easily with other elements. Some don't react at all. But, chemists have been able to make some noble gases form compounds with a few other elements.

FIGURE 3 ·····························
Camera Flashes
Argon, a noble gas, is used to produce camera flashes.

✏️ **Vocabulary** Use the word *stable* to explain why the alkali metals tend to lose 1 valence electron.

_____

_____

_____

_____

_____

_____

✏️ 🔁 **Relate Cause and Effect** Underline the cause and circle the effect in the paragraph at the right.

Metals The metals are the elements in the blue section of the periodic table in **Figure 2.** Metal atoms react by losing their valence electrons. In general, the reactivity of a metal depends on how easily its atoms lose valence electrons. The reactivity of metals decreases from left to right across the periodic table.

At the far left side of the periodic table is Group 1, the alkali metals. Each alkali metal is the most reactive element in its period. Atoms of the alkali metals have 1 valence electron. Except for lithium (Li), when a Group 1 atom loses an electron, it is left with a stable arrangement of 8 electrons in the highest energy level. These electrons are in a lower energy level than the 1 valence electron that was lost. (Lithium atoms are left with a stable arrangement of 2 electrons.) The alkali metals are so reactive that they can cause an explosion when added to water!

Nonmetals The elements in the orange section of the periodic table in **Figure 2** are the nonmetals. Nonmetal atoms become stable when they gain or share enough electrons to have 8 valence electrons. (Hydrogen atoms are left with a stable arrangement of 2 electrons.)

The nonmetals usually combine with metals by gaining electrons. Nonmetals can also combine with other nonmetals and metalloids by sharing electrons.

Atoms of Group 17, the halogens, have 7 valence electrons. A gain of one more electron gives these atoms a stable 8 electrons. The halogens react easily with other elements. **Figure 4** shows the reaction of bromine (Br), a halogen, with aluminum (Al).

900 mL
±5%

800

700

600

500

400

300

FIGURE 4 ⋯⋯⋯⋯
▷ **VIRTUAL LAB** **Reactivity of Bromine**
Aluminum reacts violently with bromine to produce aluminum bromide.

✏️ CHALLENGE What would happen if an alkali metal was combined with a halogen? Explain.

_____

_____

_____

_____

Complete the table about groups of elements in the periodic table.

Group Number	Group Name	Number of Valence Electrons	Reactivity (High/Low)
1	Alkali metals	_____	_____
17	Halogens	_____	_____
18	Noble gases	_____	_____

Metalloids The metalloids lie along the zigzag line in the periodic table, between the metals and the nonmetals. Atoms of the metalloids can either lose or share electrons when they combine with other elements. Each metalloid has some of the properties of metals and some of the properties of nonmetals.

Hydrogen Hydrogen (H) is placed in Group 1 in the periodic table because it has 1 valence electron, but hydrogen is considered to be a nonmetal. The properties of hydrogen are very different from the properties of the alkali metals. Hydrogen shares its electron when forming compounds with other nonmetals to obtain a stable arrangement of 2 electrons.

FIGURE 5 ·····················
Computer Chip
Silicon, a metalloid, is one of the most abundant elements on Earth. It is used to make computer processor chips.

 Do the Quick Lab
Element Chemistry.

🗝 Assess Your Understanding

1a. Define What are valence electrons?

_____
_____

b. Explain Why do the properties of elements change in a regular way across a period?

_____
_____
_____

c. 🔄 **Relate Cause and Effect** Explain the reactivity of the noble gases in terms of valence electrons.

_____
_____
_____
_____
_____

got it? ···

○ **I get it!** Now I know that the chemical properties of an element are determined by _____
_____

○ I need extra help with _____

Go to MY SCIENCE 🔵 COACH online for help with this subject.

Ionic Bonds

🔑 **How Do Ions Form?**

🔑 **How Are the Formulas and Names of Ionic Compounds Written?**

🔑 **What Are Properties of Ionic Compounds?**

my PLANET DiARY

FUN FACTS

The Periodic Palette

Imagine calling the colors of the rainbow cadmium, chromium, cobalt, and manganese. These may not sound like the typical colors of the rainbow to you, but they do to many artists and painters!

The "colors" listed above are transition metal elements. These metals can form compounds known as ionic compounds. Many transition metal compounds are brightly colored. They can be used to make the pigments found in oil, acrylic, and watercolor paints. For example, cadmium and chromium compounds are used for red, orange, yellow, or green paints. Cobalt and manganese compounds are used for blue and violet paints.

Communicate Write your answer to each question below. Then discuss your answers with a partner.

1. Why are transition metal compounds often used in paint pigments?

_____

_____

_____

2. Some of the compounds used in paint pigments may cause serious health problems. Do you think that using these types of paints is worth the possible health risks? Why or why not?

_____

_____

_____

▷ **PLANET DIARY** Go to **Planet Diary** to learn more about ionic compounds.

Lab zone Do the Inquiry Warm-Up *How Do Ions Form?*

Vocabulary
- ion - polyatomic ion - ionic bond - ionic compound
- chemical formula - subscript - crystal

Skills
↻ Reading: Relate Text and Visuals
△ Inquiry: Interpret Data

How Do Ions Form?

You and a friend walk past a market that sells apples for 40 cents each and pears for 50 cents each. You have 45 cents and want an apple. Your friend also has 45 cents but wants a pear. If you give your friend a nickel, she will have 50 cents and can buy a pear. You will have 40 cents left to buy an apple. Transferring the nickel gets both of you what you want. In a simple way, your actions model what can happen between atoms.

Two Atoms Talking Together

I'm about to lose an electron!

Are you sure?

I'm positive!

K   F

K⁺   F⁻

FIGURE 1 ·······························
How Ions Form
An atom that loses one of its electrons becomes a positively charged ion. The atom that gains the electron becomes a negatively charged ion.

✎ **Interpret Diagrams**
Complete the electron dot diagrams for potassium (K) and fluorine (F) before and after the electron is transferred.

····················· ✎ ·····················

↻ **Relate Text and Visuals**
Using the cartoon in **Figure 1**, explain why the potassium atom becomes positively charged and the fluorine atom becomes negatively charged.

_____

_____

_____

_____

_____

_____

Ions An **ion** (EYE ahn) is an atom or group of atoms that has an electric charge. ⌐ **When a neutral atom loses a valence electron, it loses a negative charge. It becomes a positive ion. When a neutral atom gains an electron, it gains a negative charge. It becomes a negative ion.** This is shown in **Figure 1**.

Metal atoms are likely to lose electrons. These atoms lose enough electrons to have a stable arrangement of 8 valence electrons at a lower energy level. A potassium (K) atom easily loses its 1 valence electron to become more stable. Nonmetal atoms are likely to gain electrons. These atoms gain enough electrons so that they have 8 valence electrons. A fluorine (F) atom gains 1 electron to have a stable arrangement of 8 valence electrons.

FIGURE 2 ·······················

> INTERACTIVE ART Ions

Ions have electric charges.

Common Ions and Their Charges

Name	Charge	Symbol or Formula
Lithium	1+	Li^+
Sodium	1+	Na^+
Potassium	1+	K^+
Ammonium	1+	NH_4^+
Calcium	2+	Ca^{2+}
Magnesium	2+	Mg^{2+}
Aluminum	3+	Al^{3+}
Fluoride	1–	F^-
Chloride	1–	Cl^-
Iodide	1–	I^-
Bicarbonate	1–	HCO_3^-
Nitrate	1–	NO_3^-
Oxide	2–	O^{2-}
Sulfide	2–	S^{2-}
Carbonate	2–	CO_3^{2-}
Sulfate	2–	SO_4^{2-}

Common Ions **Figure 2** lists the names of some common ions. Notice that some ions are made of several atoms. The ammonium ion is made of 1 nitrogen atom and 4 hydrogen atoms. Ions that are made of more than 1 atom are called **polyatomic ions** (pahl ee uh TAHM ik). The prefix *poly-* means "many," so *polyatomic* means "many atoms." Like other ions, polyatomic ions have an overall positive or negative charge.

Ionic Bonds When atoms that easily lose electrons react with atoms that easily gain electrons, valence electrons are transferred from one type of atom to another. The transfer gives each type of atom a more stable arrangement of electrons. Look at **Figure 3** to see how sodium atoms and chlorine atoms react to form sodium chloride (table salt).

1 The sodium atom has 1 valence electron. The chlorine atom has 7 valence electrons.

2 The valence electron of the sodium atom is transferred to the chlorine atom. Both atoms become ions. The sodium atom becomes a positive ion (Na^+). The chlorine atom becomes a negative ion (Cl^-).

3 Oppositely charged particles attract, so the positive Na^+ ion and the negative Cl^- ion attract. An **ionic bond** is the attraction between two oppositely charged ions. The resulting compound is called an **ionic compound.** It is made up of positive and negative ions. In an ionic compound, the total positive charge of all the positive ions equals the total negative charge of all the negative ions.

FIGURE 3 ···

Formation of an Ionic Bond

Follow the steps to see how an ionic bond forms between a sodium atom and a chlorine atom.

✎ **Infer Complete the electron dot diagrams for the sodium and chlorine atoms and their ions.**

▲ Sodium metal ▲ Chlorine gas

Transfer of an electron

Sodium ion Chloride ion

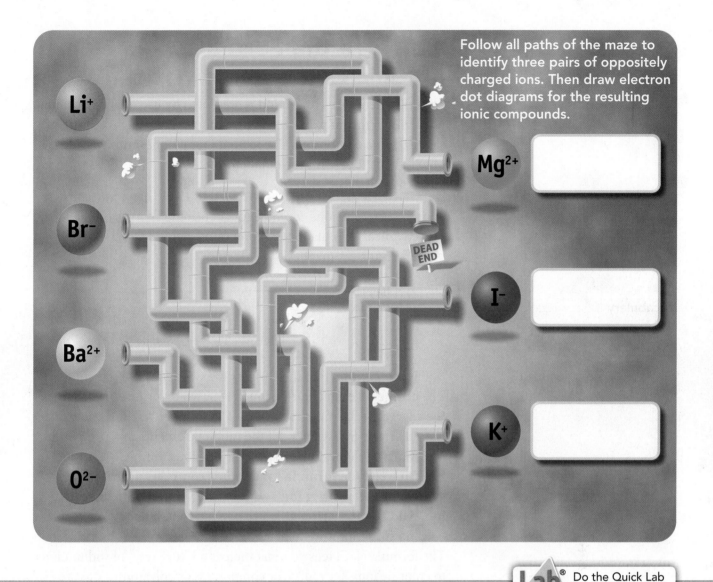

Follow all paths of the maze to identify three pairs of oppositely charged ions. Then draw electron dot diagrams for the resulting ionic compounds.

Li⁺

Br⁻

Ba²⁺

O²⁻

Mg²⁺

DEAD END

I⁻

K⁺

Lab zone® Do the Quick Lab *Ion Formation*.

🔑 Assess Your Understanding

1a. Review An atom that loses a valence electron becomes a (positive/negative) ion. An atom that gains a valence electron becomes a (positive/negative) ion.

b. Apply Concepts Write the symbols for the ions that form when potassium and iodine react to form the ionic compound potassium iodide.

_____

c. Relate Cause and Effect Why is potassium iodide electrically neutral?

_____
_____
_____
_____
_____

got_it? ....

○ **I get it!** Now I know ions form when _____
_____

○ **I need extra help with** _____

Go to **my science ⓢ coach** *online for help with this subject.*

How Are the Formulas and Names of Ionic Compounds Written?

You will often see a compound represented by its chemical formula. A **chemical formula** is a group of symbols that shows the ratio of elements in a compound. The formula for magnesium chloride is $MgCl_2$. What does this formula tell you?

Formulas of Ionic Compounds When ionic compounds form, the ions combine to balance the charges on the ions. The chemical formula for the compound reflects this balance. Look at the formula for magnesium chloride.

Chemical symbols ⟶ $MgCl_2$ ⟵ Subscript

Figure 2 shows that the charge on the magnesium ion is 2+. The charge on each chloride ion is 1−. Two chloride ions balance the charge on the magnesium ion. The number "2" in the formula is a subscript. **Subscripts** tell the ratio of elements in a compound. The ratio of magnesium ions to chloride ions in $MgCl_2$ is 1 to 2. 🔑 **To write the formula for an ionic compound, write the symbol of the positive ion and then the symbol of the negative ion. Add the subscripts that are needed to balance the charges.**

If no subscript is written, it is understood that the subscript is 1. The formula NaCl tells you that there is a 1-to-1 ratio of sodium ions to chloride ions. Formulas for compounds of polyatomic ions are written in a similar way. Calcium carbonate has the formula $CaCO_3$. There is one calcium ion (Ca^{2+}) for each carbonate ion (CO_3^{2-}).

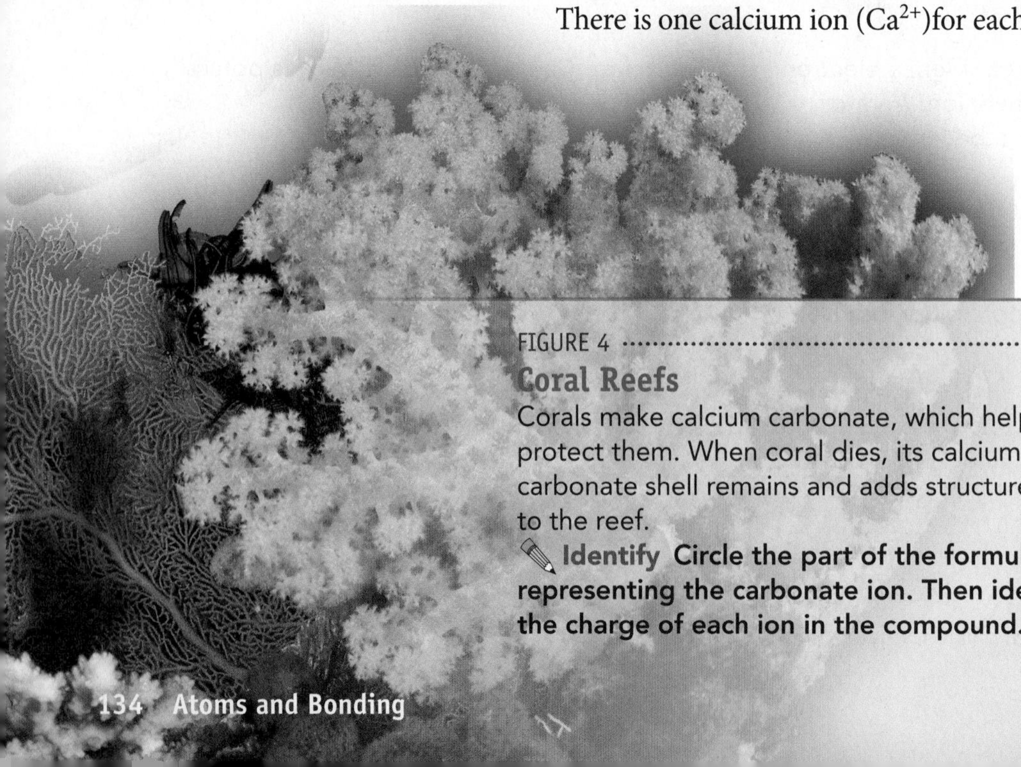

Vocabulary Choose the word that best completes the following sentence.

Mg is the _____ for magnesium.

FIGURE 4 ·······································
Coral Reefs
Corals make calcium carbonate, which helps protect them. When coral dies, its calcium carbonate shell remains and adds structure to the reef.
✎ **Identify** Circle the part of the formula representing the carbonate ion. Then identify the charge of each ion in the compound.

$CaCO_3$

Naming Ionic Compounds

Magnesium chloride, sodium bicarbonate, sodium oxide—where do these names come from? 🔑 **For an ionic compound, the name of the positive ion comes first, followed by the name of the negative ion.** The name of the positive ion is usually the name of a metal. But, a few positive polyatomic ions exist, such as the ammonium ion (NH_4^+). If the negative ion is a single element, the end of its name changes to *-ide*. For example, MgO is named magnesium oxide. If the negative ion is polyatomic, its name usually ends in *-ate* or *-ite*. Ammonium nitrate (NH_4NO_3) is a common fertilizer for plants.

did you know?

Calcium oxide (CaO), also known as lime, gives off a white light when heated. Theaters once used special lamps to focus this bright light on a single actor. So, the expression *in the limelight* describes a person who receives favorable attention.

apply it!

Chemists refer to compounds by either their names or their chemical formulas.

⚠ **Interpret Data** Use the periodic table and **Figure 2** to fill in the table.

Name	Positive Ion	Negative Ion	Formula
Magnesium chloride	Mg^{2+}	Cl^-	$MgCl_2$
Sodium bromide	___	___	___
___	___	___	Li_2O
___	Mg^{2+}	S^{2-}	___
Aluminum fluoride	___	___	___
___	___	___	KNO_3
___	NH_4^+	Cl^-	___

Do the Quick Lab
How Do You Write Ionic Names and Formulas?

🔑 **Assess Your Understanding**

2a. Explain The formula for sodium sulfide is Na_2S. Explain what this formula means.

_____

_____

_____

b. Apply Concepts Write the formula for calcium chloride. Explain how you determined this formula.

_____

_____

_____

got it?

○ **I get it!** Now I know that to write the formula for an ionic compound, _____

_____

_____

○ **I need extra help with** _____

Go to MY SCIENCE COACH *online for help with this subject.*

What Are Properties of Ionic Compounds?

Compounds have properties that are different from their component elements. You have already read about the properties of metals and nonmetals, but what are the properties of the ionic compounds that form when metals and nonmetals react? **In general, ionic compounds form hard, brittle crystals that have high melting points. They conduct electric current when dissolved in water or melted.**

Ionic Crystals Ionic compounds form solids by building up repeating patterns of ions. **Figure 5** shows a chunk of halite, which is how sodium chloride occurs naturally. Pieces of halite have a cubic shape. Equal numbers of Na^+ and Cl^- ions in halite are attracted in an alternating pattern, as shown in the diagram. The ions form an orderly, three-dimensional arrangement called a **crystal.**

Every ion in an ionic compound is attracted to ions of an opposite charge that surround it. The pattern formed by the ions is the same no matter what the size of the crystal. In a single grain of salt, the crystal pattern extends for millions of ions in every direction. Many crystals of ionic compounds are hard and brittle. This is due to the strength of their ionic bonds and the attractions among all the ions.

High Melting Points The ions in the crystal have to break apart for an ionic compound to melt. It takes a huge amount of energy to separate the ions in a crystal, because the attraction between the positive and negative ions is so great. As a result, ionic compounds have very high melting points. The melting point of sodium chloride is 801°C.

FIGURE 5 ·····················
Halite
The ions in ionic compounds are arranged in specific three-dimensional shapes called crystals. Some crystals have a cubic shape, like these crystals of halite, or sodium chloride.

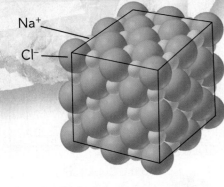

Na^+

Cl^-

apply it!

Galena, or lead sulfide (PbS), has a structure similar to that of table salt.

1 Infer The chemical formula of lead sulfide tells you that it contains _____ S^{2-} ion(s) for every Pb^{2+} ion.

2 What holds the ions together in galena?

_____

_____

3 CHALLENGE If the pattern of ions shown here for galena is expanded in every direction, how many sulfide ions would surround each lead ion? _____ How many lead ions would surround each sulfide ion? _____

S^{2-}

Pb^{2+}

FIGURE 6 ···
Glowing Pickle

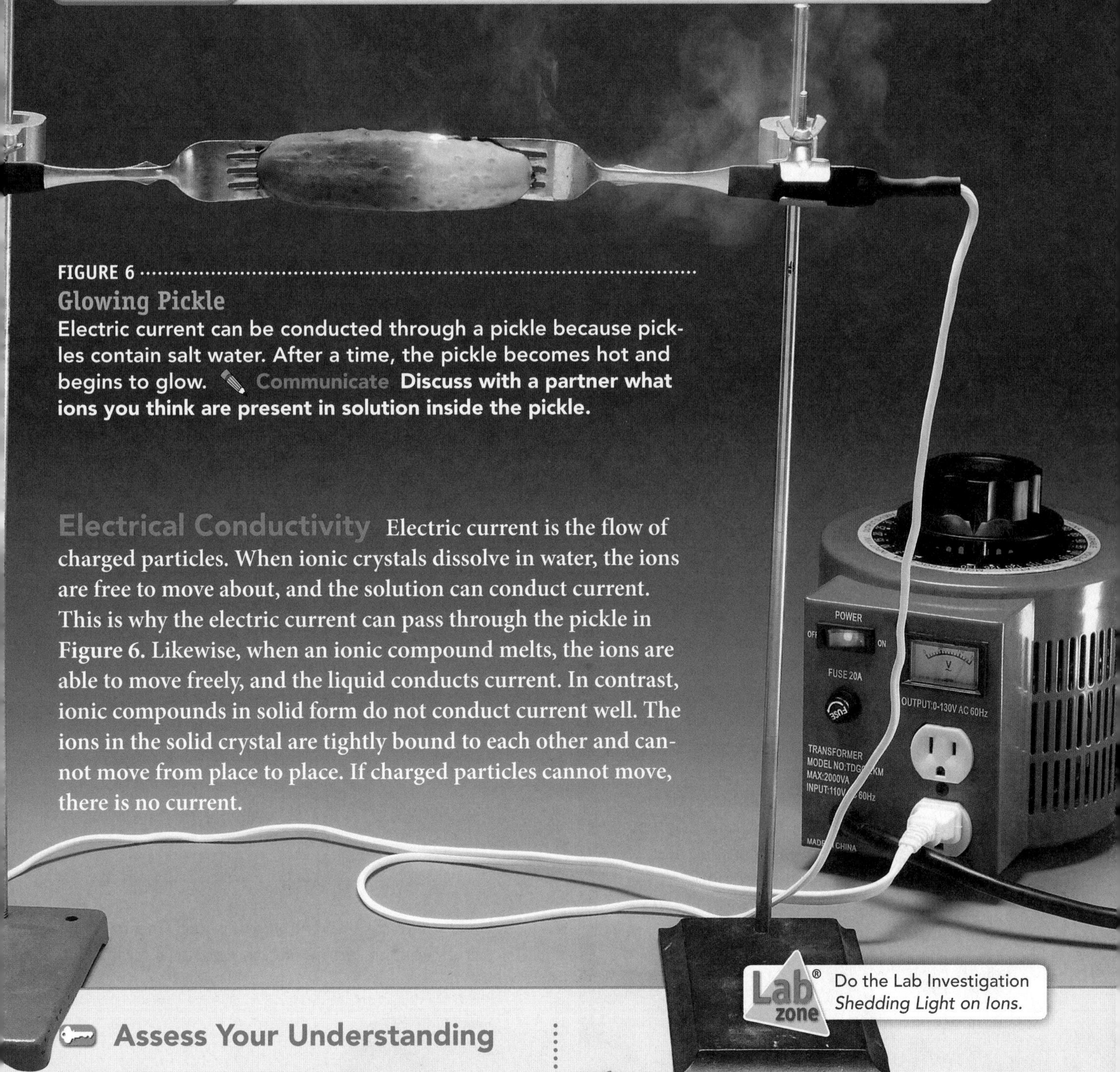

Electric current can be conducted through a pickle because pickles contain salt water. After a time, the pickle becomes hot and begins to glow. ✎ Communicate **Discuss with a partner what ions you think are present in solution inside the pickle.**

Electrical Conductivity Electric current is the flow of charged particles. When ionic crystals dissolve in water, the ions are free to move about, and the solution can conduct current. This is why the electric current can pass through the pickle in **Figure 6.** Likewise, when an ionic compound melts, the ions are able to move freely, and the liquid conducts current. In contrast, ionic compounds in solid form do not conduct current well. The ions in the solid crystal are tightly bound to each other and cannot move from place to place. If charged particles cannot move, there is no current.

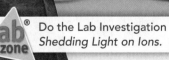

Do the Lab Investigation
Shedding Light on Ions.

🔑 Assess Your Understanding

3a. Review Ionic bonds are strong enough to cause almost all ionic compounds to be

_____ at room temperature.

b. Relate Cause and Effect Solid table salt does not conduct electric current. How does dissolving salt in water allow electric current to flow?

_____

_____

_____

got it? ······································

O **I get it!** Now I know that properties of ionic compounds include _____

_____

_____

_____

O **I need extra help with** _____

_____

Go to **MY SCIENCE** Ⓢ **COACH** online for help with this subject.

Covalent Bonds

UNLOCK THE BIG ?

🗝 **How Are Atoms Held Together in a Covalent Bond?**

🗝 **What Are Properties of Molecular Compounds?**

🗝 **How Do Bonded Atoms Become Partially Charged?**

MY PLANET DIARY

Sticky Feet

Have you ever seen a gecko climbing up a wall or running across a ceiling? Geckos seem to defy gravity. They have tiny hairs that cover the pads of their feet. These hairs branch out into hundreds of smaller structures, called *spatulae*. When a gecko climbs a wall, billions of spatulae on its feet come into contact with the surface. Scientists believe that geckos can stick to surfaces because of the billions of small attractive forces, called van der Waals forces, between the molecules of the spatulae and the molecules on the surface. Now, scientists are developing adhesives that can copy the characteristics of the spatulae.

FUN FACTS

Communicate Answer the following questions. Then discuss your answers with a partner.

1. Why is it important that billions of spatulae come into contact with the surface the gecko is climbing?

_____

_____

_____

_____

_____

_____

2. What uses do you think you could find for an adhesive that works like the gecko's foot?

_____

_____

_____

_____

_____

> **PLANET DIARY** Go to **Planet Diary** to learn more about attractions between molecules.

Lab zone Do the Inquiry Warm-Up *Covalent Bonds.*

Vocabulary
- covalent bond • molecule • double bond • triple bond
- molecular compound • nonpolar bond • polar bond

Skills
↺ Reading: Compare and Contrast
△ Inquiry: Graph

How Are Atoms Held Together in a Covalent Bond?

You and a friend walk past a bakery that sells giant chocolate chip cookies for one dollar each. But each of you has only 50 cents. If you combine your money, you can buy a cookie and split it. So, you can afford a cookie by sharing your money. Similarly, 2 atoms can form a bond by sharing electrons. The chemical bond formed when 2 atoms share electrons is called a **covalent bond.** Covalent bonds usually form between nonmetal atoms. Ionic bonds usually form when a metal combines with a nonmetal.

Electron Sharing Nonmetals can bond to other nonmetals by sharing electrons. Atoms of some nonmetals can bond with each other. **Figure 1** shows how 2 fluorine atoms can react by sharing a pair of electrons. By sharing electrons, each fluorine atom is surrounded by 8 valence electrons. ⚷ **The attractions between the shared electrons and the protons in the nucleus of each atom hold the atoms together in a covalent bond.** The 2 bonded fluorine atoms form a **molecule.** A molecule is a neutral group of atoms joined by covalent bonds.

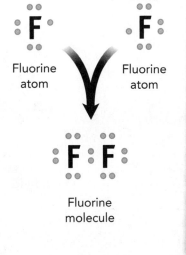

apply it!

Apply Concepts Draw electron dot diagrams to show how 2 iodine atoms bond together to form a molecule.

FIGURE 1 ....

Sharing Electrons
By sharing 2 electrons in a covalent bond, each fluorine atom gains a stable set of 8 valence electrons.

✎ **Interpret Diagrams** Circle the shared electrons that form a covalent bond between the 2 fluorine atoms.

Fluorine atom

Fluorine atom

Fluorine molecule

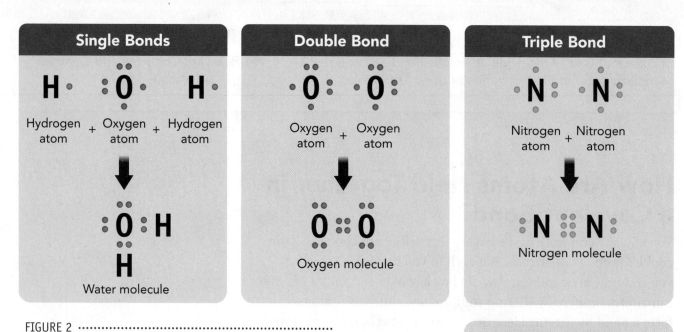

Single Bonds

Hydrogen atom + Oxygen atom + Hydrogen atom

↓

Water molecule

Double Bond

Oxygen atom + Oxygen atom

↓

Oxygen molecule

Triple Bond

Nitrogen atom + Nitrogen atom

↓

Nitrogen molecule

FIGURE 2 ···

Covalent Bonds

Atoms can form single, double, and triple covalent bonds by sharing one or more pairs of electrons.

How Many Bonds? Look at the electron dot diagrams in **Figure 2.** Count the valence electrons around each hydrogen and oxygen atom. Hydrogen has 1 valence electron. Oxygen has 6 valence electrons. In a water molecule, oxygen forms one covalent bond with each of 2 hydrogen atoms. As a result, the oxygen atom has a stable arrangement of 8 valence electrons. Each hydrogen atom forms one bond because it needs only 2 electrons to be stable.

Look at the electron dot diagram of the oxygen molecule (O_2) in **Figure 2.** This time the 2 atoms share 2 pairs of electrons, forming a **double bond.** Atoms of some elements, such as nitrogen, can share 3 pairs of electrons, forming a **triple bond.** The electron dot diagram for the nitrogen molecule (N_2) is also shown in **Figure 2.**

✎ CHALLENGE In a carbon dioxide (CO_2) molecule, the carbon atom forms a double bond with each of the 2 oxygen atoms. Draw the electron dot diagram for carbon dioxide below.

 Do the Quick Lab *Sharing Electrons.*

🔑 Assess Your Understanding

got it? ···

○ **I get it!** Now I know that the atoms in a covalent bond are held together by _____

_____

○ **I need extra help with** _____

Go to MY SCIENCE ⬤ COACH online for help with this subject.

What Are Properties of Molecular Compounds?

Water, oxygen, and sucrose (table sugar, $C_{12}H_{22}O_{11}$) are all examples of molecular compounds. A **molecular compound** is a compound that is made up of molecules. The molecules of a molecular compound contain atoms that are covalently bonded. Ionic compounds are made up of ions and do not form molecules. 🔑 **Unlike ionic compounds, molecular compounds usually do not conduct electric current when melted or dissolved in water. Also, compared to ionic compounds, molecular compounds generally have lower melting points and boiling points.**

Poor Conductivity

Most molecular compounds do not conduct electric current. Molecular compounds do not contain charged particles that are available to move, so there is no current. Have you ever noticed that some wires are insulated with plastic or rubber? These materials are made up of molecular compounds. Even as liquids, molecular compounds are poor conductors. Pure water does not conduct electric current. Neither does table sugar when it is melted or dissolved in pure water.

Low Melting Points and Boiling Points

Forces hold the molecules close to one another in a molecular solid. But the forces between molecules are much weaker than the forces between ions. Compared with an ionic solid, less heat must be added to a molecular solid to separate the molecules and change it from a solid to a liquid. For example, table salt melts at 801°C, but table sugar melts at about 190°C.

FIGURE 3 ·············

Headphones

Wires, such as the ones found on your headphones, are insulated with plastic or rubber to prevent electric current from flowing between the wires. The insulation also allows you to touch the wires without being shocked or electrocuted.

✎ **Observe** What are some other objects that have insulated wires?

_____

_____

_____

_____

do the math! Analyzing Data

Molecular and Ionic Compounds

The table shows the melting points and boiling points of a few molecular compounds and ionic compounds.

Substance	Formula	Melting Point (°C)	Boiling Point (°C)
Calcium chloride	$CaCl_2$	775	1,935
Isopropyl alcohol	C_3H_8O	–87.9	82.3
Octane	C_8H_{18}	–56.8	125.6
Sodium chloride	NaCl	800.7	1,465
Water	H_2O	0	100

Molecular compound   Ionic compound

1 **Graph** In the space below, draw a bar graph of the melting points of these compounds. Arrange the bars in order of increasing melting point. Label each bar with the chemical formula of the compound.

2 The melting points of molecular compounds are (lower/higher) than those of ionic compounds.

3 The boiling points of molecular compounds are (lower/higher) than those of ionic compounds.

4 **Predict** Ammonia (NH_3) has a melting point of –78°C and a boiling point of –34°C. These data suggest that ammonia is a(n) (molecular/ionic) compound.

Melting Points of Molecular and Ionic Compounds

Melting Point (°C)
900
800
700
600
500
400
300
200
100
0
–100
–200
Substance

Lab zone® Do the Quick Lab *Properties of Molecular Compounds.*

Assess Your Understanding

got it?

O I get it! Now I know that properties of molecular compounds include ____________________

____

____

O I need extra help with ____________________

Go to MY SCIENCE COACH *online for help with this subject.*

How Do Bonded Atoms Become Partially Charged?

Have you ever played tug-of-war? If you have, you know that when one team pulls the rope with more force than the other team, the rope moves toward the side of the stronger team. The same is true of electrons in a covalent bond. Atoms of some elements pull more strongly on the shared electrons of a covalent bond than do atoms of other elements. As a result, the electrons are shared unequally. 🔑 **Unequal sharing of electrons causes covalently bonded atoms to have slight electric charges.**

Nonpolar Bonds and Polar Bonds If 2 atoms pull equally on the electrons, neither atom becomes charged. This happens when identical atoms are bonded. A covalent bond in which electrons are shared equally is a **nonpolar bond.** The hydrogen molecule (H_2) shown in **Figure 4** has a nonpolar bond.

When electrons in a covalent bond are shared unequally, the atom with the stronger pull gains a slightly negative charge. The atom with the weaker pull gains a slightly positive charge. A covalent bond in which electrons are shared unequally is a **polar bond.** Hydrogen fluoride (HF), also shown in **Figure 4,** has a polar bond.

✏️ **Compare and Contrast**
In a nonpolar bond electrons are shared (equally/unequally).
In a polar bond electrons are shared (equally/unequally).

FIGURE 4 ·······························

▷ **ART IN MOTION** **Nonpolar and Polar Bonds**
Hydrogen forms a nonpolar bond with another hydrogen atom. In hydrogen fluoride, fluorine attracts electrons more strongly than hydrogen does. The bond formed is polar.

Round 1: H_2

Round 2: HF

✏️ **Communicate** Imagine you're a sportscaster. Write a commentary describing each of the "tug-of-war" matchups below.

Round 1: Hydrogen (H_2)

_____
_____
_____
_____

Round 2: Hydrogen Fluoride (HF)

_____
_____
_____
_____

143

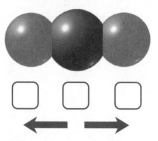

Nonpolar Molecule
Carbon dioxide

Opposite pulling cancels.

Polar Molecule
Water

Electrons pulled
toward oxygen

FIGURE 5 ································

Nonpolar and Polar Molecules

Both carbon dioxide and water molecules contain polar bonds. However, only water is a polar molecule.

✎ **Interpret Diagrams** Draw a positive (+) sign next to the atoms that gain a slight positive charge. Draw a negative (–) sign next to the atoms that gain a slight negative charge.

Polar Bonds in Molecules A molecule is polar if it has a positively charged end and a negatively charged end. However, not all molecules containing polar bonds are polar overall. In a carbon dioxide molecule, the oxygen atoms attract electrons more strongly than the carbon atom does. The bonds between the oxygen and carbon atoms are polar. But, as you can see in **Figure 5,** a carbon dioxide molecule has a straight-line shape. The two oxygen atoms pull with equal strength in opposite directions. The attractions cancel out, so the molecule is nonpolar.

A water molecule, with its two polar bonds, is itself polar. As you can see in **Figure 5,** a water molecule has a bent shape. The two hydrogen atoms are at one end of the molecule. The oxygen atom is at the other end of the molecule. The oxygen atom attracts electrons more strongly than do the hydrogen atoms. As a result, the end of the molecule with the oxygen atom has a slight negative charge. The end of the molecule with the hydrogen atoms has a slight positive charge.

EXPLORE
THE BIG
?

A Sea of Bonding

How can bonding determine the properties of a substance?

FIGURE 6 ·······················

▶ INTERACTIVE ART The Dead Sea is a saltwater lake in the Middle East. It is so salty that neither fish nor plants can survive in it. The water contains many dissolved compounds, including sodium chloride, magnesium chloride, and potassium chloride.

✎ **Review** Answer the questions about water and sodium chloride.

Water (H_2O)

Water is an example of a(n) (ionic/molecular) compound.

This type of bond forms when _____
_____
_____

Properties of these compounds
include _____
_____
_____
_____

Close-up of salt

Attractions Between Molecules

Opposite charges attract. Polar molecules are connected to each other by weak attractions between their slight negative and positive charges. These attractions are called van der Waals forces. The negatively charged oxygen ends of the polar water molecules attract the positively charged hydrogen ends of nearby water molecules. Van der Waals forces pull water molecules toward each other. They are also the reason a gecko's feet can grip onto smooth surfaces, such as glass.

The properties of polar and nonpolar compounds are different because of differences in attractions between their molecules. The melting point and boiling point of water are much higher than the melting point and boiling point of oxygen. The attractions between the polar water molecules require more energy to overcome than the attractions between the nonpolar oxygen molecules.

Sodium Chloride (NaCl)

Sodium chloride is an example of a(n) (ionic/molecular) compound.

This type of bond forms when _____
_____
_____

Properties of these compounds include _____
_____
_____
_____

Assess Your Understanding

1a. Review What type of bonds are formed when atoms share electrons unequally?

_____

b. Predict Would carbon dioxide or water have a higher boiling point? Explain.

_____
_____
_____
_____
_____
_____

c. ANSWER THE BIG ? How can bonding determine the properties of a substance?

_____
_____
_____
_____
_____
_____
_____
_____
_____
_____
_____

got it? ....

○ **I get it!** Now I know that some atoms in covalent bonds become slightly negative or slightly positive when _____
_____
_____

○ **I need extra help with** _____
_____

Go to MY SCIENCE ⓢ COACH *online for help with this subject.*

LESSON

4 Bonding in Metals

UNLOCK THE BIG ?

🔑 **What Is the Structure of a Metal Crystal?**

🔑 **What Are Properties of Metals?**

my planet DiaRY

DISCOVERY

Superconductors

In 1911, physicist Heike Kamerlingh Onnes made a remarkable discovery. When he cooled mercury to −269°C (4 kelvins), the mercury no longer resisted the flow of electric current! The cooled mercury became the world's first superconductor. A superconductor is a material that has no resistance to the flow of electric current.

Certain metals and alloys become superconductors as they are cooled to very low temperatures. This means they can carry electric currents for long periods of time without losing energy as heat. Superconductors can also be used to produce very powerful magnetic fields. These magnetic fields can be used to levitate and move high-speed trains.

Communicate Write your answers to each question below. Then discuss your answers with a partner.

1. How is a superconductor different from a regular conductor?

_____

_____

_____

_____

2. Power lines lose 10 to 15 percent of the electric current they carry to heat. Why might scientists want to create superconducting power lines?

_____

_____

_____

_____

> PLANET DIARY Go to **Planet Diary** to learn more about metals.

 Do the Inquiry Warm-Up *Are They "Steel" the Same?*

Vocabulary
- metallic bond
- alloy

Skills
- Reading: Identify the Main Idea
- Inquiry: Classify

What Is the Structure of a Metal Crystal?

The properties of solid metals can be explained by the structure of metal atoms and the bonding among those atoms. When metal atoms combine chemically with atoms of other elements, they usually lose valence electrons. They then become positively charged metal ions. Metal atoms lose electrons easily because they do not hold onto their valence electrons very strongly.

The loosely held valence electrons in metal atoms result in a type of bonding that happens in metals. Most metals are crystalline solids. **A metal crystal is composed of closely packed, positively charged metal ions. The valence electrons drift among the ions.** Each metal ion is held in the crystal by a **metallic bond**—an attraction between a positive metal ion and the electrons surrounding it. **Figure 1** illustrates the metallic bonds that hold together aluminum foil.

FIGURE 1 ·······················
Metallic Bonding
The positively charged metal ions are embedded in a "sea" of valence electrons.

✎ **Infer** Why would nonmetals be unlikely to have the type of bonding shown here?

_____

_____

_____

Do the Quick Lab
Metal Crystals.

🔑 Assess Your Understanding

got it? ···

○ **I get it!** Now I know that a metal crystal consists of _____

_____

○ **I need extra help with** _____

Go to MY SCIENCE ⓢ COACH online for help with this subject.

What Are Properties of Metals?

You know a piece of metal when you see it. It's usually hard, dense, and shiny. Almost all metals are solids at room temperature. They can be hammered into sheets or drawn out into thin wires. Electronics such as stereos, computers, and MP3 players have metal parts because metals conduct electric current. Metallic bonding explains many of the common physical properties of metals.

🔑 **Properties of metals include a shiny luster, and high levels of malleability, ductility, electrical conductivity, and thermal conductivity.** Each of these properties is related to the behavior of valence electrons in metal atoms.

Luster Some of the parts of the motorcycle shown in **Figure 2** are covered in chromium, which is shiny. Polished metals have a shiny and reflective luster, called metallic luster. The luster of a metal is due to its valence electrons. When light strikes these electrons, they absorb the light and then re-emit the light.

✏️ **Identify the Main Idea**
Underline the main idea of this section on the properties of metals. As you read, circle the supporting details.

The fender protects the rider from dirt and debris. Metals can be used to form a fender because they are

Metal fins cool a motorcycle by _____ heat to the outside.

Malleability and Ductility

Metals are ductile. They can be bent easily and pulled into thin strands or wires. Metals are also malleable. They can be rolled into thin sheets, as with aluminum foil, or beaten into complex shapes. Metals act this way because the positive metal ions are attracted to the loose electrons all around them rather than to other metal ions. These ions can be made to change position. However, the metallic bonds between the ion and the surrounding electrons keep the metal ions from breaking apart from one another.

Thermal Conductivity

Thermal energy is the total energy of motion of all the particles in an object. Thermal energy flows from warmer matter to cooler matter. The greater energy of the particles in the warmer parts of the material is transferred to the particles in the cooler parts. This transfer of thermal energy is known as heat. Metals conduct heat easily because the valence electrons within a metal are free to move. Electrons in the warmer part of the metal can transfer energy to electrons in the cooler part of the metal.

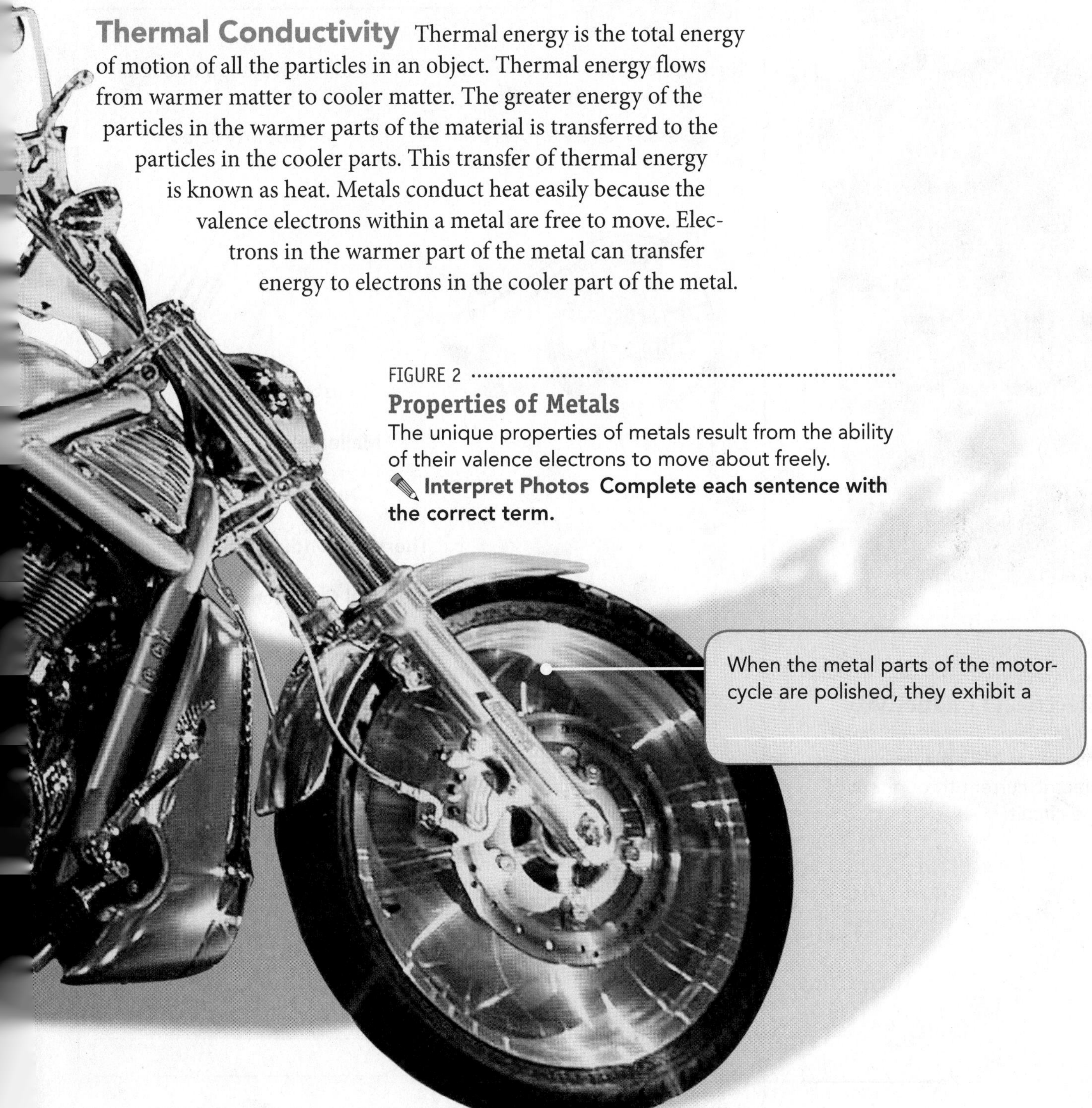

FIGURE 2 ·································

Properties of Metals

The unique properties of metals result from the ability of their valence electrons to move about freely.

✎ **Interpret Photos Complete each sentence with the correct term.**

> When the metal parts of the motorcycle are polished, they exhibit a

Electrical Conductivity Charged particles that are free to move can conduct an electric current. Metals conduct electric current easily because the valence electrons in a metal can move freely among the atoms. Electrical wires are made out of metal. Circuit boards, such as the one shown in **Figure 3,** contain metal strips that conduct electric current throughout the circuit.

Many objects that are made out of metal take advantage of one or more properties of metals.

1 ⚠ **Classify** Draw arrows from each physical property listed below to the object or objects you think best exhibit that particular property.

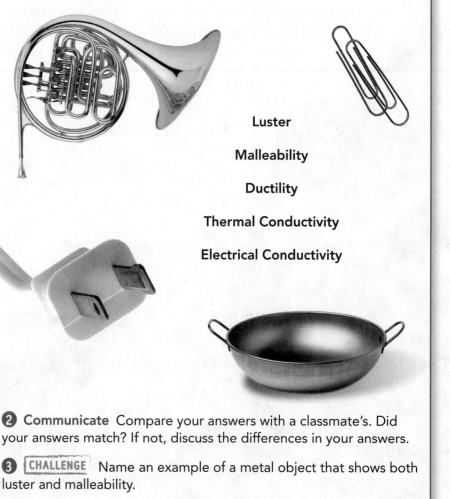

Luster

Malleability

Ductility

Thermal Conductivity

Electrical Conductivity

2 Communicate Compare your answers with a classmate's. Did your answers match? If not, discuss the differences in your answers.

3 [CHALLENGE] Name an example of a metal object that shows both luster and malleability.

_____

_____

_____

FIGURE 3 ·······················
Electrical Conductivity
Metal strips on a circuit board inside this MP3 player conduct electric current throughout the circuit.

Alloys Very few of the "metals" you use every day are made up of just one element. Most of the metallic objects you see and use are made of alloys. An alloy is a mixture made of two or more elements, at least one of which is a metal. Alloys are generally stronger and less reactive than the pure metals from which they are made.

Pure gold is shiny, but it is soft and easily bent. For that reason, gold jewelry is made of an alloy of gold mixed with a harder element, such as copper or silver. Gold alloys are much harder than pure gold but still retain its beauty and shine.

Iron is a strong metal, but iron objects rust when they are exposed to air and water. For this reason, iron is often alloyed with one or more other elements to make steel. Objects made of iron alloys, such as the shark suit worn by the diver in Figure 4, are much stronger than iron and resist rust much better. Forks and spoons made of stainless steel can be washed over and over again without rusting. That's because stainless steel—an alloy of iron, carbon, nickel, and chromium—does not react with air and water as iron does.

FIGURE 4
Alloys
A steel suit prevents the diver from being injured by a shark.
✎ **List** What other objects do you think contain steel?

_____

_____

Lab zone®   Do the Quick Lab
What Do Metals Do?

🔑 Assess Your Understanding

1a. Identify What accounts for the properties of metals?

_____

_____

b. Explain Explain why metals are good conductors of electric current.

_____

_____

c. Apply Concepts Why is it safer to use a non-metal mixing spoon when cooking something on the stove?

_____

_____

_____

_____

_____

_____

got it?

○ I get it! Now I know that properties of metals include _____

_____

○ I need extra help with _____

Go to **MY SCIENCE** 💬 **COACH** online for help with this subject.

151

Study Guide

REVIEW THE BIG

Compared to molecular compounds, ionic compounds have _____ melting points.

Ionic compounds conduct electric current when _____

LESSON 1 Atoms, Bonding, and the Periodic Table

🔑 The number of valence electrons in each atom of an element helps determine the chemical properties of that element.

Vocabulary
- valence electron
- electron dot diagram
- chemical bond

·C·

Carbon

LESSON 2 Ionic Bonds

🔑 When a neutral atom loses or gains a valence electron, it becomes an ion.

🔑 For an ionic compound, the name of the negative ion follows the name of the positive ion.

🔑 Ionic compounds have high melting points.

Vocabulary
- ion • polyatomic ion • ionic bond
- ionic compound • chemical formula
- subscript • crystal

LESSON 3 Covalent Bonds

🔑 Attractions between the shared electrons and the protons in the nucleus of each atom hold the atoms together in a covalent bond.

🔑 Molecular compounds have low melting points and do not conduct electric current.

🔑 Unequal sharing of electrons causes bonded atoms to have slight electric charges.

Vocabulary
- covalent bond • molecule • double bond • triple bond
- molecular compound • nonpolar bond • polar bond

LESSON 4 Bonding in Metals

🔑 A metal crystal is composed of closely packed, positively charged metal ions. The valence electrons drift among the ions.

🔑 Properties of metals include a shiny luster, and high levels of malleability, ductility, electrical conductivity, and thermal conductivity.

Vocabulary
- metallic bond
- alloy

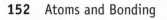

Review and Assessment

LESSON 1 **Atoms, Bonding, and the Periodic Table**

1. An electron dot diagram shows an atom's number of

   a. protons.
   b. electrons.
   c. valence electrons.
   d. chemical bonds.

2. When atoms react, they form a chemical bond, which is defined as _____
   _____
   _____

Use the diagrams to answer Questions 3 and 4.

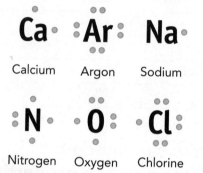

Ca· :Är: Na·
Calcium   Argon   Sodium

:N· ·O: ·Cl:
Nitrogen   Oxygen   Chlorine

3. **Infer** Which of these elements can become stable by losing 1 electron? Explain.
   _____
   _____
   _____

4. **Draw Conclusions** Which of these elements is least likely to react with other elements? Explain.
   _____
   _____

5. Write About It Go to your local grocery store and observe how the products on the shelves are organized. Write a paragraph comparing how food products are organized in a grocery store and how elements are organized in the periodic table.

LESSON 2 **Ionic Bonds**

6. When an atom loses or gains electrons, it becomes a(n)

   a. ion.
   b. formula.
   c. crystal.
   d. subscript.

7. Magnesium chloride is an example of an ionic compound, which is a compound composed of
   _____

8. **Classify** Based on their chemical formulas, which of these compounds is not likely to be an ionic compound: KBr, SO_2, or $AlCl_3$? Explain your answer.
   _____
   _____
   _____

9. **Interpret Tables** Use the periodic table to find the number of valence electrons for calcium (Ca), aluminum (Al), rubidium (Rb), oxygen (O), sulfur (S), and iodine (I). Then use that information to predict the formula for each of the following compounds: calcium oxide, aluminum iodide, rubidium sulfide, and aluminum oxide.
   _____
   _____
   _____
   _____

10. Write About It Pretend that you are the size of an atom and you are observing a reaction between a potassium ion and a fluorine atom. Describe how an ionic bond forms as the atoms react. Tell what happens to the valence electrons in each atom and how each atom is changed by losing or gaining electrons.

Covalent Bonds

11. A covalent bond in which electrons are shared equally is called a

    a. double bond.   **b.** triple bond.

    c. polar bond.   **d.** nonpolar bond.

12. The formulas N_2, H_2O, and CO_2 all represent molecules, which are defined as _____

_____

_____

13. Infer A carbon atom can form four covalent bonds. How many valence electrons does a carbon atom have?

_____

_____

14. Classify Identify each molecule below as either a polar molecule or a nonpolar molecule. Explain your reasoning.

   Oxygen   **Carbon dioxide**

_____

_____

_____

_____

_____

_____

_____

_____

_____

Bonding in Metals

15. The metal atoms in iron are held together by

    a. ionic bonds.   **b.** polar bonds.

    c. covalent bonds.   **d.** metallic bonds.

16. Polished metals have a metallic luster, which means that _____

_____

17. Apply Concepts Why does an aluminum horseshoe bend but not break when a blacksmith pounds it into shape with a hammer?

_____

_____

_____

_____

_____

_____

APPLY
THE BIG
? **How can bonding determine the properties of a substance?**

18. An ice cube and a scoop of table salt are left outside on a warm, sunny day. Explain why the ice cube melts and the salt does not.

_____

_____

_____

_____

Standardized Test Prep

Multiple Choice

Circle the letter of the best answer.

1. The table below lists some ions and their charges.

Ions and Their Charges		
Name	**Charge**	**Symbol/Formula**
Sodium	1+	Na^+
Calcium	2+	Ca^{2+}
Chloride	1–	Cl^-
Phosphate	3–	PO_4^{3-}

How many sodium ions are needed to balance the charge of one phosphate ion?

A 1
B 2
C 3
D 4

2. The chemical formula for a glucose molecule is $C_6H_{12}O_6$. The subscripts represent the

A mass of each element.
B number of atoms of each element in a glucose molecule.
C total number of bonds made by each atom.
D number of valence electrons in each atom.

3. Elements that have the same number of valence electrons are

A within the same group of the periodic table.
B within the same period of the periodic table.
C called noble gases.
D called metalloids.

4. When an atom loses an electron, it

A becomes a negative ion.
B becomes a positive ion.
C forms a covalent bond.
D gains a proton.

5. All of the following are characteristics that result from metallic bonding except

A the tendency to form hard, brittle crystals.
B the ability to conduct electric current.
C the ability to be hammered into sheets.
D luster.

Constructed Response

Use the electron dot diagrams to help you answer Question 6. Write your answer on a separate sheet of paper.

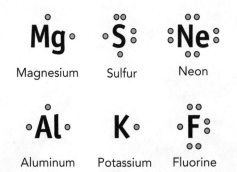

Magnesium   Sulfur   Neon

Aluminum   Potassium   Fluorine

6. Predict the formula for the compounds, if any, that would form from each of the following combinations of elements: magnesium and fluorine, aluminum and sulfur, and potassium and neon. If a compound is unlikely to form, explain the reason why.

Pharmacists
Chemists at Work

Interested in science—specifically in chemistry? Your local drugstore pharmacist is a highly trained chemist.

Pharmacists work with medications. All pharmacists earn an advanced degree in pharmacy. They must also take an exam in their state before they can receive their license.

Retail pharmacists dispense medications from behind a pharmacy counter at a drugstore. They work with customers to make sure the customers' medications are safe for them to take. This means knowing how medications interact with each other, and which are safe to take at the same time.

But drugstore pharmacies aren't the only places you'll find pharmacists. Research pharmacists develop and test new medications in labs. These medicines may improve and save lives, lives of people you know.

Research It Find out more about what a research pharmacist or a retail pharmacist does, and create an informational poster about this person's work.

Pharmacists are trained to be experts in handling medications. ▶

THE SUPERHERO OF GLUES

It bonds instantly to put together a broken dish, close a hole in a fish's skin, or stick a ton of concrete to a metal beam! Magic? No, it's cyanoacrylate, a special glue. Just three square centimeters of cyanoacrylate can hold more than one ton of just about anything to any surface.

Cyanoacrylate ($C_5H_5NO_2(l)$) forms strong bonds when it comes into contact with hydroxide ions ($OH-(g)$), found in water. Almost the moment you squeeze it out of the tube, the adhesive comes into contact with water vapor in the air and hardens, changing from liquid to solid.

Cyanoacrylate's powerful electron-attracting groups form chains of molecules, linked together. These chains form a rigid, plastic net that holds any molecules it comes into contact with! You have one super sticky situation.

Design It Design a cartoon strip explaining how the cyanoacrylate molecule forms chains to produce super bonds.

◀ Cyanoacrylate glue is used to attach a researcher's tag to a loggerhead sea turtle.

Sci-Fi Metal

Scientists in California have produced an amorphous, or glassy, metal that acts like plastic but is stronger than titanium. To produce the metal, elements are mixed and melted together, and then cooled very quickly.

A glassy metal is stronger than other metals because its atoms do not cool into a crystalline pattern. Instead, it has a random arrangement of atoms, which makes it able to transfer energy faster and last longer than other metals.

Research It Research the advantages and disadvantages of using glassy metals. What impact might glassy metals have on industry and society?

▲ NASA has used amorphous metal, which has a mirrored surface, to make solar wind collector tiles.

HOW DO BEES MAKE HONEY?

How is matter conserved in a chemical reaction?

Honeybees drink nectar from flowers. They store the nectar in a honey sac found inside their bodies. Nectar begins changing into honey in the honey sac. Nectar is mostly water, which evaporates during the honey-making process.

▶ **UNTAMED SCIENCE** Watch the **Untamed Science** video to learn more about chemical reactions.

After collecting nectar, the honeybees return to the hive where they spit the nectar into the mouths of house bees. Chemicals in the mouths of the house bees continue changing the nectar into honey until it is ready to be stored in the honeycomb.

Draw Conclusions Explain why bees must collect more nectar than actual honey that is produced.

_____

_____

_____

Chemical Reactions

5 Getting Started

Check Your Understanding

1. **Background** Read the paragraph below and then answer the question.

Alex is doing an experiment to see how vinegar reacts with **ionic compounds.** He measures the **mass** of a sample of baking soda. Alex records the measurement in his lab book next to the **chemical formula** for baking soda, $NaHCO_3$.

An **ionic compound** consists of positive and negative ions.

Mass is the amount of material in an object.

A **chemical formula** shows the ratio of elements in a compound.

- Which substance is an ionic compound in the experiment that Alex is conducting?

> **MY READING WEB** If you had trouble completing the question above, visit **My Reading Web** and type in *Chemical Reactions*.

Vocabulary Skill

Identify Multiple Meanings Some familiar words have more than one meaning. Words you use every day may have different meanings in science.

Word	Everyday Meaning	Scientific Meaning
matter	*n.* a subject of discussion, concern, or action **Example:** We had an important *matter* to discuss in the meeting.	*n.* anything that has mass and takes up space **Example:** Solids, liquids, and gases are states of *matter*.
product	*n.* anything that is made or created **Example:** Milk and cheese are dairy *products*.	*n.* a substance formed as a result of a chemical reaction **Example:** In a chemical reaction, substances can combine or split up to form *products*.

2. **Quick Check** Circle the sentence below that uses the scientific meaning of the word *product*.
   - She brought napkins and other paper **products** to the picnic.
   - Table salt is the **product** of the reaction of sodium and chlorine.

chemical change

precipitate

open system

replacement

Chapter Preview

LESSON 1
- physical change
- chemical change
- reactant
- product
- precipitate
- exothermic reaction
- endothermic reaction

↺ **Relate Cause and Effect**
△ **Graph**

LESSON 2
- chemical equation
- law of conservation of mass
- open system
- closed system
- coefficient
- synthesis
- decomposition
- replacement

↺ **Summarize**
△ **Make Models**

LESSON 3
- activation energy
- concentration
- catalyst
- enzyme
- inhibitor

↺ **Ask Questions**
△ **Predict**

> **VOCAB FLASH CARDS** For extra help with vocabulary, visit **Vocab Flash Cards** and type in *Chemical Reactions.*

Observing Chemical Change

🔑 How Can Changes in Matter Be Described?

🔑 How Do You Identify a Chemical Reaction?

MY PLANET DIARY

Chemistry in the Kitchen

Teen chef Fatoumata Dembele knows that chemical reactions are an important part of cooking great food. In fact, Fatoumata is so skilled at using chemistry in the kitchen that she won an award for her recipes.

Fatoumata knows that to prepare some foods, such as eggs, adding heat is required. Other foods, such as gelatin, need to have heat removed to taste best. Fatoumata says you have to keep a close eye on food while it's cooking. A good chef always pays attention to signs of change. For example, when you cook meat, the color is what tells you when it's ready. A raw steak is red, but a medium steak should be dark brown on the outside and pink in the center. Fatoumata prefers her steak well done. She knows it's ready when the meat is brown all the way through. For chefs like Fatoumata, there is one particular property that matters the most. It's the taste!

Write your answers to the questions below.

1. Energy is required for chemical reactions to take place. What form of energy is used in cooking?

_____

2. Think of something you've cooked before. What changes did you observe in the food?

_____
_____
_____

> PLANET DIARY Go to **Planet Diary** to learn more about chemical changes.

Lab zone® Do the Inquiry Warm-Up *What Happens When Chemicals React?*

Vocabulary

- physical change • chemical change
- reactant • product • precipitate
- exothermic reaction • endothermic reaction

Skills

↺ Reading: Relate Cause and Effect

△ Inquiry: Graph

How Can Changes in Matter Be Described?

Picture yourself frying an egg. You crack open the shell, and the yolk and egg white spill into the pan. As the egg heats up, the white changes from a clear liquid to a white solid. The egg, the pan, and the stove are all examples of matter. Recall that matter is anything that has mass and takes up space. An important part of chemistry is describing matter.

Properties of Matter Matter is often described by its characteristics, or properties, and how it changes. There are two kinds of properties of matter—physical properties and chemical properties.

How would you describe the penny in **Figure 1A**? It is solid, shiny, and hard. A physical property is a characteristic of a substance that can be observed without changing the substance into another substance. The temperature at which a solid melts is a physical property. Color, texture, density, and conductivity are other physical properties of matter.

A chemical property is a characteristic of a substance that describes its ability to change into other substances. To observe the chemical properties of a substance, you must try to change it into another substance. For example, **Figure 1B** shows a penny that has turned green. This color change demonstrates a chemical property of the penny's copper coating. When copper is exposed to air, it reacts over time to form a dull, crusty solid. Another chemical property is a material's ability to burn in the presence of oxygen. This property is called flammability.

FIGURE 1 ·····················

Properties of Copper
Pennies are coated with copper.

✎ **Complete the following tasks.**

1. **Classify** Check off which properties of copper are physical properties and which are chemical properties.

2. **Communicate** Add two properties to the list and ask a classmate to classify them as physical or chemical.

Copper

Property	Physical	Chemical
• Reddish color	☐	☐
• Reacts with oxygen	☐	☐
• Smooth texture	☐	☐
• Conducts heat	☐	☐
• Not flammable	☐	☐
• _____	☐	☐
• _____	☐	☐

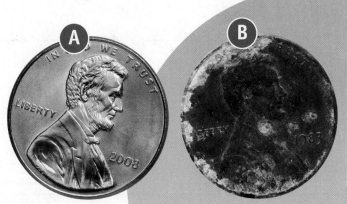

163

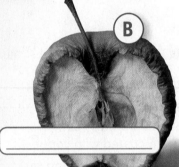

Changes in Matter Like properties of matter, there are two types of changes in matter. 🔑 **Changes in matter can be described in terms of physical changes and chemical changes.** A **physical change** is any change that alters the form or appearance of a substance but does not change it into another substance. When you cut an apple in half, as shown in **Figure 2A,** you cause a physical change. In a physical change, some of the physical properties of the material may be altered, but the chemical composition remains the same. Bending, crushing, and cutting are all physical changes. Changes in the state of matter, such as melting, freezing, and boiling, are also physical changes.

Sometimes when matter changes, its chemical composition is changed. For example, when a cut apple is left out in the air, it turns brown, as shown in **Figure 2B**. Compounds in the apple react with the oxygen in the air to form new compounds. A change in matter that produces one or more new substances is a **chemical change,** or chemical reaction. In a chemical change, the atoms rearrange to form new substances. When a substance undergoes a chemical change, it results in different physical properties as well. Burning and rusting are both chemical changes. Substances that undergo the chemical changes are called **reactants.** The new substances that form are the **products.**

FIGURE 2 ·····················

▶ **INTERACTIVE ART** **Changes in Matter**

Matter can undergo both physical and chemical changes.

✎ **Identify** Label each apple with the type of change it has undergone.

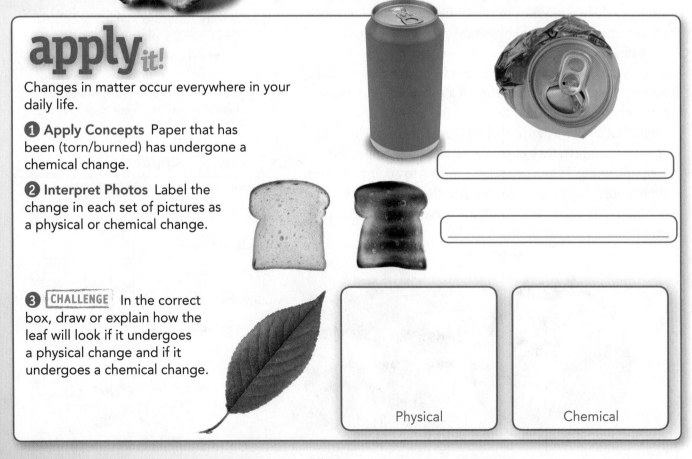

apply it!

Changes in matter occur everywhere in your daily life.

❶ **Apply Concepts** Paper that has been (torn/burned) has undergone a chemical change.

❷ **Interpret Photos** Label the change in each set of pictures as a physical or chemical change.

❸ **CHALLENGE** In the correct box, draw or explain how the leaf will look if it undergoes a physical change and if it undergoes a chemical change.

Physical

Chemical

Bonding and Chemical Change Chemical changes occur when existing bonds break and new bonds form. As a result, new substances are produced. Atoms form bonds when they share or transfer electrons. The reaction pictured in **Figure 3** involves both the breaking of shared bonds and the transfer of electrons.

Oxygen gas (O_2) in the air consists of molecules made up of two oxygen atoms bonded together. These bonds break when oxygen reacts with magnesium (Mg) and a new ionic bond forms. The compound magnesium oxide (MgO) is produced. Magnesium oxide, a white powder, has properties that differ from those of either shiny magnesium or invisible oxygen gas. For example, while magnesium melts at 650°C, magnesium oxide melts at 2,800°C.

⟲ **Relate Cause and Effect**
Find and underline the effect caused by breaking and forming bonds.

FIGURE 3 ·····························
Breaking and Making Bonds
✎ **Summarize** On the lines below the diagrams, describe what happens to the bonds in each of the steps as oxygen reacts with magnesium.

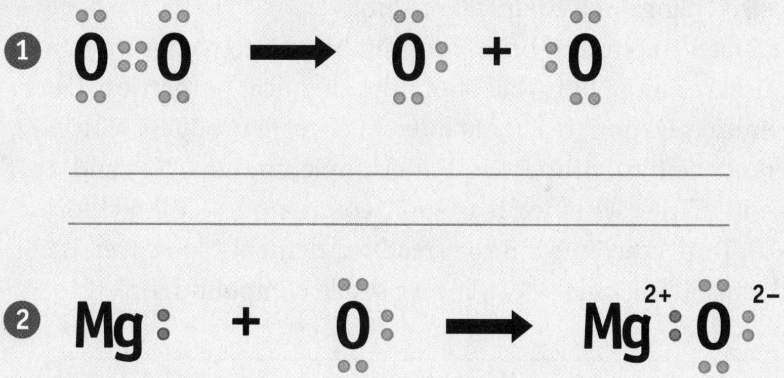

① O⬝⬝O → O⬝ + ⬝O

② Mg⬝ + ⬝O⬝ → Mg^{2+}⬝O^{2-}

Lab Do the Quick Lab
zone *Observing Change.*

🔑 **Assess Your Understanding**

1a. Review The freezing point of water is a (physical/chemical) property. The ability of oxygen to react with iron to cause rust is a (physical/chemical) property.

b. Pose Questions When silver coins are found in ancient shipwrecks, they are coated with a black crust. Ask a question that could help you determine whether the silver underwent a chemical change or physical change. Explain.

_____

_____

_____

_____

got it?

○ **I get it!** Now I know that two ways changes in matter can be described are _____

_____

_____

_____

○ **I need extra help with** _____

Go to MY SCIENCE 🗨 COACH *online for help with this subject.*

How Do You Identify a Chemical Reaction?

Look at the images in **Figure 4**. Even without reading the caption, you probably can tell that each image shows a chemical reaction. How can you tell when a chemical reaction occurs? 🗝 **Chemical reactions involve changes in properties and changes in energy that you can often observe.**

Changes in Properties One way to detect chemical reactions is to observe changes in the physical properties of the materials. Changes in properties result when new substances form. For instance, formation of a precipitate, gas production, and a color change are all possible evidence that a chemical reaction has taken place. Many times, physical properties such as texture and hardness may also change in a chemical reaction.

Changes in physical properties can be easy to recognize in a chemical reaction, but what about the chemical properties? During a chemical reaction, reactants interact to form products with different chemical properties. For example, sodium (Na) and chlorine (Cl_2) react to form an ionic compound, sodium chloride (NaCl). Both reactants are very reactive elements. However, the product, sodium chloride, is a very stable compound.

Vocabulary Identify Multiple Meanings Precipitation can mean rain, snow, or hail. In chemistry, precipitation is the formation of a solid from

_____

_____

① Formation of a Precipitate
The mixing of two liquids may form a precipitate. A **precipitate** (pree SIP uh tayt) is a solid that forms from liquids during a chemical reaction. For example, the precipitate seen in this curdled milk has formed from the liquids milk and lemon juice.

FIGURE 4 ···
Evidence of Chemical Reactions
Many kinds of change provide evidence that a chemical reaction has occurred.

✎ **Design Experiments** Describe how you would test the best method for separating the precipitate from the liquid in curdled milk.

_____

_____

_____

_____

_____

_____

_____

Although you may observe a change in matter, the change does not always indicate that a chemical reaction has taken place. Sometimes physical changes give similar results. For example, when water boils, the gas bubbles you see are made of molecules of water, just as the liquid was. Boiling is a physical change. The only sure evidence of a chemical reaction is that one or more new substances are produced.

2 Gas Production

Another observable change is the formation of a gas from solid or liquid reactants. Often, the gas formed can be seen as bubbles.

✎ **Observe** Bread dough rises from gas bubbles produced when yeast reacts with sugar. What evidence in a slice of bread shows the presence of gas?

_____
_____
_____
_____
_____

3 Color Change

A color change can signal that a new substance has formed. For example, avocados turn brown when they react with oxygen in the air.

✎ **Apply Concepts** Draw or describe evidence of a chemical reaction you have observed in food or in other types of matter. Label the evidence as a color change, formation of a precipitate, or gas production.

✎ **Relate Evidence and Explanation** Adding food coloring to water causes a color change. Is this evidence of a chemical reaction? Explain.

_____
_____
_____
_____
_____
_____
_____

Changes in Energy Recall that a chemical reaction occurs when bonds break and new bonds form. Breaking bonds between atoms or ions requires energy, while forming bonds releases energy.

In an **exothermic reaction** (ek soh THUR mik), the energy released as the products form is greater than the energy required to break the bonds of the reactants. The energy is usually released as heat. For example, some stoves use natural gas. When natural gas burns, it releases heat. This heat is used to cook your food. Similarly, the reaction between oxygen and other fuels that produce fire, such as wood, coal, oil, or the wax of the candle shown in **Figure 5,** release energy in the form of light and heat.

In an **endothermic reaction** (en doh THUR mik), more energy is required to break the bonds of the reactants than is released by the formation of the products. The energy can be absorbed from nearby matter. When energy is absorbed, it causes the surroundings to become cooler. In **Figure 5,** baking soda undergoes an endothermic reaction when it is mixed with vinegar. The reaction absorbs heat from its surroundings, so the reaction feels cold. Not all endothermic reactions result in a temperature decrease. Many endothermic reactions occur only when heat is constantly added, as when you fry an egg. Heat must be applied throughout the entire process in order for the reactions that cook the egg to continue.

FIGURE 5

▷ **VIRTUAL LAB** **Exothermic and Endothermic Reactions**
Chemical reactions either absorb energy or release energy.

✎ **Complete the following tasks.**

1. **Interpret Photos** Shade in the arrow that indicates the direction the net energy is moving for each reaction.

2. **Infer** How might each reaction feel if you were to put your hands near it?

_____

_____

do the math! Analyzing Data

A student adds magnesium oxide to hydrochloric acid. She measures the temperature of the reaction every minute. Her data are recorded in the table.

1 **Graph** Plot the data from the table onto the graph. Then name the graph.

2 **Interpret Data** Is the reaction endothermic or exothermic? Explain.

_____
_____
_____
_____
_____
_____

Time (min)	Temperature (°C)
0	20
1	24
2	27
3	29
4	29

3 **Read Graphs** In which time interval did the temperature increase the most?

_____

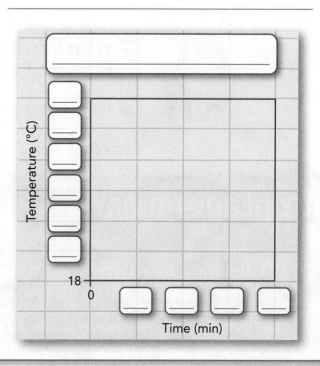

Temperature (°C)

18
0

Time (min)

Lab zone ® Do the Lab Investigation *Where's the Evidence?*

🔑 Assess Your Understanding

2a. List What changes in physical properties can be used as evidence that a chemical reaction has occurred?

_____
_____
_____

b. Apply Concepts What evidence of a chemical change is observed when rust forms on iron?

_____
_____

c. Compare and Contrast How are endothermic and exothermic reactions the same? How are they different?

_____
_____
_____
_____
_____
_____
_____
_____

got it? ·

○ **I get it!** Now I know that two kinds of changes you can observe when chemical reactions occur are

_____

○ **I need extra help with** _____

Go to MY SCIENCE ⓢ COACH *online for help with this subject.*

169

Describing Chemical Reactions

🔑 **What Information Does a Chemical Equation Contain?**

🔑 **How Is Mass Conserved During a Chemical Reaction?**

🔑 **What Are Three Types of Chemical Reactions?**

MY PLANET DIARY

Lifesaving Reactions

What moves faster than 300 km/h, inflates in less than a second, and saves lives? An airbag, of course! Did you know that the "air" in an airbag is made by a chemical reaction? A compound called sodium azide (NaN_3) breaks down into sodium metal (Na) and nitrogen gas (N_2). The nitrogen gas fills the airbag and cushions the passengers in an accident.

It's important that the correct amount of sodium azide is used. The mass of sodium azide in the airbag before the collision will equal the mass of sodium and nitrogen that is made by the reaction. If too little or too much nitrogen gas is made, the airbag will not inflate properly.

FUN FACTS

Write your answer to the question below.

What might happen if an airbag doesn't contain the correct amount of sodium azide?

_____

_____

_____

_____

_____

▷ **PLANET DIARY** Go to **Planet Diary** to learn more about the law of conservation of mass.

Lab zone® Do the Inquiry Warm-Up *Did You Lose Anything?*

What Information Does a Chemical Equation Contain?

Cell phone text messages, like the one shown in **Figure 1,** use symbols and abbreviations to express ideas in shorter form. A type of shorthand is used in chemistry, too. A **chemical equation** is a way to show a chemical reaction, using symbols instead of words. Chemical equations are shorter than sentences, but they contain plenty of information. In chemical equations, chemical formulas and other symbols are used to summarize a reaction.

Vocabulary

- chemical equation • law of conservation of mass
- open system • closed system • coefficient
- synthesis • decomposition • replacement

Skills

🔊 Reading: Summarize

△ Inquiry: Make Models

FIGURE 1 ⋯⋯⋯⋯⋯⋯⋯⋯⋯⋯⋯⋯

Symbols and Abbreviations

Text messages, like chemical equations, let you express ideas in shorter form.

✎ **Interpret Photos** Translate the text message using complete words and sentences.

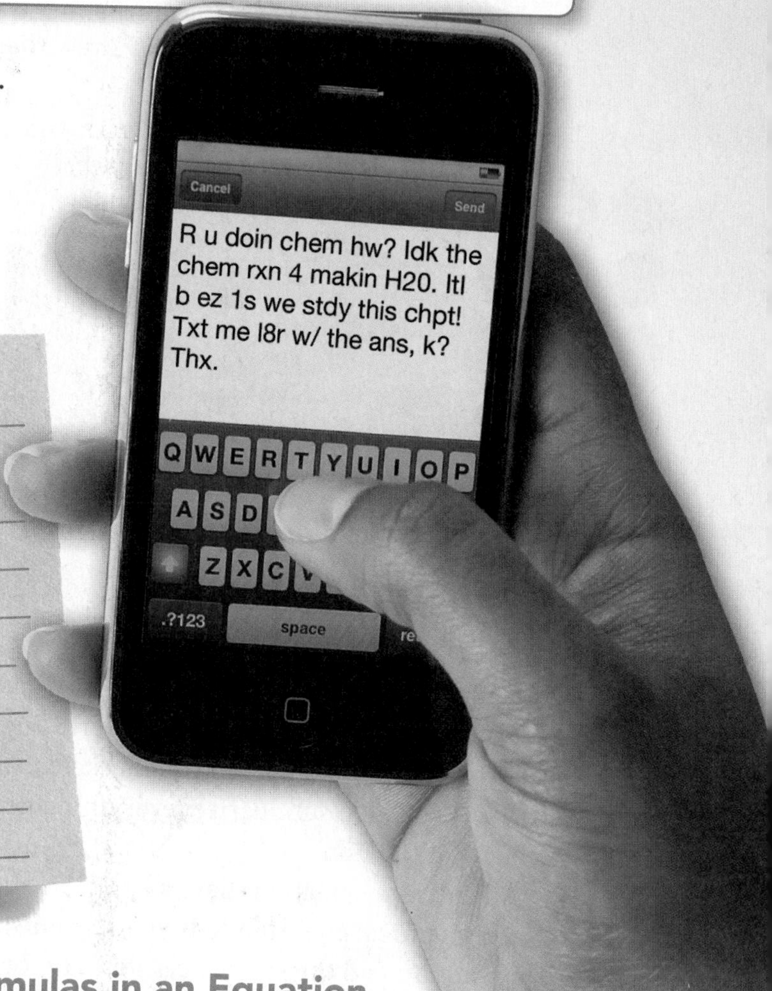

_____

_____

_____

_____

_____

_____

_____

_____

_____

Text message on phone reads:
R u doin chem hw? Idk the chem rxn 4 makin H20. Itl b ez 1s we stdy this chpt! Txt me l8r w/ the ans, k? Thx.

Formulas in an Equation

You may recall that a chemical formula is a combination of symbols that represents the elements in a compound. For example, CO_2 is the formula for carbon dioxide. The formula tells you that the ratio of carbon atoms to oxygen atoms in this compound is 1 to 2. Carbon dioxide is a molecular compound. Each carbon dioxide molecule has 1 carbon atom and 2 oxygen atoms. **Figure 2** lists the formulas of other familiar compounds.

FIGURE 2 ⋯⋯⋯⋯⋯⋯⋯⋯⋯⋯⋯⋯

Chemical Formulas

The formula of a compound identifies the elements in the compound and the ratio in which their atoms or ions are present.

✎ **Interpret Tables** Complete the table by filling in the missing chemical formulas.

Formulas of Familiar Compounds

Compound	Formula
Propane	C_3H_8
Sugar (sucrose)	$C_{12}H_{22}O_{11}$
Rubbing alcohol	C_3H_8O
Ammonia	NH_3
Baking soda	$NaHCO_3$
Water	_____
Carbon dioxide	_____
Sodium chloride	_____

171

FIGURE 3 ··

Modeling a Chemical Equation

Like a skateboard, a chemical equation has a basic structure.

▲ **Make Models** **Complete the equation by filling in the number of the skateboard parts shown. Determine the number of complete skateboards that can be made and draw them as the product.**

_____ wheels   +   _____ trucks   +   _____ decks   ➡   _____ skateboards

Structure of an Equation

Suppose you are building a skateboard. What parts do you need? How many of each part are necessary to build a complete skateboard? **Figure 3** summarizes everything you need to build several skateboards. Similarly, a chemical equation summarizes everything needed to carry out a chemical reaction.

All chemical equations have a basic structure that is followed. 🔑 **A chemical equation tells you the substances you start with in a reaction and the substances that are formed at the end.** The substances you have at the beginning are the reactants. When the reaction is complete, you have new substances, called the products.

The formulas for the reactants are written on the left, followed by an arrow. You read the arrow as "yields," or "reacts to form." The formulas for the products are written to the right of the arrow. When there are two or more reactants, they are separated by plus signs. In a similar way, plus signs are used to separate two or more products. Below is the general structure of a chemical equation.

$$\text{Reactant + Reactant} \rightarrow \text{Product + Product}$$

The number of reactants and products can vary. Some reactions have only one reactant or product. Other reactions have two, three, or more reactants or products. For example, the reaction that occurs when limestone, or calcium carbonate ($CaCO_3$), is heated has one reactant and two products (CaO and CO_2).

$$CaCO_3 \rightarrow CaO + CO_2$$

apply it!

Molecules of nitrogen (N_2) and hydrogen (H_2) react to form ammonia (NH_3).

① Identify Indicate the number of H_2 and N_2 molecules needed to yield two molecules of NH_3.

② Make Models Draw the correct number of reactant molecules in the boxes on the left side of the equation.

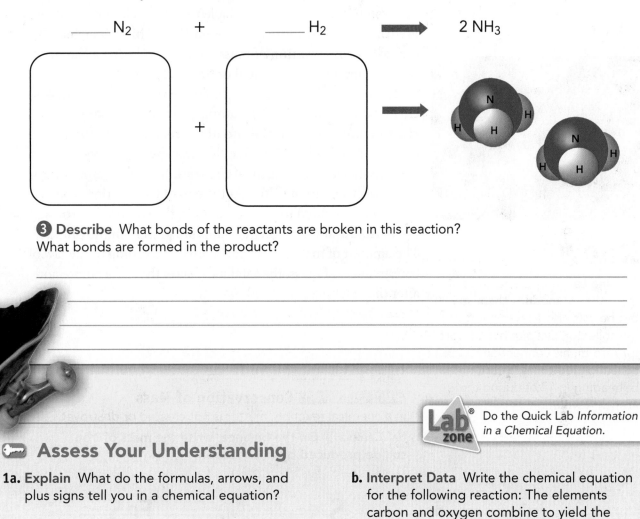

_____ N_2 + _____ H_2 ⟶ 2 NH_3

③ Describe What bonds of the reactants are broken in this reaction? What bonds are formed in the product?

_____

_____

_____

_____

_____

Lab zone® Do the Quick Lab *Information in a Chemical Equation.*

🔑 Assess Your Understanding

1a. Explain What do the formulas, arrows, and plus signs tell you in a chemical equation?

_____

_____

_____

_____

_____

b. Interpret Data Write the chemical equation for the following reaction: The elements carbon and oxygen combine to yield the compound carbon dioxide.

_____

_____

_____

got it? •

○ **I get it!** Now I know that a chemical equation tells you _____

_____

○ **I need extra help with** _____

Go to MY SCIENCE Ⓢ COACH *online for help with this subject.*

How Is Mass Conserved During a Chemical Reaction?

Look at the reaction below in **Figure 4.** Iron and sulfur can react to form iron sulfide (FeS). Can you predict the mass of iron sulfide, knowing the mass of the reactants? It might help you to know about a principle first demonstrated by the French chemist Antoine Lavoisier in 1774. This principle, called the law of conservation of mass, states that during a chemical reaction, matter is not created or destroyed.

The idea of atoms explains the conservation of mass. 🔑 **In a chemical reaction, all of the atoms present at the start of the reaction are present at the end of the reaction.** Atoms are not created or destroyed. However, they may be rearranged to form new substances. Look again at **Figure 4.** Suppose 1 atom of iron reacts with 1 atom of sulfur. At the end of the reaction, you have 1 iron atom bonded to 1 sulfur atom in the compound iron sulfide (FeS). All the atoms in the reactants are present in the products. The amount of matter does not change. According to the law of conservation of mass, the total mass stays the same before and after the reaction.

did you know? ....

Antoine Lavoisier is known as the father of modern chemistry, but he was also a lawyer and a tax collector. Despite his support for reform, his connection to tax collection led to his unfortunate beheading in 1794 during the French Revolution.

FIGURE 4 ·······································

> **INTERACTIVE ART** **Conservation of Mass**
In a chemical reaction, matter is not created or destroyed.
✏️ **Calculate** On the balance, write the mass of iron sulfide produced by this reaction.

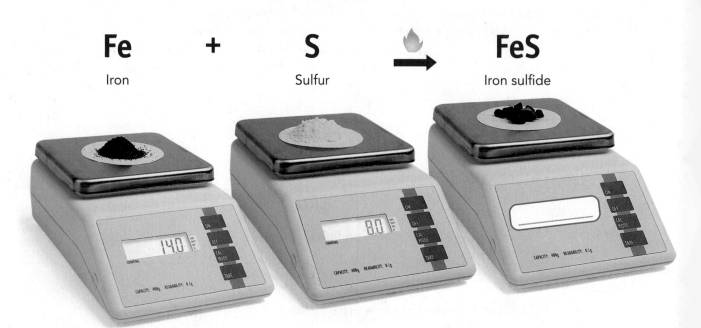

| Fe | + | S | → | FeS |
| Iron | | Sulfur | | Iron sulfide |

Open and Closed Systems

At first glance, some reactions may seem to violate the principle of conservation of mass. It's not always easy to measure all the matter involved in a reaction. For example, if you burn a match, oxygen comes into the reaction from the surrounding air, but how much? Likewise, the products escape into the air. Again, how much?

A fish bowl is an example of an open system. It contains different types of matter that are interacting with each other. In an **open system,** matter can enter from or escape to the surroundings. If you want to measure all the matter before and after a reaction, you have to be able to contain it. In a **closed system,** matter does not enter or leave. A chemical reaction that occurs inside a sealed, airtight container is a closed system. The enclosed ecosphere shown in **Figure 5** doesn't allow any mass to enter or escape.

FIGURE 5 ·······························

Open and Closed Systems

Matter cannot enter or leave a closed system, as it can in an open system.

✎ **Complete the following tasks.**

1. **Identify** Label each system as open or closed.

2. **Design Experiments** Which system would you use to demonstrate conservation of mass? Why?

_____

_____

_____

_____

3. [CHALLENGE] Why do you think the fish bowl above is considered a system, but an empty fish bowl is not?

_____

_____

_____

Balancing Chemical Equations

The principle of conservation of mass means that the total number of atoms of each element in the reactants must equal the total number of atoms of each element in the products. To be accurate, a chemical equation must show the same number of atoms of each element on both sides of the equation. Chemists say an equation is balanced when conservation of mass is correctly shown. How can you write a balanced chemical equation?

STEP 1 **Write the Equation** Suppose you want to write a balanced chemical equation for the reaction between hydrogen and oxygen that forms water. To begin, write the correct chemical formulas for both reactants and the product. Place the reactants, H_2 and O_2, on the left side of the arrow, separated by a plus sign. Then write the product, H_2O, on the right side of the arrow.

Hydrogen   Oxygen   Water

STEP 2 **Count the Atoms** Count the number of atoms of each element on each side of the equation. Recall that a subscript tells you the ratio of elements in a compound.

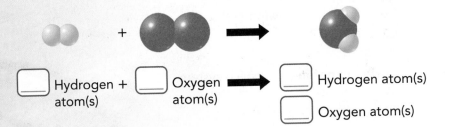

Hydrogen + atom(s)   Oxygen atom(s)   Hydrogen atom(s)   Oxygen atom(s)

After counting, you find 2 atoms of oxygen in the reactants but only 1 atom of oxygen in the product. How can the number of oxygen atoms on both sides of the equation be made equal? You cannot change the formula for water to H_2O_2 because H_2O_2 is the formula for hydrogen peroxide, a completely different compound. So how can you show that mass is conserved?

STEP 3 **Use Coefficients to Balance Atoms** To balance the equation, use coefficients. A **coefficient** (koh uh FISH unt) is a number placed in front of a chemical formula in an equation. It tells you the amount of a reactant or a product that takes part in a reaction. The coefficient applies to every atom of the formula it is in front of. If the coefficient is 1, you don't need to write it.

Balance the number of oxygen atoms by changing the coefficient of H_2O to 2. Again, count the number of atoms on each side of the equation.

🖊

Summarize Describe the steps to balancing a chemical equation.

_____

_____

_____

_____

_____

_____

_____

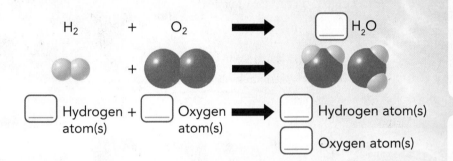

Balancing the oxygen atoms "unbalances" the number of hydrogen atoms. There are now 2 hydrogen atoms in the reactants and 4 in the product. How can you balance the hydrogen? Try changing the coefficient of H_2 to 2. Then, count the atoms again.

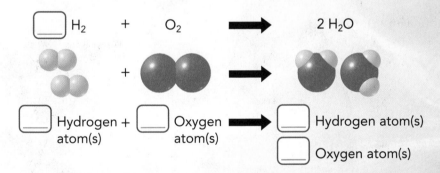

STEP 4 **Look Back and Check** Is the number of atoms of each element in the reactants equal to the number of atoms of each element in the products? If so, mass is conserved and the equation is balanced. The balanced equation tells you 2 hydrogen molecules react with 1 oxygen molecule to yield 2 water molecules.

do the
math! Sample Problem

Apply Concepts Use the sample problem in the blue box below to help you balance the following equations.

❶ $KClO_3 \rightarrow KCl + O_2$

_____

❷ $NaBr + Cl_2 \rightarrow NaCl + Br_2$

_____

_____

❸ $Na + Cl_2 \rightarrow NaCl$

_____

❶ Write the equation.
$Mg + O_2 \rightarrow MgO$

❷ Count the atoms.
$Mg + O_2 \rightarrow MgO$
  1   2   1 1

❸ Use coefficients to balance.
$2 Mg + O_2 \rightarrow 2 MgO$
  2   2   2 2

❹ Look back and check.

How Can Chemical Reactions Generate *SPEED*?

How is matter conserved in a chemical reaction?

FIGURE 6 ··

> **INTERACTIVE ART** One day, you might be able to drink the exhaust from your car! Sounds gross, right? Well, it could be possible with hydrogen fuel cells. Hydrogen fuel cells use a chemical reaction between hydrogen and oxygen to generate energy for running a car. In the process, water is produced.

✎ **Review** Use what you've learned about chemical reactions to answer questions about fuel cells.

1 **Endothermic or Exothermic?**

The reaction in a fuel cell is used to power cars and other devices. Is it an endothermic or exothermic reaction? Explain.

_____

_____

_____

_____

_____

2 **Conservation of Mass**

Inside a fuel cell, hydrogen is converted into H^+ ions. These ions combine with oxygen to produce energy for the car and water as exhaust. Describe how the fuel cell obeys the law of conservation of mass.

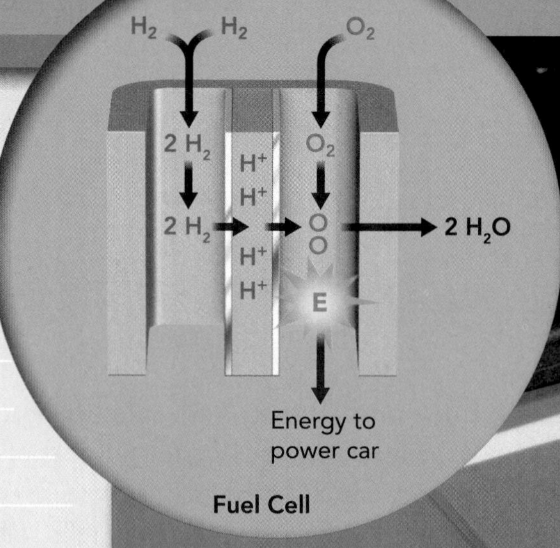

_____

_____

_____

_____

_____

_____

_____

H_2 H_2 O_2

$2 H_2$ H^+ O_2
          H^+
$2 H_2$ $\rightarrow$ $2 H_2O$
          H^+
          H^+ **E**

Energy to power car

Fuel Cell

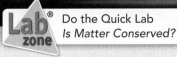

Do the Quick Lab
Is Matter Conserved?

🔑 Assess Your Understanding

2a. Infer If the total mass of the products in a reaction is 90 grams, what was the total mass of the reactants?

_____

b. Apply Concepts Balance the equations.

- $Al + CuO \rightarrow Al_2O_3 + Cu$
- $Fe_2O_3 + C \rightarrow Fe + CO_2$
- $SO_2 + O_2 \rightarrow SO_3$

_____
_____
_____
_____

c. ANSWER **THE BIG ?** How is matter conserved in a chemical reaction?

_____
_____
_____
_____
_____
_____
_____
_____

③ Properties of Matter

Hydrogen fuel cells power missions in space. Describe why the product of fuel cells would be more beneficial to space missions than that of other fuels.

_____
_____
_____
_____
_____
_____
_____

④ Balance the Chemical Equation

Hydrogen must be obtained from decomposing fuels like methane (CH_4). Balance the equation for generating hydrogen for fuel cells.

$$CH_4 + H_2O \rightarrow CO + H_2$$

got it? ······································

○ **I get it!** Now I know that the masses of reactants and products must be _____

_____

○ **I need extra help with** _____

Go to **MY SCIENCE** ⓢ **COACH** online for help with this subject.

What Are Three Types of Chemical Reactions?

In a chemical reaction, substances may combine to make a more complex substance. They may break apart to make simpler substances. They may even exchange parts. In each case, new substances are formed. 🔑 **Three types of chemical reactions are synthesis, decomposition, and replacement.**

Synthesis Some musicians use a machine called a synthesizer. A synthesizer combines different electronic sounds to make music. To synthesize is to put things together. In chemistry, when two or more elements or compounds combine to make a more complex substance, the reaction is classified as **synthesis** (SIN thuh sis). The reaction of phosphorus with oxygen is a synthesis reaction.

$$P_4 + 3\,O_2 \rightarrow P_4O_6$$

Decomposition In contrast to a synthesis reaction, a **decomposition** reaction occurs when compounds break down into simpler products. You probably have a bottle of hydrogen peroxide (H_2O_2) in your house to clean cuts. If you keep such a bottle for a very long time, you'll have water instead. Hydrogen peroxide decomposes into water and oxygen gas.

$$2\,H_2O_2 \rightarrow 2\,H_2O + O_2$$

Replacement When one element replaces another element in a compound, or if two elements in different compounds trade places, the reaction is called a **replacement.** Look at this example.

$$2\,Cu_2O + C \rightarrow 4\,Cu + CO_2$$

Copper metal is obtained by heating copper oxide with carbon. The carbon replaces the copper in the compound with oxygen.

The reaction between copper oxide and carbon is called a *single* replacement reaction because one element, carbon, replaces another element, copper, in the compound. In a *double* replacement reaction, elements in a compound appear to trade places with the elements in another compound. The following reaction is an example of a double replacement.

$$FeS + 2\,HCl \rightarrow FeCl_2 + H_2S$$

apply it!

Aluminum (Al) reacts with silver tarnish (Ag_2S) to yield pure silver (Ag) in a baking soda solution.

$$3\,Ag_2S + 2\,Al \rightarrow 6\,Ag + Al_2S_3$$

1 Classify What type of reaction is this?

_____

_____

2 Interpret Data Which element replaces another in the reaction?

_____

_____

_____

3 CHALLENGE Use information from the reaction to design an experiment that could be used to remove the tarnish (Ag_2S) from a silver fork.

_____

_____

_____

_____

_____

_____

_____

_____

FIGURE 7 181

Types of Reactions

✎ **Complete the following tasks.**

1. Interpret Diagrams Label each type of reaction represented.

2. Explain How are synthesis and decomposition reactions related to each other?

_____

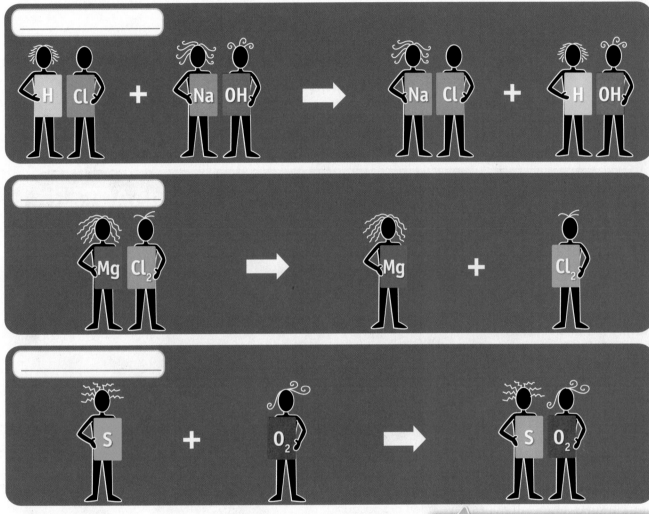

🗝 Assess Your Understanding

3a. Classify What type of chemical reaction is shown in the chemical equation below?

$$Zn + 2 HCl \rightarrow H_2 + ZnCl_2$$

_____

_____

b. Draw Conclusions The elements iron and oxygen can react to form the compound iron oxide. What type of reaction is this? Explain.

_____

_____

_____

 Do the Quick Lab *Categories of Chemical Reactions.*

got it? ....

○ **I get it!** Now I know that three types of chemical reactions are _____

_____

○ **I need extra help with** _____

Go to **my science** 🅢 **coach** *online for help with this subject.*

181

Controlling Chemical Reactions

🔑 **How Do Reactions Get Started?**

🔑 **What Affects the Rate of a Chemical Reaction?**

my PLANET DiARY

DISASTER

Up in Flames

On May 6, 1937, the *Hindenburg* airship was consumed by flames while landing at Lakehurst Naval Air Station in New Jersey. Thirty-five of the 97 people on board and one person on the ground died in the accident.

The cause of the fire, which destroyed the ship within one minute, is still unknown. Most people now believe that an electrical spark started the fire. However, several theories have been proposed to explain what caught fire first. One theory states that the spark ignited the flammable hydrogen inside the blimp. Another theory proposes that the paint on the fabric covering the ship caught fire first, setting off a reaction in the hydrogen.

Write your answer to the task below.

The *Hindenburg* could fly because the hydrogen that filled it was "lighter than air." Yet, hydrogen is incredibly flammable. Describe your own design for the ideal air transport machine.

_____

_____

_____

_____

_____

Lab zone ® Do the Inquiry Warm-Up *Can You Speed Up or Slow Down a Reaction?*

▷ **PLANET DIARY** Go to **Planet Diary** to learn more about controlling chemical reactions.

Vocabulary
- activation energy
- concentration • catalyst
- enzyme • inhibitor

Skills
- Reading: Ask Questions
- Inquiry: Predict

How Do Reactions Get Started?

Suppose you're a snowboarder, like the one shown in **Figure 1.** You know that the only way to ride down the mountain is to first get to the top. One way to get there is by riding the chairlift. Once you reach the top of the mountain, you can get off the lift and enjoy the ride down. If you never get to the top, you will never be able to go down the mountain.

Activation Energy Chemical reactions can be like snowboarding. A reaction won't begin until the reactants have enough energy to push them to the "top of the mountain." The energy is used to break the chemical bonds of the reactants. Then the atoms form the new bonds of the products. **Activation energy** is the minimum amount of energy needed to start a chemical reaction. ⚷ **All chemical reactions need a certain amount of activation energy to get started.** Usually, once a few molecules react, the rest will quickly follow. The first few reactions provide the activation energy for more molecules to react.

Hydrogen and oxygen can react to form water. However, if you just mix the two gases together, nothing happens. For the reaction to start, activation energy must be added. An electric spark or adding heat can provide that energy. A few of the hydrogen and oxygen molecules will react, producing energy. That energy will provide the activation energy needed for even more molecules to react.

⟲ **Ask Questions** Is it clear where chemical reactions get activation energy from? Write a question about this topic that you want answered.

_____

_____

_____

_____

_____

FIGURE 1 ··········
Activation Energy
✎ A chemical reaction needs a push to the "top of the mountain" to get started.

1. **Infer** Place an arrow at the point where enough activation energy has been added to start the reaction.

2. **Interpret Diagrams** Where does the snowboarder get the activation energy needed to reach the top of the mountain?

_____

Graphing Changes in Energy

Every chemical reaction needs activation energy to start. Whether or not a reaction still needs more energy from the environment to keep going depends on whether it is exothermic or endothermic.

Exothermic reactions follow the pattern you can see in **Figure 2A.** The dotted line marks the energy of the reactants before the reaction begins. The peak on the graph shows the activation energy. Notice that at the end of the reaction, the products have less energy than the reactants. This type of reaction results in a release of energy. The burning of fuels, such as wood, natural gas, or oil, is an example of an exothermic reaction.

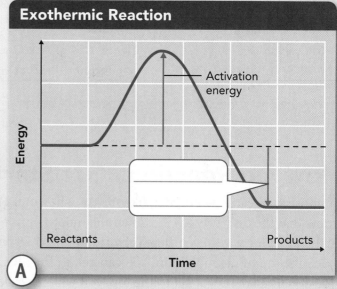

Exothermic Reaction

A

FIGURE 2 ··

▶ ART IN MOTION Graphs of Exothermic and Endothermic Reactions

Each of the graphs shows the amount of energy before and after the reaction.

✎ **Read Graphs** On each graph, label whether energy is absorbed or released.

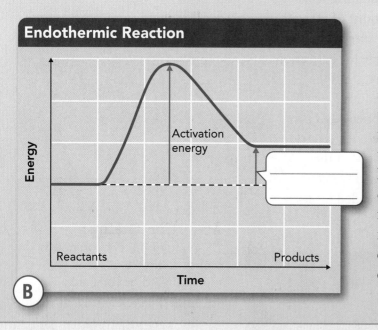

Endothermic Reaction

B

Now look at the graph of an endothermic reaction in **Figure 2B.** Endothermic reactions also need activation energy to get started. In addition, they need energy to continue. Notice that the energy of the products is greater than the energy of the reactants. This means that the reaction must continually absorb energy to keep going. Some endothermic reactions draw energy from the surroundings, leaving the area feeling cold. However, most endothermic reactions require continuous energy. For example, cooking a hamburger requires adding energy constantly until the meat is done.

Lab zone®

Do the Quick Lab Modeling Activation Energy.

🔑 Assess Your Understanding

got it? ···

O **I get it!** Now I know that in order for reactions to get started _____

_____

O I need extra help with _____

Go to MY SCIENCE ⓢ COACH online for help with this subject.

What Affects the Rate of a Chemical Reaction?

Chemical reactions don't all occur at the same rate. Some, like explosions, are very fast. Others, like the rusting of iron in air, are slow. A particular reaction can occur at different rates depending on the conditions.

If you want to make a chemical reaction happen faster, the particles of the reactants need to collide either more quickly or with more energy. Also, if more particles are available to react, the reaction will happen faster. To slow down a reaction, you need to do the opposite. **Factors that can affect rates of reactions include surface area, temperature, concentration, and the presence of catalysts and inhibitors.**

Surface Area Look at the burning building in **Figure 3**. It used to be a sugar factory. The factory exploded when sugar dust ignited in the air above the stored piles of sugar. Although the sugar itself doesn't react violently in air, the dust can. This difference is related to surface area. When a piece of solid substance reacts with a liquid or gas, only the particles on the surface of the solid come into contact with the other reactant. If you break the solid into smaller pieces, more particles are exposed to the surface and the reaction happens faster. Speeding up a reaction by increasing surface area can be dangerous, but it can also be useful. For example, chewing your food breaks it into smaller pieces that your body can digest more easily and quickly.

FIGURE 3 ·······
Surface Area and Reaction Rate
Sugar dust can react quickly because it has a greater surface area than a pile of sugar. A chemical reaction that moves quickly can cause an explosion.

do the math!

To find the surface area of a cube with 2-cm-long sides, find the area of each face of the cube.

Area = Length × Width

$4 \text{ cm}^2 = 2 \text{ cm} \times 2 \text{ cm}$

Then add them together.

$4 \text{ cm}^2 + 4 \text{ cm}^2 + 4 \text{ cm}^2 + 4 \text{ cm}^2 + 4 \text{ cm}^2 + 4 \text{ cm}^2 = 24 \text{ cm}^2$

Imagine cutting the cube in half. Find the surface area of each half. Add the values together to get the total surface area.

_____

_____

_____

_____

_____

_____

A chemical reaction takes place in glow sticks. Changing the temperature affects the rate of the reaction.

1 Relate Cause and Effect When the temperature increases, the rate of a chemical reaction (increases/decreases).

2 Predict The brightness of a glow stick's light is affected by temperature. What would happen if the glow stick were placed in boiling water?

_____

_____

_____

3 CHALLENGE The military uses glow sticks for lighting at night. Suggest a method for storing them during the day to maximize their use at night.

_____

_____

_____

_____

_____

_____

Temperature Changing the temperature of a chemical reaction also affects the reaction rate. When you heat a substance, its particles move faster. Faster-moving particles have more energy, which helps reactants get over the activation energy barrier more quickly. Also, faster-moving particles come in contact more often, giving more chances for a reaction to happen.

In contrast, reducing temperature slows down reaction rates. For example, milk contains bacteria, which carry out thousands of chemical reactions as they live and reproduce. You store milk and other foods in the refrigerator because keeping foods cold slows down those reactions, so your foods stay fresh longer.

Concentration Another way to increase the rate of a chemical reaction is to increase the concentration of the reactants. **Concentration** is the amount of a substance in a given volume. For example, adding a small spoonful of sugar to a cup of tea will make it sweet. Adding a large spoonful of sugar makes the tea even sweeter. The cup of tea with more sugar has a greater concentration of sugar molecules.

Increasing the concentration of reactants supplies more particles to react. Look at the tower of bubbles in **Figure 4.** This is the product of the decomposition reaction of a 35 percent hydrogen peroxide solution in water. Hydrogen peroxide that you buy at your local drug store is usually between 3 percent and 12 percent. The high concentration of hydrogen peroxide solution used in this reaction will release huge amounts of oxygen gas more quickly than a lower concentration would.

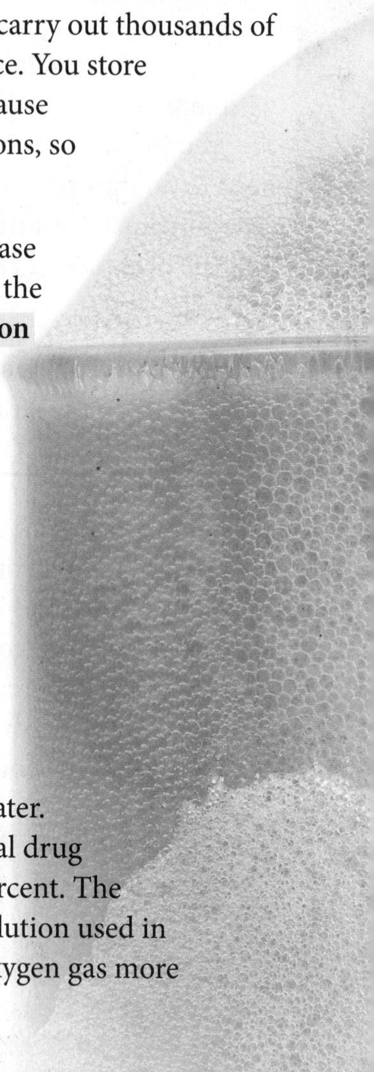

FIGURE 4 ·······································

Elephant Toothpaste

This reaction is nicknamed "elephant toothpaste" because of the enormous amount of bubbles it produces.

✎ **Predict How would using a lower concentration of hydrogen peroxide affect the rate of reaction?**

_____

_____

_____

Catalysts and Inhibitors Another way to control the rate of a reaction is to change the activation energy needed. A **catalyst** (KAT uh list) increases the reaction rate by lowering the activation energy needed. Although catalysts affect a reaction's rate, they are not permanently changed by a reaction and are not considered reactants.

Many chemical reactions can normally only happen at temperatures that would kill living things. Yet, some of these reactions are necessary for life. The cells in your body contain thousands of biological catalysts called **enzymes** (EN zymz) that help these reactions occur at body temperature. Each one is specific to only one chemical reaction. Enzymes provide a surface on which reactions can take place. Since enzymes bring reactant molecules close together, chemical reactions using enzymes require less activation energy and can happen at lower temperatures.

Sometimes it is more useful to slow down a reaction rather than speed it up. A material used to decrease the rate of a chemical reaction is an **inhibitor.** Inhibitors called preservatives are added to food to prevent spoiling.

FIGURE 5 ··

Catalysts

Adding a catalyst speeds up a chemical reaction.

✏️ **Graph** Draw and label the energy graph for the same chemical reaction when using a catalyst.

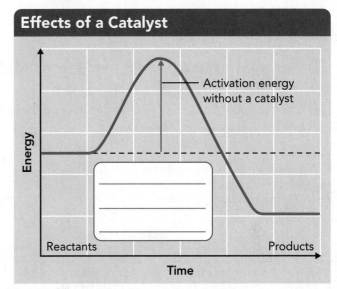

Effects of a Catalyst

Energy

Activation energy without a catalyst

Reactants

Products

Time

Lab zone ® Do the Quick Lab *Effect of Temperature on Chemical Reactions.*

🔑 Assess Your Understanding

1a. Describe To slow down a reaction, you can (increase/decrease) the concentration of the reactants.

b. Compare and Contrast What would react more quickly in the air, a pile of grain or a cloud of grain dust? Explain.

_____

_____

c. Explain How do enzymes speed up chemical reactions in your body?

_____

_____

_____

_____

_____

_____

got it? ··

O **I get it!** Now I know that the rate of a chemical reaction can be affected by_____

_____

_____

O **I need extra help with** _____

Go to MY SCIENCE Ⓢ COACH *online for help with this subject.*

187

REVIEW
THE BIG
?

The total mass before a chemical reaction equals _____

_____.

LESSON 1 **Observing Chemical Change**

🔑 Changes in matter can be described in terms of physical changes and chemical changes.

🔑 Chemical reactions involve changes in properties and changes in energy that you can often observe.

Vocabulary
- physical change • chemical change
- reactant • product • precipitate
- exothermic reaction • endothermic reaction

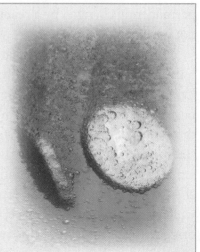

LESSON 2 **Describing Chemical Reactions**

🔑 A chemical equation tells you the substances you start with in a reaction and the substances that are formed at the end.

🔑 In a chemical reaction, all of the atoms present at the start of the reaction are present at the end of the reaction.

🔑 Three types of chemical reactions are synthesis, decomposition, and replacement.

Vocabulary
- chemical equation • law of conservation of mass
- open system • closed system • coefficient
- synthesis • decomposition • replacement

$$2\ H_2 \quad + \quad O_2 \quad \longrightarrow \quad 2\ H_2O$$

LESSON 3 **Controlling Chemical Reactions**

🔑 All chemical reactions need a certain amount of activation energy to get started.

🔑 Factors that can affect rates of reactions include surface area, temperature, concentration, and the presence of catalysts and inhibitors.

Vocabulary
- activation energy
- concentration
- catalyst
- enzyme
- inhibitor

 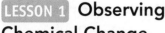
Review and Assessment

LESSON 1 Observing
Chemical Change

1. Which of the following results in a chemical
change in matter?

  a. bending a straw **b.** boiling water

  c. braiding hair **d.** burning wood

2. A solid that forms from liquids in a chemical

reaction is called a(n)_____

3. Interpret Photos What evidence in the photo
below tells you that a chemical reaction may
have occurred?

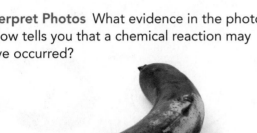

_____

_____

4. Solve Problems Steel that is exposed to water
and salt rusts quickly. If you were a shipbuilder,
how would you protect a new ship? Explain.

_____

_____

_____

_____

_____

5. 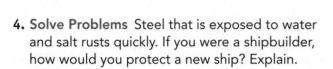 **Write About It** Suppose you have an Internet
friend who is studying chemistry just like you
are. Your friend claims the change from liquid
water to water vapor is a chemical change.
Write a brief e-mail that might convince your
friend otherwise.

LESSON 2 Describing
Chemical Reactions

6. How can you balance a chemical equation?

  a. Change the coefficients.

  b. Change the products.

  c. Change the reactants.

  d. Change the subscripts.

7. In an open system, such as a campfire, matter

can _____

_____

8. Classify Identify each of the balanced
equations below as synthesis, decomposition,
or replacement.

$2\ Al + Fe_2O_3 \rightarrow 2\ Fe + Al_2O_3$

_____

$2\ Ag + S \rightarrow Ag_2S$

_____

$CaCO_3 \rightarrow CaO + CO_2$

_____

9. Calculate Water decomposes into hydrogen
(H_2) and oxygen (O_2) when an electric current
is applied. How many grams of water must
decompose to produce 2 grams of hydrogen
and 16 grams of oxygen?

_____

_____

10. math! Balance the equations.

$MgO + HBr \rightarrow MgBr_2 + H_2O$

$N_2 + O_2 \rightarrow N_2O_5$

$C_2H_4 + O_2 \rightarrow CO_2 + H_2O$

$Fe + HCl \rightarrow FeCl_2 + H_2$

LESSON 3 Controlling Chemical Reactions

11. In general, what happens when you increase the temperature of a reaction?

   a. The heat destroys the reactants.

   b. The rate of the reaction decreases.

   c. The rate of the reaction increases.

   d. The rate of the reaction stays the same.

Graphs A and B represent the same chemical reaction under different conditions. Use the graphs to answer Questions 12 and 13.

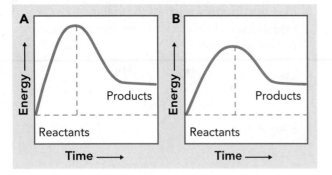

12. Interpret Data How does the energy of the products compare with the energy of the reactants?

_____

_____

_____

_____

13. Apply Concepts What change in condition might account for the lower activation energy barrier in the second graph? Explain.

_____

_____

_____

_____

 How is matter conserved in a chemical reaction?

14. Rust forms when iron metal (Fe) reacts with oxygen (O_2) to produce iron oxide (Fe_2O_3). Write a balanced equation for this reaction. Suppose you find the mass of an iron object, let it rust, and measure the mass again. Predict whether the mass will increase, decrease, or stay the same. Explain your answer in terms of the law of conservation of mass.

_____

_____

_____

_____

_____

_____

_____

_____

_____

_____

_____

_____

_____

_____

Standardized Test Prep

Multiple Choice

Circle the letter of the best answer.

1. The diagram below represents molecules of two different elements. The elements react chemically to produce a compound.

The diagram represents an

A   endothermic reaction in which energy is absorbed.

B   endothermic reaction in which energy is released.

C   exothermic reaction in which energy is absorbed.

D   exothermic reaction in which energy is released.

2. Which of the following is the **best** evidence for a chemical reaction?

A   change in temperature

B   change of state

C   formation of a new substance

D   gas bubbles

3. Which shows a balanced chemical equation for the decomposition of aluminum oxide (Al_2O_3)?

A $Al_2O_3 \rightarrow 2\,Al + O_2$

B $Al_2O_3 \rightarrow 2\,Al + 3\,O_2$

C $2\,Al_2O_3 \rightarrow 4\,Al + O_2$

D $2\,Al_2O_3 \rightarrow 4\,Al + 3\,O_2$

4. Which of the following would increase the rate of reaction?

A   maintain a constant temperature

B   increase the concentration of the reactants

C   increase the activation energy

D   add an inhibitor

5. Which equation describes a synthesis reaction?

A $2\,Na + Cl_2 \rightarrow 2\,NaCl$

B $Mg + CuSO_4 \rightarrow MgSO_4 + Cu$

C $2\,KI \rightarrow 2\,K + I_2$

D $CH_4 + 2\,O_2 \rightarrow CO_2 + 2\,H_2O$

Constructed Response

Use the table below and your knowledge of science to help you answer Question 6. Write your answer on a separate sheet of paper.

Compound	Formula
Carbon dioxide	CO_2
Methane	CH_4
Oxygen	O_2
Water	H_2O

6. The main compound of natural gas is methane. When methane reacts with oxygen gas, carbon dioxide and water vapor are produced. Write a balanced equation for this reaction. Explain why the burning of methane is a chemical change, not a physical change. Does this change absorb heat or release heat?

LOOK, MA, WARM HANDS

Winter to many means braving shorter days and blasts of frosty air. Along with heavy clothes, gloves and thick socks, reusable hand warmers can help battle the chill.

Sodium acetate is a salt used in many things, including salt and vinegar chips. The solution in a sodium acetate heat pad is supersaturated. Flexing a metal disk within the heat pad causes a few sodium acetate molecules to come out of solution and form crystals. This causes an exothermic change, which brings the temperature of the solution up to 54°C. (Room temperature is about 22°C.) Placing the heat pad in boiling water causes the crystals to dissolve and become a solution again, so that you can reuse the heat pad. You add heat to dissolve the crystals. When they come out of solution, into their solid state, they release that heat.

So the next time your hands are cold on a chilly day, use a portable warmer and take advantage of the exothermic change!

Design It Design an experiment to determine whether rock salt produces an exothermic or endothermic change when it is placed on icy roads and driveways.

Safe Moist Heating Pad

To Activate   place pad on flat surface and flex metal disc in corner

To Recharge   place pad on top of cloth in boiling water for 15 minutes or until all crystals are dissolved

note: if crystals form while pad is cooling, recharge

◀ Reusable sodium acetate heat pads use a change of state to generate heat.

Museum of Science

CAN YOU BE CLEAN AND GREEN?

It seems that everything is labeled with something "green" these days. Cleaning products are no exception, but can you make sure that you are both clean and "green"?

The best way to buy green is to read the ingredients list. In order to understand the ingredients and the claims, it helps to know how a product works and what the ingredients do. Detergents and soap work because they contain chemicals called surfactants. Surfactants are long, chain-like molecules. One end of the chain has a strong attraction to oil and dirt, and binds with them. The other end has a strong attraction to water, and binds with water molecules to wash the oil and dirt away. Today, many detergents use petroleum as a basis for surfactants. Petroleum is a nonrenewable resource that can pollute water sources. Some detergents use vegetable oils instead. These oils are renewable resources. Products that use them are more environmentally friendly than those that use petroleum-based surfactants.

Design It Some consumers fight going "green" because they think these products won't work as well. Design a test to compare how well a biodegradable detergent works with one that uses petroleum.

HOW DID THIS SINKHOLE APPEAR?

THE BIG ?

What determines the properties of a solution?

You might be wondering, "What is a sinkhole?" A sinkhole forms when the ground suddenly collapses. Sometimes sinkholes are caused by human activities like mining or by broken water pipes. In this photograph, divers are exploring a sinkhole that happened naturally when the underground rock, called limestone, mixed with slightly acidic water. The water actually dissolved the rock!

 Infer Do you think this sinkhole appeared suddenly or gradually over time? Explain your reasoning.

_____

_____

_____

_____

_____

> UNTAMED SCIENCE Watch the **Untamed Science** video to learn more about solutions.

Acids, Bases, and Solutions

6 Getting Started

Check Your Understanding

1. **Background** Read the paragraph below and then answer the question.

> When we breathe, we take in oxygen (O_2) and exhale carbon dioxide (CO_2). The bonds between the oxygen atoms in O_2 are **nonpolar bonds.** The bonds between the carbon and oxygen atoms in CO_2 are **polar bonds.** However, carbon dioxide is a nonpolar molecule.

> A covalent bond in which electrons are shared equally is a **nonpolar bond.**
>
> A covalent bond in which electrons are shared unequally is a **polar bond.**

- Carbon monoxide (CO) is an air pollutant. What type of bonds are in carbon monoxide?

_____

> MY READING WEB If you had trouble completing the question above, visit **My Reading Web** and type in *Acids, Bases, and Solutions.*

Vocabulary Skill

Identify Related Word Forms You can expand your vocabulary by learning the related forms of a word. For example, the common verb *to bake* is related to the noun *baker* and the adjective *baked.*

Verb	Noun	Adjective
indicate to show; to point	**indicator** something that shows or points to	**indicative** serving as a sign; showing
saturate to fill up as much as possible	**saturation** the condition of holding as much as possible	**saturated** to be full; to hold as much as is possible

2. **Quick Check** Review the words related to *saturate*. Complete the following sentences with the correct form of the word.

- The _____ sponge could hold no more water.

- He continued to add water to the point of _____

solution

solute

colloid

saturated solution

Chapter Preview

LESSON 1
- solution
- solvent
- solute
- colloid
- suspension

🔁 **Identify Supporting Evidence**
🔺 **Interpret Data**

LESSON 2
- dilute solution
- concentrated solution
- solubility
- saturated solution

🔁 **Identify the Main Idea**
🔺 **Calculate**

LESSON 3
- acid
- corrosive
- indicator
- base

🔁 **Summarize**
🔺 **Predict**

LESSON 4
- hydrogen ion (H$^+$)
- hydroxide ion (OH$^-$)
- pH scale
- neutralization
- salt

🔁 **Relate Cause and Effect**
🔺 **Measure**

▷ **VOCAB FLASH CARDS** For extra help with vocabulary, visit **Vocab Flash Cards** and type in *Acids, Bases, and Solutions.*

1 Understanding Solutions

- **How Are Mixtures Classified?**

- **How Does a Solution Form?**

MY PLANET DIARY

MISCONCEPTION

Killer Quicksand?

Misconception: You may have watched scenes in a movie like the one below. It's a common misconception that if you fall into a pit of quicksand, it is nearly impossible to escape its muddy clutches.

Fact: Although it is real, quicksand is not as deadly as it's often made out to be. Quicksand is a mixture of sand and water and is rarely more than a few feet deep. It forms when too much water mixes with loose sand. Water molecules surround the individual grains of sand, reducing the friction between them. The sand grains easily slide past each other and can no longer support any weight.

Fortunately, a human body is less dense than quicksand, which means you can float on it. By relaxing and lying on your back, you'll eventually float to the top.

Write your answer to the question below.

Quicksand can be frightening until you understand how it works. Describe something that seemed scary to you until you learned more about it.

_____

_____

_____

_____

_____

_____

_____

_____

> PLANET DIARY Go to **Planet Diary** to learn more about solutions.

 Do the Inquiry Warm-Up *What Makes a Mixture a Solution?*

Vocabulary
- solution • solvent
- solute • colloid
- suspension

Skills
Reading: Identify Supporting Evidence
Inquiry: Interpret Data

How Are Mixtures Classified?

What do peanut butter, lemonade, and salad dressing have in common? All of these are examples of different types of mixtures. 🗝 **A mixture is classified as a solution, colloid, or suspension based on the size of its largest particles.**

Solutions Grape juice is one example of a mixture called a solution. A **solution** is a mixture containing a solvent and at least one solute and has the same properties throughout. The **solvent** is the part of a solution usually present in the largest amount. It dissolves the other substances. The **solute** is the substance that is dissolved by the solvent. Solutes can be gases, liquids, or solids. Water is the solvent in grape juice. Sugar and other ingredients are the solutes. A solution has the same properties throughout. It contains solute, molecules or ions that are too small to see.

Water as a Solvent In many common solutions, the solvent is water. Water dissolves so many substances that it is often called the "universal solvent." Life depends on water solutions. Nutrients used by plants are dissolved in water in the soil. Water is the solvent in blood, saliva, sweat, urine, and tears.

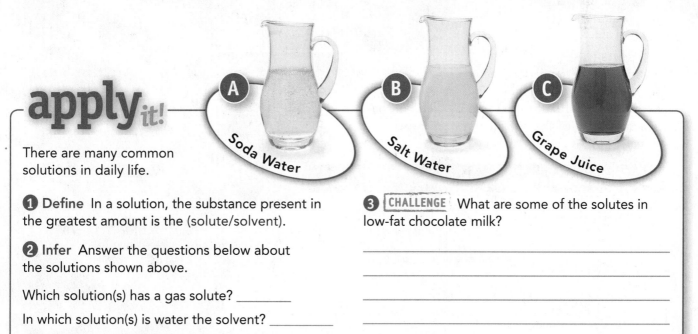

apply it!

There are many common solutions in daily life.

❶ **Define** In a solution, the substance present in the greatest amount is the (solute/solvent).

❷ **Infer** Answer the questions below about the solutions shown above.

Which solution(s) has a gas solute? _____

In which solution(s) is water the solvent? _____

Which solution(s) has two or more solutes? _____

❸ **CHALLENGE** What are some of the solutes in low-fat chocolate milk?

_____

_____

_____

_____

Identify Supporting Evidence Underline evidence in the text that shows water is not the only solvent.

Other Solvents Although water is the most common solvent, it is certainly not the only one. Many solutions are made with solvents other than water, as shown in the table in **Figure 1.** For example, gasoline is a solution of several different liquid fuels. Solvents don't even have to be liquids. A solution may be a combination of gases, liquids, or solids. Air is an example of a solution that is made up of nitrogen, oxygen, and other gases. Solutions can even be made up of solids. Metal alloys like bronze, brass, and steel are solutions of different solid elements.

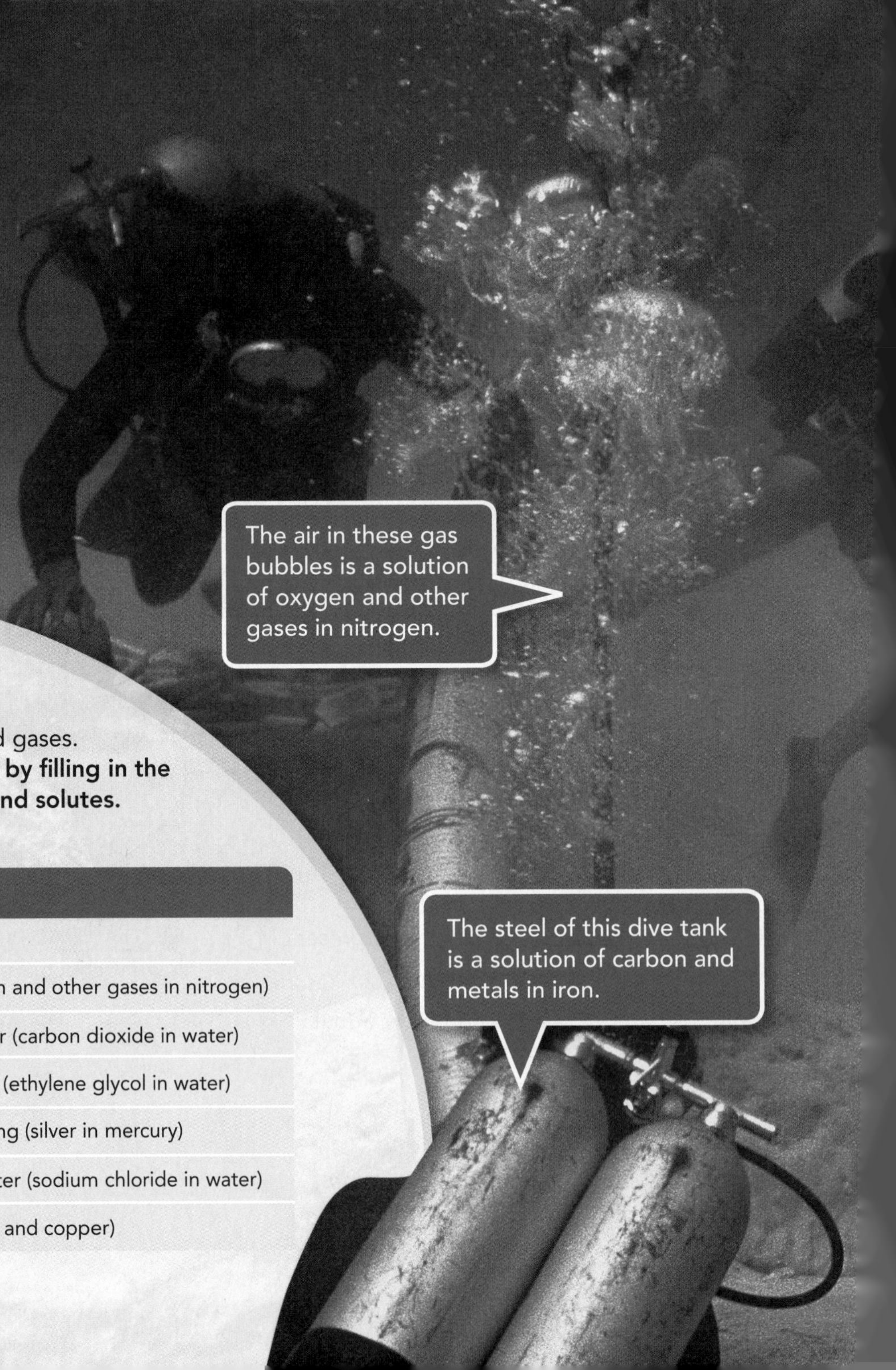

Sea water is a solution of sodium chloride and other compounds in water.

The air in these gas bubbles is a solution of oxygen and other gases in nitrogen.

The steel of this dive tank is a solution of carbon and metals in iron.

FIGURE 1

Solutions

Solutions can be made from any combination of solids, liquids, and gases.

Identify Complete the table by filling in the state of matter of the solvents and solutes.

Common Solutions

Solute	Solvent	Solution
_____	_____	Air (oxygen and other gases in nitrogen)
_____	_____	Soda water (carbon dioxide in water)
Liquid	_____	Antifreeze (ethylene glycol in water)
_____	Liquid	Dental filling (silver in mercury)
_____	_____	Ocean water (sodium chloride in water)
Solid	_____	Brass (zinc and copper)

Colloids Not all mixtures are solutions. As shown in **Figure 2,** a **colloid** (KAHL oyd) is a mixture containing small, undissolved particles that do not settle out. The particles in a colloid are too small to be seen without a microscope, yet they are large enough to scatter a beam of light. For example, fog is a colloid that is made up of water droplets in air. Fog scatters the headlight beams of cars. Milk, shaving cream, and smoke are some other examples of colloids. Because they scatter light, most colloids are not clear, unlike many solutions.

Suspensions If you tried to mix sand in water, you would find that the sand never dissolves completely, no matter how much you stir it. Sand and water make up a suspension. A **suspension** (suh SPEN shun) is a mixture in which particles can be seen and easily separated by settling or filtration. Unlike a solution, a suspension does not have the same properties throughout. It contains visible particles that are larger than the particles in solutions or colloids.

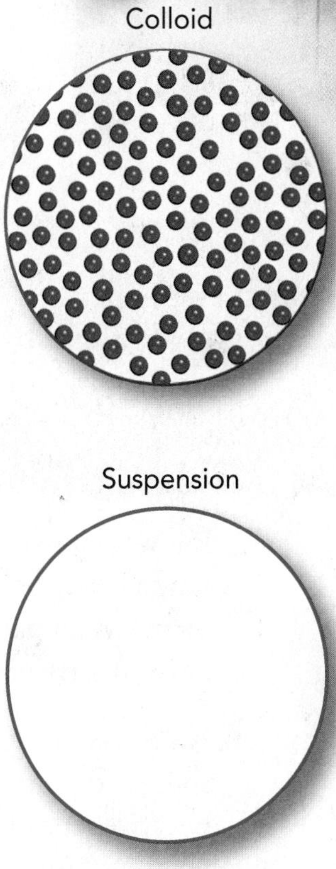

Colloid

Suspension

FIGURE 2 ···························
Colloids and Suspensions
Colloids and suspensions are classified by the size of their particles.

✏ **Interpret Diagrams** In the circle, draw the particles of a suspension.

Do the Quick Lab
Scattered Light.

🔑 **Assess Your Understanding**

1a. Review What is a solution?

_____
_____
_____

b. Compare and Contrast How are colloids and suspensions different from solutions?

_____
_____

c. Infer Suppose you mix food coloring in water to make it blue. Have you made a solution or a suspension? Explain.

_____
_____
_____
_____
_____
_____

got it? ···

O **I get it!** Now I know that classifying mixtures as solutions, colloids, and suspensions is based on _____

_____

O I need extra help with _____

Go to MY SCIENCE ⓢ COACH online for help with this subject.

How Does a Solution Form?

If it were possible to see the particles of a solution, you could see how a solute behaves when it's mixed in a solution. 🔑 **A solution forms when particles of the solute separate from each other and become surrounded by particles of the solvent.**

Ionic and Molecular Solutes **Figure 3** shows an ionic solid, sodium chloride (NaCl), mixed with water. The positive and negative ions of the solute are attracted to the partially charged polar water molecules. Eventually, water molecules will surround all of the ions and the solid crystal will be completely dissolved.

Molecular compounds, such as table sugar, break up into individual neutral molecules in water. The polar water molecules attract the polar sugar molecules. This causes the sugar molecules to move away from each other. The covalent bonds within the molecules remain unbroken.

FIGURE 3 ·······························

▶ INTERACTIVE ART

Forming a Solution

✏ **Sequence** Explain what occurs as sodium chloride, an ionic solid, dissolves in water.

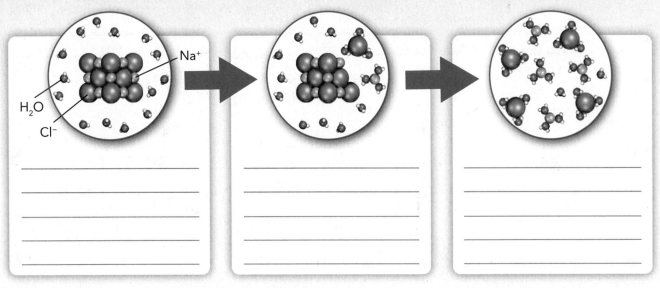

do the math! Analyzing Data

Airplane de-icing fluids are typically solutions of ethylene glycol in water. The freezing point of pure water is 0°C.

1 **Explain** How is the percent of ethylene glycol in de-icing fluid related to water's freezing point?

_____
_____
_____

2 **Read Graphs** How much does a 45% solution of de-icing fluid lower the freezing point of water?

_____
_____

3 **Interpret Data** Would you allow a plane to take off in −20°C weather if it were de-iced with a solution of 30% ethylene glycol? Explain.

_____
_____

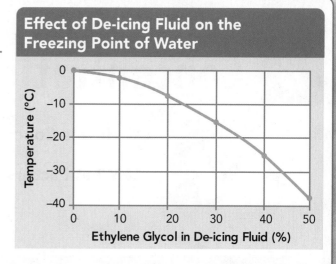

Effect of De-icing Fluid on the Freezing Point of Water

Temperature (°C) vs. Ethylene Glycol in De-icing Fluid (%)

Solutes and Conductivity

How could you find out if the solute of a water solution was salt or sugar? Ionic compounds in water conduct electric current, but a solution of molecular compounds may not. If ions are present, electric current will flow and you'll know the solute is salt.

Effects of Solutes

Solutes raise the boiling point of a solution above that of the solvent. As the temperature of a liquid rises, the molecules gain energy and escape as gas. In a liquid solution, the solute particles prevent the solvent molecules' escape. The temperature must go above the boiling point of the solvent in order for the solution to boil. However, the temperature increases only slightly and is not enough to cook food faster.

Solutes lower the freezing point of a solution below that of the solvent alone. When pure liquid water freezes at 0°C, the molecules pack together to form crystals of ice. In a solution, the solute particles get in the way of the water molecules forming ice crystals. The temperature must drop below 0°C in order for the solution to freeze.

 Lab zone | ® Do the Lab Investigation _Speedy Solutions._

🔑 Assess Your Understanding

2. Apply Concepts Why is salt sprinkled on icy roads and sidewalks?

_____
_____
_____
_____
_____

got it? ....

○ **I get it!** Now I know that in a solution the particles of solute _____

_____

○ **I need extra help with** _____

_Go to_ MY SCIENCE ⑤ COACH _online for help with this subject._

Concentration and Solubility

UNLOCK THE BIG ?

🔑 **How Is Concentration Changed?**

🔑 **What Factors Affect Solubility?**

my planet Diary

Even Whales Get the Bends

Decompression sickness, or "the bends" as it's commonly known, is a fear for many scuba divers. Under the extreme pressure of the deep ocean, nitrogen and other gases from the air dissolve in a diver's body tissues. If the diver rises too quickly, the sudden decrease in pressure causes the dissolved gas to bubble out of the tissue. The bubbles can enter a blood vessel and cause intense pain, and sometimes more severe injury.

But what if the diver is a whale? Previously, it was thought that whales did not suffer from the bends. Scientists have discovered evidence in beached whales of nitrogen bubbles expanding and damaging vital organs. It is believed that sonar waves from nearby ships may have frightened the whales, causing them to surface too quickly. This can result in the bends.

Write your answers to the questions below.

1. Scientists have found small gashes in the bones of whale fossils, which are a sign of the bends. What conclusions can you draw from these fossils?

_____

_____

_____

_____

_____

2. Scuba diving is a popular activity. Would you scuba dive knowing the risks of getting the bends?

_____

_____

_____

_____

▶ PLANET DIARY Go to **Planet Diary** to learn more about solubility.

Lab zone® Do the Inquiry Warm-Up *Does It Dissolve?*

Vocabulary

- dilute solution
- concentrated solution
- solubility
- saturated solution

Skills

🔄 **Reading:** Identify the Main Idea
🔺 **Inquiry:** Calculate

How Is Concentration Changed?

Have you ever had maple syrup on your pancakes? You probably know that it's made from the sap of maple trees. Is something that sweet really made in a tree? Well, not exactly.

The sap of a maple tree and maple syrup differ in their concentrations. That is, they differ in the amount of solute (sugar and other compounds) dissolved in a certain amount of solvent (water). A **dilute solution** is a mixture that has only a little solute dissolved in a certain amount of solvent. A **concentrated solution** is a mixture that has a lot of solute dissolved in the solvent. The sap is a dilute solution and the syrup is a concentrated solution.

Changing Concentration How is sap turned into syrup? 🔑 **You can change the concentration of a solution by adding solute. You can also change it by adding or removing solvent.** For example, water is removed from the dilute sap to make the more concentrated syrup.

> ✏️ **Vocabulary Identify Related Word Forms** To *concentrate* is the verb form of the adjective *concentrated*. Write a sentence about solutions using the verb *concentrate*.
>
> _____
> _____
> _____
> _____
> _____

FIGURE 1 ·······················

Changing the Concentration of a Solution

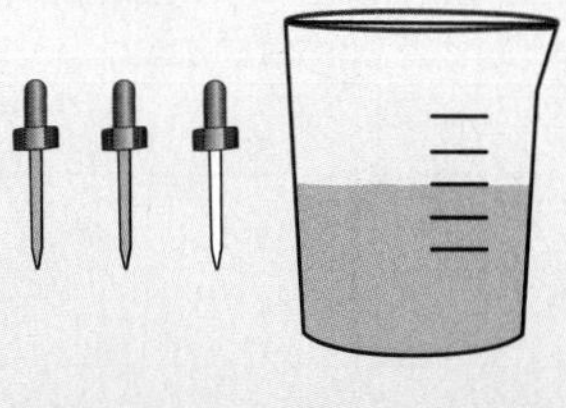

🖊️ The solution above is made with two droppers of coloring.

1. **Apply Concepts** Show two ways you can make a more concentrated solution by shading in the droppers and water level you would use.

2. **Explain** Describe your methods on the lines.

A

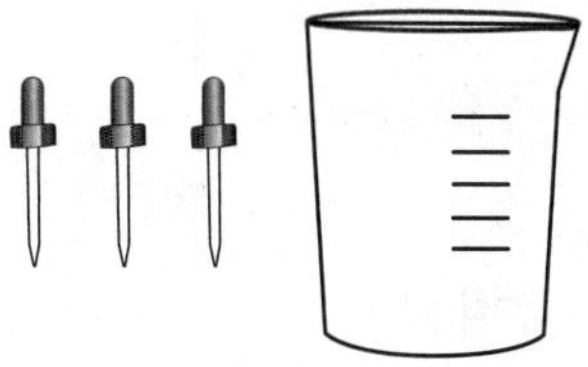

B

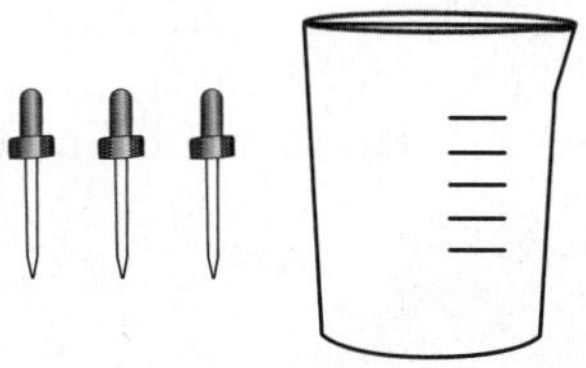

Calculating Concentration You know that maple syrup is more concentrated than maple sap. What is the actual concentration of either solution? To determine the concentration of a solution, compare the amount of solute to the total amount of solution. You can report concentration as the percent of solute in solution by volume or mass.

do the math! Sample Problem

To calculate concentration, compare the amount of solute to the amount of solution. For example, if a 100-gram solution contains 10 grams of solute, its concentration is 10% by weight.

$$\frac{10\ g}{100\ g} \times 100\% = 10\%$$

Calculate Determine the concentration of the contact solution.

_____

_____

_____

10.7 grams hydrogen peroxide
355 grams solution

Contact Solution

10.7 grams hydrogen peroxide
355 grams solution

 Do the Quick Lab
Measuring Concentration.

🔑 Assess Your Understanding

1a. Describe What is a concentrated solution?

_____

_____

_____

b. Calculate Find the concentration of a solution with 30 grams of solute in 250 grams of solution.

_____

c. CHALLENGE Solution A has twice as much solute as Solution B. Is it possible for the solutions to have the same concentration? Explain.

_____

_____

_____

_____

_____

got it? ....

○ **I get it!** Now I know that the concentration of a solution can be changed by _____

_____

○ **I need extra help with** _____

Go to **MY SCIENCE** 🔵 **COACH** *online for help with this subject.*

What Factors Affect Solubility?

Suppose you add sugar to a cup of hot tea. Is there a limit to how sweet you can make the tea? Yes, at some point, no more sugar will dissolve. **Solubility** is a measure of how much solute can dissolve in a solvent at a given temperature. 🔑 **Factors that can affect the solubility of a substance include pressure, the type of solvent, and temperature.**

When you've added so much solute that no more dissolves, you have a **saturated solution.** If you can continue to dissolve more solute in a solution, then the solution is unsaturated.

Working With Solubility Look at the table in **Figure 2.** It compares the solubilities of familiar compounds in 100 grams of water at 20°C. You can see that only 9.6 grams of baking soda will dissolve in these conditions. However, 204 grams of table sugar will dissolve in the same amount of water at the same temperature.

Solubility can be used to help identify a substance. It is a characteristic property of matter. Suppose you had a white powder that looked like table salt or sugar. Since you never taste unknown substances, how could you identify the powder? You could measure its solubility in 100 grams of water at 20°C. Then compare the results to the data in **Figure 2** to identify the substance.

Solubility in 100 g of Water at 20°C	
Compound	Solubility (g)
Baking soda (sodium bicarbonate, $NaHCO_3$)	9.6
Table salt (sodium chloride, NaCl)	35.9
Table sugar (sucrose, $C_{12}H_{22}O_{11}$)	204

FIGURE 2 ·····

Solubility

Pickling requires saturated solutions of salt in water.

✎ Calculate **Using the table, determine the amount of sodium chloride you would need to make pickles using 500 grams of water.**

_____

_____

Factors Affecting Solubility

You have already read that there is a limit to solubility. By changing certain conditions, you can change a substance's solubility.

Pressure The solubility of a gas solute in a liquid solvent increases as the pressure of the gas over the solution increases. To increase the carbon dioxide concentration in soda water, the gas is added to the liquid under high pressure. Opening the bottle or can reduces the pressure. The escaping gas makes the fizzing sound you hear.

Scuba divers must be aware of the effects of pressure on gases if they want to avoid decompression sickness. Under water, divers breathe from tanks of compressed air. The air dissolves in their blood in greater amounts as they dive deeper. If divers return to the surface too quickly, the gases can bubble out of solution. The bubbles can block blood flow. Divers double over in pain, which is why you may have heard this condition called "the bends."

Solvents Sometimes you just can't make a solution because the solute and solvent are not compatible, as shown in **Figure 3**. This happens with motor oil and water. Have you ever tried to mix oil and water? If so, you've seen how quickly they separate into layers after you stop mixing them. Oil and water separate because water is a polar compound and oil is nonpolar. Some polar and nonpolar compounds do not mix very well.

For liquid solutions, ionic and polar compounds usually dissolve in polar solvents. Nonpolar compounds do not usually dissolve in very polar solvents, but they will dissolve in nonpolar solvents.

did you know?

The popping sound you hear when you crack your knuckles is dissolved gas coming out of the fluid between the joints because of a decrease in pressure. That's why you can't crack the same knuckle twice in a row. You have to wait a few minutes for the gas to dissolve back into the fluid.

◀ Polar water mixed with nonpolar motor oil

FIGURE 3

Solvents and Solubility

Some polar and nonpolar compounds form layers when they are mixed together.

✎ CHALLENGE **Determine which of these liquids are polar and which are nonpolar by the way they form layers or mix together. The first answer is given.**

A. Polar

B. _____

C. _____

D. _____

E. _____

F. _____

Temperature For most solid solutes, solubility increases as temperature increases. For example, the solubility of table sugar in 100 grams of water at 0°C is 180 grams. However, the solubility increases to 231 grams at 25°C and 487 grams at 100°C.

Cooks use this increased solubility of sugar to make candy. At room temperature, not enough sugar for candy can dissolve in the water. Solutions must be heated for all the sugar to dissolve.

When heated, a solution can dissolve more solute than it can at cooler temperatures. If a heated, saturated solution cools slowly, the extra solute may remain dissolved to become a supersaturated solution. It has more dissolved solute than is predicted by its solubility at the given temperature. If you disturb a supersaturated solution, the extra solute will quickly come out of solution. You can see an example of a supersaturated solution in **Figure 4.**

Unlike most solids, gases become less soluble when the temperature goes up. For example, more carbon dioxide can dissolve in cold water than in hot water. If you open a warm bottle of soda water, carbon dioxide escapes the liquid in greater amounts than if the soda water had been chilled. Why does a warm soda taste "flat" when it's opened? It contains less gas. If you like soda water that's very fizzy, open it when it's cold!

FIGURE 4 ⋯⋯⋯⋯⋯⋯⋯⋯⋯⋯⋯⋯⋯⋯⋯⋯
Supersaturated Solution
Dropping a crystal of solute into a supersaturated solution causes the extra solute to rapidly come out of solution.

⋯⋯⋯⋯⋯⋯⋯⋯✎⋯⋯⋯⋯⋯⋯⋯⋯
Identify the Main Idea
Underline the sentences on this page that explain how increasing temperature affects the solubility of both solid and gas solutes.

apply it!

Crystallized honey, a supersaturated solution, can be more than 70 percent sugar.

1 Calculate How many grams of sugar could be in 50 grams of crystallized honey?

_____

_____

2 Develop Hypotheses How would you explain why certain types of honey rarely crystallize?

_____

_____

3 CHALLENGE Is there a way to turn crystallized honey back into liquid honey? Explain.

_____

_____

_____

_____

Cooking With Chemistry

What determines the properties of a solution?

FIGURE 5 ···

> INTERACTIVE ART At the Solutions Shack Diner, solutions are found everywhere on the menu. In order to serve his customers, the chef must know about the properties of solutions.

✎ **Solve Problems** Use what you know about the properties of solutions to help the chef in the kitchen.

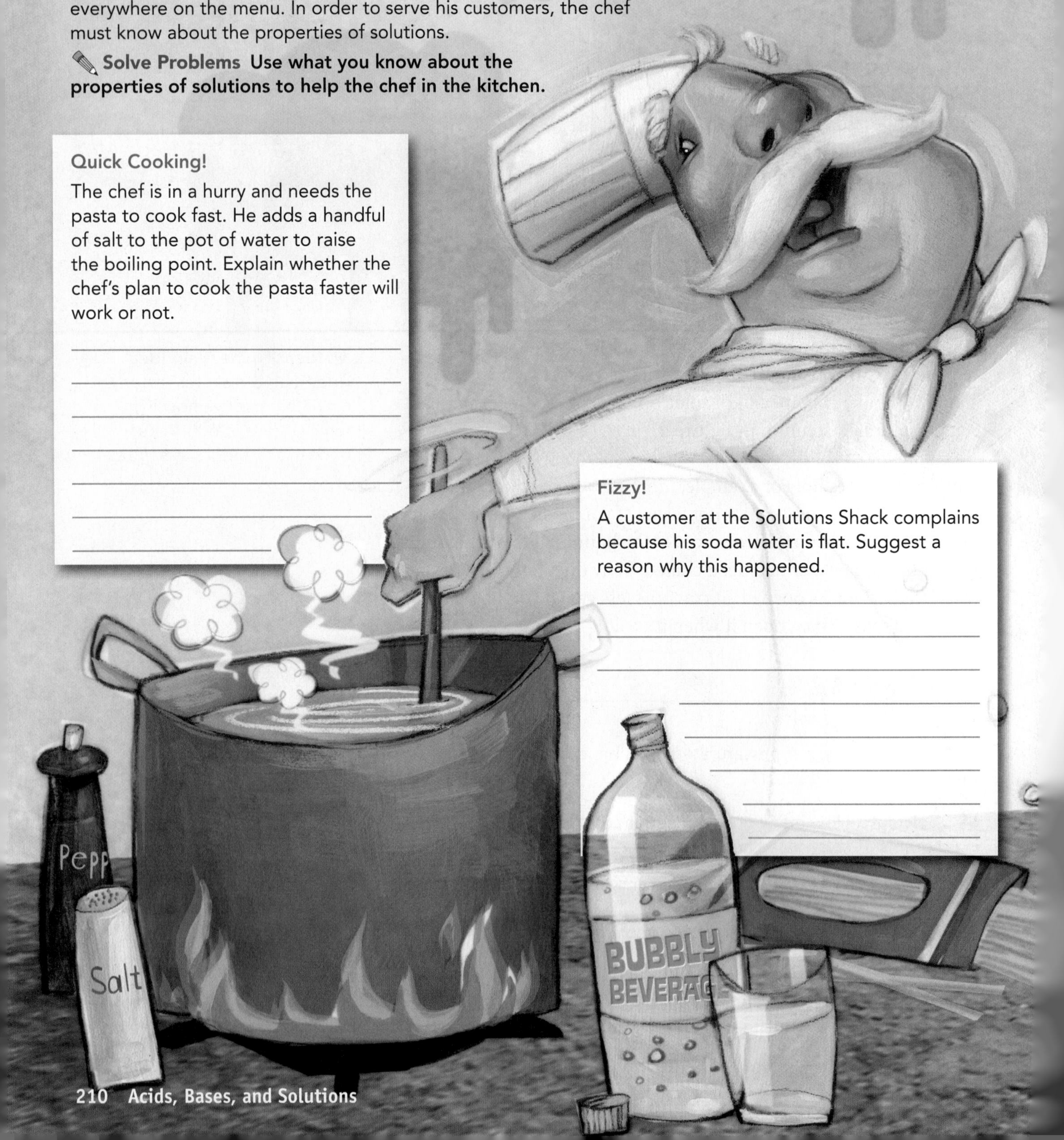

Quick Cooking!

The chef is in a hurry and needs the pasta to cook fast. He adds a handful of salt to the pot of water to raise the boiling point. Explain whether the chef's plan to cook the pasta faster will work or not.

_____

_____

_____

_____

_____

_____

_____

Fizzy!

A customer at the Solutions Shack complains because his soda water is flat. Suggest a reason why this happened.

_____

_____

_____

_____

_____

Mix It Up!

The chef is making salad dressing with vinegar, olive oil, and pepper, but the ingredients are not mixing together. Why?

_____

_____

_____

_____

_____

Yum!

The chef makes the best iced tea. His secret is to make it exactly 15 percent sugar by mass. If he wants to make 3,000 grams of iced tea, how many grams of sugar should he use?

- ○ 200 grams
- ○ 20,000 grams
- ○ 450 grams
- ○ 45,000 grams

Lab zone ® Do the Quick Lab
Predicting Rates of Solubility.

🔑 Assess Your Understanding

2a. Review How can you tell when a solution is saturated?

_____

_____

b. Control Variables You are given two white powdery substances. How would you use solubility to identify them?

_____

_____

_____

_____

_____

_____

_____

_____

c. ANSWER THE BIG **?** What determines the properties of a solution?

_____

_____

_____

_____

_____

_____

_____

_____

got it? ....

○ **I get it!** Now I know that the solubility of a substance can be affected by _____

_____

_____

○ **I need extra help with** _____

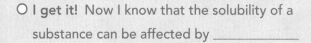

Go to MY SCIENCE ⓢ COACH *online for help with this subject.*

Describing Acids and Bases

UNLOCK THE BIG ?

🔑 **What Are the Properties of Acids?**

🔑 **What Are the Properties of Bases?**

my planet Diary

VOICES FROM HISTORY

Bog Bodies

Even in Shakespeare's time it was known that tanning, the process of making leather, helps preserve body tissues. Hundreds of years later, the body of a 2,300-year-old man was found in the peat bogs of Europe. The man is a bog body. Bog bodies are the remains of human bodies that have been preserved in the highly acidic conditions of peat bogs.

The bog acids are similar in strength to vinegar. They naturally pickle the human bodies. The lack of oxygen and cold temperatures of Northern Europe cause the acids to saturate body tissues before they decay. As a result, the organs, hair, and skin are all preserved. The acids dissolve the bones of the bog bodies, but details like tattoos and fingerprints can still be seen on some of the bodies.

> GRAVE DIGGER. ...A tanner will last you nine year.
>
> HAMLET. Why he, more than another?
>
> GRAVE DIGGER. Why, sir, his hide is so tanned with his trade that he will keep out water a great while, and your water is a sore decayer of your...dead body.
>
> —Shakespeare, *Hamlet*

Write your answers to the questions below.

1. Hypothesize why bog acids react differently with the bones of the bodies than they do with the organs, hair, and skin.

_____

_____

_____

_____

_____

2. How are pickles similar to bog bodies?

_____

_____

> **PLANET DIARY** Go to **Planet Diary** to learn more about acids.

Lab zone® Do the Inquiry Warm-Up *What Color Does Litmus Paper Turn?*

Vocabulary
- acid • corrosive
- indicator • base

Skills
↻ Reading: Summarize
△ Inquiry: Predict

What Are the Properties of Acids?

Have you had any fruit to eat recently? If so, an acid was probably part of your meal. Many common items contain acids. **Acids** are compounds with specific characteristic properties. ⚷ **An acid reacts with metals and carbonates, tastes sour, and turns blue litmus paper red.**

Acids are an important part of our lives. Folic acid, found in green, leafy vegetables, is important for cell growth. Hydrochloric acid in your stomach helps with digestion. Phosphoric acid is used to make plant fertilizers. Sulfuric acid drives many types of batteries, giving it the nickname "battery acid."

Reactions With Metals Acids react with certain metals to produce hydrogen gas. Platinum and gold don't react with most acids, but copper, zinc, and iron do. When they react, the metals seem to disappear in the solution. This is one reason acids are described as **corrosive,** meaning they "wear away" other materials.

The purity of precious metals can be determined using acids. **Figure 1** shows a touchstone, which is used to test the purity of gold. The gold object is scraped on the touchstone. Then, acid is poured onto the streak. The more gas bubbles the streak produces, the lower the purity of the gold.

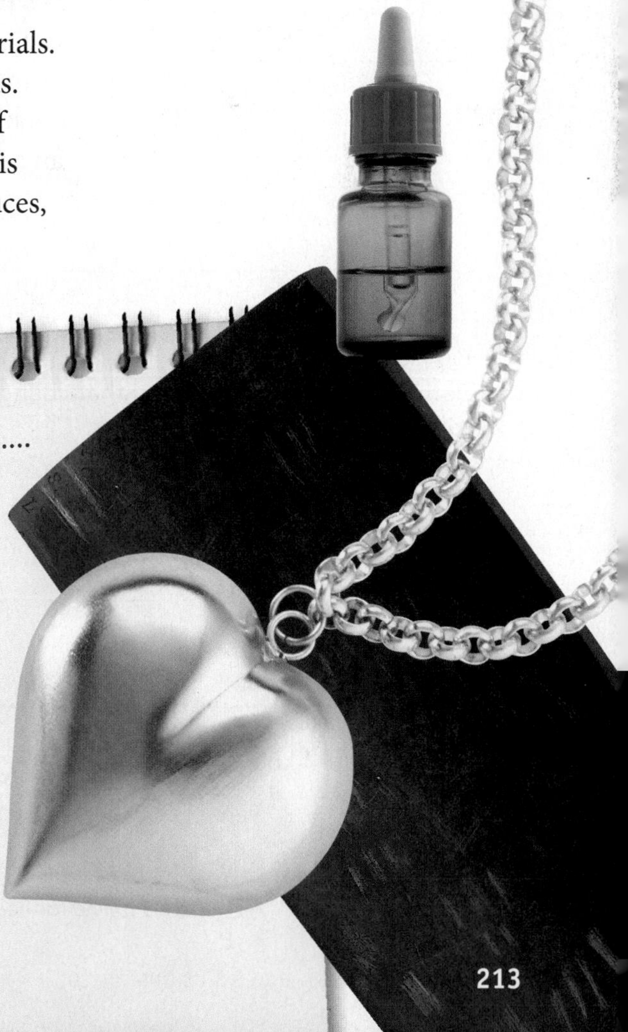

FIGURE 1 ·······
Reaction With Metals
Acids are used to test the purity of precious metals.

✎ **Infer** What could you determine about a gold necklace that bubbles when it is exposed to an acid?

_____

_____

_____

_____

Reactions With Carbonates

Acids also react with carbonate ions. Carbonate ions contain carbon and oxygen atoms bonded together with an overall negative charge (CO_3^{2-}). One product of the reaction of an acid with a carbonate is the gas carbon dioxide.

Objects that contain carbonate ions include seashells, eggshells, chalk, and limestone. The sculpture shown in **Figure 2** is carved from limestone. Geologists use this property of acids to identify rocks. If carbon dioxide gas is produced when dilute acid is poured on a rock's surface, then the rock could be made of limestone.

Sour Taste

If you've ever tasted a lemon, you've had firsthand experience with the sour taste of acids. Citrus fruits, such as lemons, grapefruit, and oranges, all contain citric acid. Other foods such as vinegar and tomatoes also contain acids.

Although sour taste is a characteristic of many acids, it is not one you should use to identify a compound as an acid. Scientists don't taste chemicals. It is never safe to taste unknown chemicals.

Reactions With Indicators

Chemists use indicators to test for acids. Litmus paper is an example of an **indicator,** a compound that changes color when it comes in contact with an acid. Acids turn blue litmus paper red.

FIGURE 2 ·······················

Reactions With Carbonates
Acids react with the carbonates in limestone.

✎ **Predict** **Describe what a geologist would observe if she poured acid on the sculpture.**

_____

_____

_____

_____

_____

▲ Blue litmus paper turns red in the presence of acid

Do the Quick Lab *Properties of Acids.*

🔑 Assess Your Understanding

1a. Define What is a compound that changes color in an acid called?

○ metal ○ indicator ○ carbonate

b. Explain Why are acids described as corrosive?

_____

_____

c. Draw Conclusions How might you tell if a food contains an acid?

_____

_____

_____

_____

gotit? ···

○ **I get it!** Now I know that the properties of acids include _____

_____

○ **I need extra help with** _____

Go to **MY SCIENCE COACH** online for help with this subject.

What Are the Properties of Bases?

Bases are another group of compounds that can be identified by their common properties. **A base tastes bitter, feels slippery, and turns red litmus paper blue.** The properties of bases are often described as the "opposite" of acids. Bases have many uses. Ammonia is used in fertilizers and household cleaners. Baking soda is a base called sodium bicarbonate, which causes baked goods to rise.

▲ Cocoa beans

Bitter Taste Have you ever tasted tonic water? The base, quinine, causes the slightly bitter taste. Bases taste bitter. Other foods that contain bases include bitter melon, almonds, and cocoa beans, like those shown above.

Slippery Feel Bases have a slippery feel. Many soaps and detergents contain bases. The slippery feeling of your shampoo is a property of the bases it contains.

Just as you avoid tasting an unknown substance, you wouldn't want to touch one either. Strong bases can irritate your skin. A safer way to identify bases is by their other properties.

Summarize What are some uses of bases?

_____
_____
_____
_____
_____

FIGURE 3 ......

Acid and Base Properties

✎ **Classify** Draw an arrow from each item to the word "acid" or "base" that describes its properties.

Window cleaner   Limes

(ACID)   (BASE)

Vinegar   Dish soap

215

Reactions of Bases Unlike acids, bases don't react with metals. They also don't react with carbonates to form carbon dioxide gas. The lack of a reaction can be a useful property in identifying bases. If you know that a compound doesn't react with metals, you know something about it. For example, you know the compound is probably not an acid. Another important property of bases is how they react with acids in a type of chemical reaction called neutralization, in which acids and bases deactivate one another.

Reactions With Indicators Since litmus paper can be used to test acids, it can be used to test bases, too, as shown in **Figure 4**. Unlike acids, however, bases turn red litmus paper blue. An easy way to remember this is to think of the letter *b*. **B**ases turn litmus paper **b**lue.

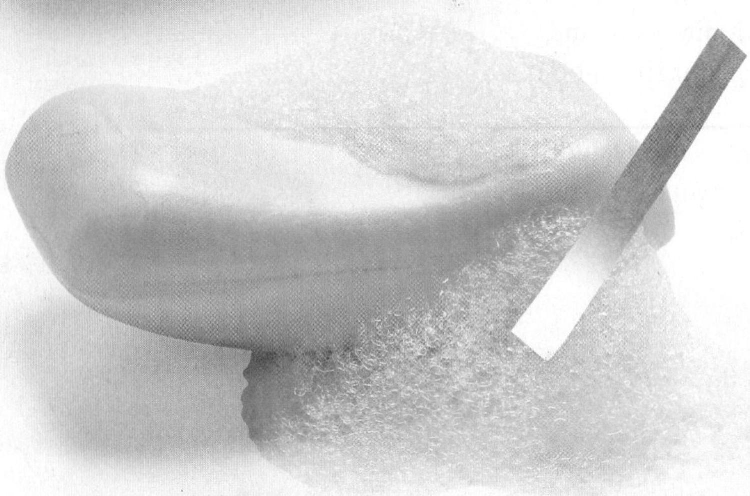

FIGURE 4 ···

Litmus Paper
Litmus paper is used to test if a substance is an acid or a base.

✎ **Look at the apple and soap photos to complete the following tasks.**

1. **Predict** Color or label each strip of litmus paper with the color you would expect to see from the substance.

2. **Infer** What would you infer about a substance that did not change the color of red or blue litmus paper?

_____

_____

FIGURE 5 ···

Properties of Acids and Bases
✎ **Compare and Contrast** Complete the table of properties of acids and bases.

Properties	Acids	Bases
Reaction with metals		
Reaction with carbonates		
Taste		
Reaction with litmus paper		
Uses		

apply it!

Bee venom is slightly acidic, but wasp venom is closer to neutral, meaning it's not an acid or a base. Pure water is another neutral substance.

1 **Predict** Bee venom would taste (bitter/sour).

2 **Apply Concepts** How would bee venom and wasp venom react with litmus paper?

_____

_____

_____

_____

3 CHALLENGE One suggestion for treating a bee sting is cleaning it with vinegar. Is this a cure that you would try? Explain.

_____

_____

_____

Lab zone® Do the Quick Lab *Properties of Bases.*

🔑 Assess Your Understanding

2a. Review The properties of bases are often considered (identical/opposite) to acids.

b. Apply Concepts In what products are you most likely to find bases in your home?

_____

_____

_____

_____

c. Pose Questions The color of hydrangea flowers depends on the amount of acid or base in the soil. Write a question that helps you determine the cause of a pink hydrangea.

_____

_____

_____

_____

_____

got it? ....

○ **I get it!** Now I know that the properties of bases include _____

_____

○ **I need extra help with** _____

Go to MY SCIENCE ⓢ COACH *online for help with this subject.*

4 Acids and Bases in Solution

UNLOCK THE BIG ?

🔑 **What Ions Do Acids and Bases Form in Water?**

🔑 **What Are the Products of Neutralization?**

my pLaneT DiaRY

FUN FACT

Ocean Stingers

You've probably heard of venomous animals like rattlesnakes and black widow spiders. Did you know that some of the most venomous creatures in the world are jellyfish? Some jellyfish stings can permanently scar and even kill their victims. Jellyfish use their venom to stun and paralyze both prey and predators, including humans. A jellyfish sting can quickly turn a day at the beach into a dash to the hospital. Luckily, most jellyfish stings can be easily treated. The venom of some jellyfish contains bases. Bases can be neutralized, or deactivated, by an acid. The best way to treat some jellyfish stings is to rinse the affected area with vinegar. Vinegar is a solution containing acetic acid, which is a weak acid that safe for your skin.

Write your answers to the questions below.

1. Stings from other kinds of animals can be acidic. How might you treat a sting that contains an acid?

_____

_____

_____

_____

2. Since jellyfish are nearly invisible, most people never know they're in danger. What advice would you give to a person planning on spending a day at the beach?

_____

_____

_____

▶ PLANET DIARY Go to **Planet Diary** to learn more about neutralization.

Lab zone® Do the Inquiry Warm-Up *What Can Cabbage Juice Tell You?*

Vocabulary
- hydrogen ion (H⁺)   • hydroxide ion (OH⁻)
- pH scale   • neutralization   • salt

Skills
↺ Reading: Relate Cause and Effect
△ Inquiry: Measure

What Ions Do Acids and Bases Form in Water?

A chemist pours hydrochloric acid into a beaker. Then she slowly adds a base, sodium hydroxide, to the acid. What happens when these two chemicals mix? To answer this question, you must know what happens to acids and bases in solution.

Acids in Solution   **Figure 1** lists some common acids. Notice that each formula begins with the letter H, the symbol for hydrogen. In a solution with water, most acids separate into hydrogen ions and negative ions. A **hydrogen ion (H⁺)** is an atom of hydrogen that has lost its electron. In the case of hydrochloric acid, for example, hydrogen ions and chloride ions form.

$$HCl \rightarrow H^+ + Cl^-$$

The production of hydrogen ions helps define an acid. 🔑 **An acid produces hydrogen ions (H⁺) in water.** These hydrogen ions are responsible for corroding metals and turning blue litmus paper red. Acids may be strong or weak. Strength refers to how well the acid dissociates, or separates, into ions in water. As shown in **Figure 2,** molecules of a strong acid, such as nitric acid, dissociate to form hydrogen ions in solution. With a weak acid, like acetic acid, very few particles separate to form ions in solution.

FIGURE 1 ·····················
Common Acids
The table lists some common acids.

Acid	Formula
Hydrochloric acid	HCl
Nitric acid	HNO_3
Sulfuric acid	H_2SO_4
Acetic acid	$HC_2H_3O_2$

FIGURE 2 ···
Strength of Acids
In solution, strong acids act differently than weak acids do.

✎ **Compare and Contrast** In the empty beaker, use the key to draw how ions of acetic acid would act in solution.

Strong Acid

Weak Acid

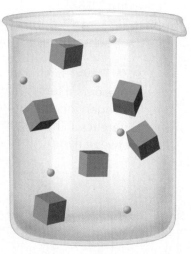

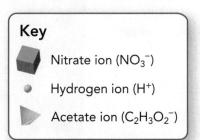

Key
- Nitrate ion (NO_3^-)
- Hydrogen ion (H⁺)
- Acetate ion ($C_2H_3O_2^-$)

Bases in Solution

Look at the table in **Figure 3**. Many of the bases shown are made of positive ions combined with hydroxide ions. The **hydroxide ion (OH⁻)** is a negative ion made of oxygen and hydrogen. When some bases dissolve in water, they separate into positive ions and hydroxide ions. Look, for example, at what happens to sodium hydroxide in water.

$$NaOH \rightarrow Na^+ + OH^-$$

Not every base contains hydroxide ions. For example, ammonia (NH_3) does not. In solution, ammonia reacts with water to form hydroxide ions.

$$NH_3 + H_2O \rightarrow NH_4^+ + OH^-$$

Notice that both reactions produce negative hydroxide ions. 🔑 **A base produces hydroxide ions (OH⁻) in water.** Hydroxide ions are responsible for the bitter taste and slippery feel of bases, and for turning red litmus paper blue. Strong bases, like sodium hydroxide, readily produce hydroxide ions in water. Weak bases, such as ammonia, do not.

Measuring pH

To determine the strength of an acid or base, chemists use a scale called pH. As shown in **Figure 4,** the **pH scale** ranges from 0 to 14. It expresses the concentration of hydrogen ions in a solution.

The most acidic substances are found at the low end of the scale, while basic substances are found at the high end. A low pH tells you that the concentration of hydrogen ions is high and the concentration of hydroxide ions is low. A high pH tells you that the opposite is true.

You can find the pH of a solution using indicator paper, which changes a different color for each pH value. Matching the color of the paper with the colors on the scale tells you the solution's pH. A pH lower than 7 is acidic. A pH higher than 7 is basic. If the pH is 7, the solution is neutral, meaning it's neither an acid nor a base.

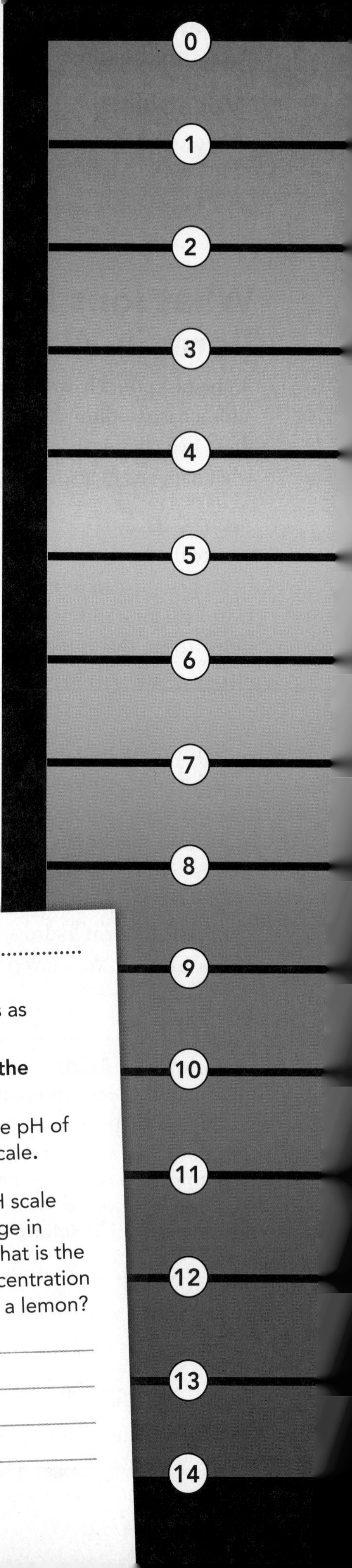

Base	Formula
Sodium hydroxide	NaOH
Potassium hydroxide	KOH
Calcium hydroxide	$Ca(OH)_2$
Aluminum hydroxide	$Al(OH)_3$
Ammonia	NH_3
Calcium oxide	CaO

FIGURE 3 ·······················
Common Bases

FIGURE 4 ··
▶ INTERACTIVE ART **The pH Scale**
The pH scale helps classify solutions as acidic or basic.

✎ **Use the pH scale to complete the following tasks**.

1. ◢**Measure** Find the approximate pH of each substance shown on the scale.

2. CHALLENGE Each unit of the pH scale represents a tenfold (10x) change in hydrogen ion concentration. What is the difference in hydrogen ion concentration between hydrochloric acid and a lemon?

_____

_____

_____

_____

0
1
2
3
4
5
6
7
8
9
10
11
12
13
14

Hydrochloric acid

pH = _____

Lemon

pH = _____

Vinegar

pH = _____

Banana

pH = _____

Pure water

pH = _____

Blood

pH = _____

Baking soda

pH = _____

Antacid

pH = _____

Drain cleaner

pH = _____

apply it!

You can predict the pH of an acid or base using its properties.

1 Estimate Place each item on the pH scale below.

A Soap   **B** Tomato   **C** Ammonia

2 Classify Add your own item to the pH scale based on properties you've experienced.

| 0 | 1 | 2 | 3 | 4 | 5 | 6 | 7 | 8 | 9 | 10 | 11 | 12 | 13 | 14 |

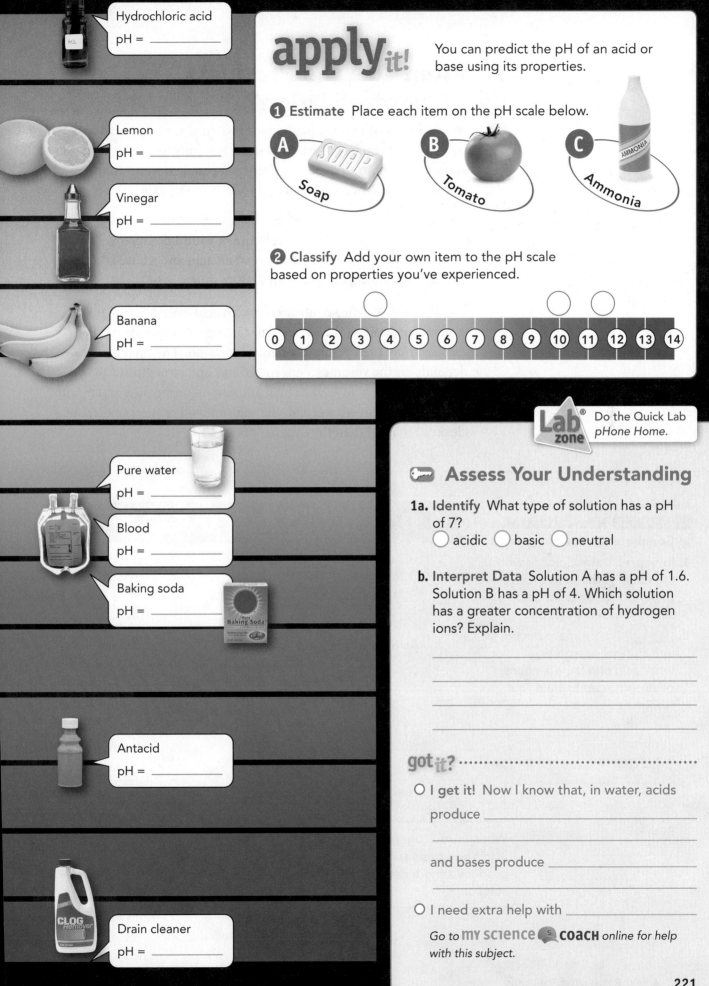

Lab zone

Do the Quick Lab *pHone Home.*

Assess Your Understanding

1a. Identify What type of solution has a pH of 7?

○ acidic ○ basic ○ neutral

b. Interpret Data Solution A has a pH of 1.6. Solution B has a pH of 4. Which solution has a greater concentration of hydrogen ions? Explain.

_____

_____

_____

_____

got it?

○ **I get it!** Now I know that, in water, acids produce _____

_____

and bases produce _____

_____

○ **I need extra help with** _____

Go to **MY SCIENCE COACH** *online for help with this subject.*

What Are the Products of Neutralization?

Are you curious about what happens when you mix an acid and a base? Would you be surprised to learn it results in salt water? Look at the equation for the reaction between equal concentrations and amounts of hydrochloric acid and sodium hydroxide.

$$HCl + NaOH \rightarrow H_2O + Na^+ + Cl^-$$

If you tested the pH of the mixture, it would be close to 7, or neutral. In fact, a reaction between an acid and a base is called **neutralization** (noo truh lih ZAY shun).

Reactants After neutralization, an acid-base mixture is not as acidic or basic as the individual starting solutions were. The reaction may even result in a neutral solution. The final pH depends on the volumes, concentrations, and strengths of the reactants. For example, if a small amount of strong base reacts with a large amount of strong acid, the solution will remain acidic, but closer to neutral than the original pH.

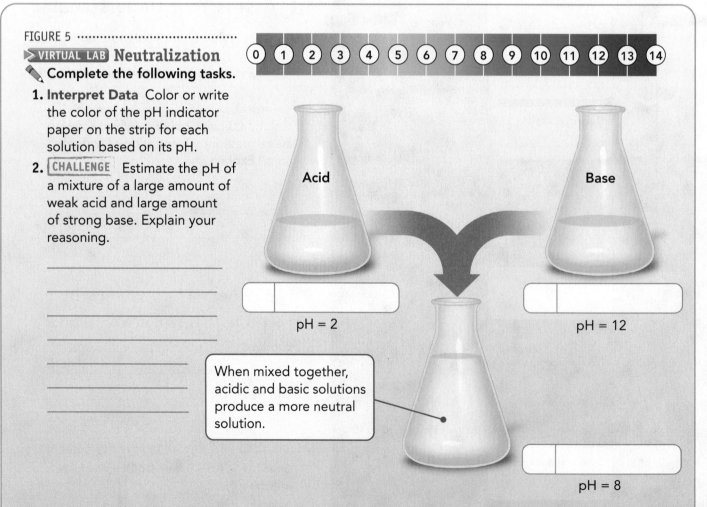

FIGURE 5 ·······························

> VIRTUAL LAB **Neutralization**

✎ **Complete the following tasks.**

1. **Interpret Data** Color or write the color of the pH indicator paper on the strip for each solution based on its pH.

2. CHALLENGE Estimate the pH of a mixture of a large amount of weak acid and large amount of strong base. Explain your reasoning.

Acid

Base

pH = 2

pH = 12

When mixed together, acidic and basic solutions produce a more neutral solution.

pH = 8

Products

"Salt" may be the familiar name of the stuff you sprinkle on food, but to a chemist, the word refers to a specific group of compounds. A **salt** is any ionic compound that can be made from a neutralization reaction. A salt is made from the positive ion of a base and the negative ion of an acid.

Look at the equation for the neutralization reaction of nitric acid with potassium hydroxide that forms potassium nitrate salt.

$$HNO_3 + KOH \rightarrow H_2O + K^+ + NO_3^-$$
(acid)   (base)   (water)   (salt)

🔑 **In a neutralization reaction, an acid reacts with a base to produce a salt and water.** Some common salts are shown in the table in **Figure 6.**

> ✎ **Relate Cause and Effect**
> Choose all of the following that result from neutralization.
> ○ Water is produced.
> ○ pH of the product is closer to 7 than the reactants' pH.
> ○ Acids turn into bases.

FIGURE 6 ·······

Common Salts

The table lists common salts produced from neutralization reactions.

✎ **Interpret Tables** Complete the table with the formula for each salt.

Common Salts			
Salt	Neutralization reaction	Salt formula	Use
Sodium chloride	$NaOH + HCl \longrightarrow H_2O + Na^+ + Cl^-$	_____	Table salt
Potassium iodide	$KOH + HI \longrightarrow H_2O + K^+ + I^-$	_____	Disinfectants
Potassium chloride	$KOH + HCl \longrightarrow H_2O + K^+ + Cl^-$	_____	Salt substitute
Calcium carbonate	$Ca(OH)_2 + H_2CO_3 \longrightarrow 2 H_2O + Ca^{2+} + CO_3^{2-}$	_____	Limestone

 ® Do the Quick Lab
The Antacid Test.

🔑 **Assess Your Understanding**

2a. Define How is the scientific meaning of salt different from the common meaning of salt?

_____

_____

_____

_____

b. Make Generalizations Is the pH of an acid-base neutralization always 7? Why or why not?

_____

_____

_____

_____

got it? ·······

○ **I get it!** Now I know that a neutralization reaction produces _____

_____

○ **I need extra help with** _____

Go to **my science** ⓢ **coach** *online for help with this subject.*

Solutions contain a _____ and at least one _____ . The solubility of a substance depends on _____ .

LESSON 1 Understanding Solutions

🔑 A mixture is classified as a solution, colloid, or suspension based on the size of its largest particles.

🔑 A solution forms when particles of the solute separate from each other and become surrounded by particles of the solvent.

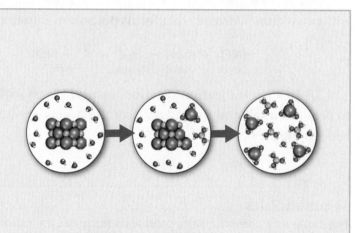

Vocabulary
- solution • solvent • solute
- colloid • suspension

LESSON 2 Concentration and Solubility

🔑 You can change the concentration of a solution by adding solute. You can also change it by adding or removing solvent.

🔑 Factors that can affect the solubility of a substance include pressure, the type of solvent, and temperature.

Vocabulary
- dilute solution • concentrated solution
- solubility • saturated solution

LESSON 3 Describing Acids and Bases

🔑 An acid reacts with metals and carbonates, tastes sour, and turns blue litmus paper red.

🔑 A base tastes bitter, feels slippery, and turns red litmus paper blue.

Vocabulary
- acid • corrosive • indicator • base

LESSON 4 Acids and Bases in Solution

🔑 An acid produces hydrogen ions (H^+) in water.

🔑 A base produces hydroxide ions (OH^-) in water.

🔑 In a neutralization reaction, an acid reacts with a base to produce a salt and water.

Vocabulary
- hydrogen ion (H^+) • hydroxide ion (OH^-)
- pH scale • neutralization • salt

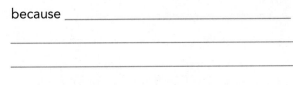
Review and Assessment

LESSON 1 Understanding Solutions

1. Which of the following is an example of a solution?

   a. fog   **b.** soda water

   c. milk   **d.** mud

2. A mixture of pepper and water is a suspension

because _____

_____

_____

3. Apply Concepts The table below shows the main components of Earth's atmosphere. What is the solvent in air? What are the solutes?

Composition of Earth's Atmosphere	
Compound	**Percent Volume**
Argon (Ar)	0.93
Carbon dioxide (CO_2)	0.03
Nitrogen (N_2)	78.08
Oxygen (O_2)	20.95
Water vapor (H_2O)	0 to 3

_____

_____

_____

_____

4. Predict Suppose you put equal amounts of pure water and salt water into separate ice cube trays of the same size and shape. What would you expect to happen when you put both trays in the freezer? Explain.

_____

_____

_____

_____

_____

LESSON 2 Concentration and Solubility

5. How can you increase the concentration of a solution?

   a. add solute   **b.** increase temperature

   c. add solvent   **d.** decrease pressure

6. Most gases become more soluble in liquid as

the temperature _____

7. Interpret Diagrams Which of the diagrams below shows a dilute solution? Which one shows a concentrated solution? Explain.

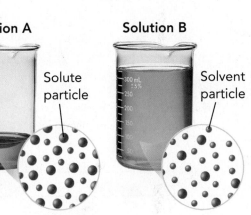

Solution A   Solution B

Solute particle   Solvent particle

_____

_____

_____

_____

_____

_____

_____

8. math! The concentration of a water and alcohol solution is 25 percent alcohol by volume. Calculate what the volume of alcohol would be in 200 mL of the solution.

LESSON 3 Describing Acids and Bases

9. Which of the following is a property of bases?

   a. sour taste

   b. slippery feel

   c. turns blue litmus paper red

   d. reacts with some metals

10. Litmus paper is an example of an indicator

because _____

_____

11. **Classify** Which of the following substances contain bases? Explain your reasoning.

   Lemon   Tonic Water   Soap

_____

_____

_____

_____

12. **Design Experiments** Acid rain forms when carbon dioxide (CO_2) in the air reacts with rainwater. How could you test if rain in your town was acid rain?

_____

_____

_____

_____

13. **Write About It** A bottle of acid is missing from the chemistry lab. Design a "Missing Acid" poster describing the properties of the acid. Include examples of tests that could be done to check if a bottle that is found contains acid.

LESSON 4 Acids and Bases in Solution

14. What is an ion called that is made of hydrogen and oxygen?

   a. an acid   **b.** a base

   c. a hydrogen ion **d.** a hydroxide ion

15. In water, acids separate into _____

_____

_____

_____

16. **Apply Concepts** Suppose you have a solution that is either an acid or a base. It doesn't react with any metals. Is the pH of the solution more likely to be 4 or 9? Explain.

_____

_____

_____

_____

APPLY THE BIG ? **What determines the properties of a solution?**

17. You are given three beakers of unknown liquids. One beaker contains pure water. One contains salt water. One contains sugar water. Without tasting the liquids, how could you identify the liquid in each beaker?

_____

_____

_____

_____

_____

_____

_____

_____

Standardized Test Prep

Multiple Choice

Circle the letter of the best answer.

1. The graph below shows how the solubility of potassium chloride (KCl) in water changes with temperature.

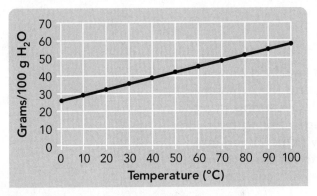

Thirty grams of potassium chloride are dissolved in 100 grams of water at 60°C. Which *best* describes the solution?

A saturated	**B** supersaturated
C unsaturated	**D** acidic

2. Which of the following pH values indicates a solution with the highest concentration of hydrogen ions?

   A pH = 1
   B pH = 2
   C pH = 7
   D pH = 14

3. Three sugar cubes are placed in a beaker containing 50 milliliters of water at 20°C. Which action would speed up the rate at which the sugar cubes dissolve in the water?

   A Use less water.
   B Transfer the contents to a larger beaker.
   C Cool the water and sugar cubes to 5°C.
   D Heat and stir the contents of the beaker.

4. A scientist observes that an unknown solution turns blue litmus paper red and reacts with zinc to produce hydrogen gas. Which of the following *best* describes the unknown solution?

   A a colloid
   B an acid
   C a base
   D a suspension

5. Why is dissolving table salt in water an example of a physical change?

   A Neither of the substances changes into a new substance.
   B The salt cannot be separated from the water.
   C The water cannot become saturated with salt.
   D A physical change occurs whenever a substance is mixed with water.

Constructed Response

Use the diagram below and your knowledge of science to help you answer Question 6. Write your answer on a separate sheet of paper.

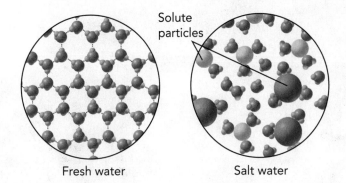

Fresh water   Salt water

6. At temperatures below 0°C, fresh water on the surface of a lake is frozen while a nearby body of salt water is not frozen. Explain this observation in terms of what happens to water molecules when water freezes.

LIMESTONE AND ACID DRAINAGE

Sport Meets Science

Fifteen-year-old Luke Andraka likes to go kayaking on the Cheat River in West Virginia. On a trip during the summer of 2007, he did more than paddle around. Observing that the water in some areas was orange, Luke began asking questions. He learned that acid runoff from a nearby mine flowed into the stream. The acid changed the chemistry of the stream, causing dead zones, where plants and shellfish could not live and the color of the water changed.

This gave Luke an idea for his science fair project. Luke knew that limestone can neutralize acid rain. He hypothesized that adding limestone to the water could reverse the effects of the runoff from the mine. He experimented to see whether adding small pieces of limestone would work better than adding large pieces of limestone. He proved that limestone could raise the pH level in the stream and clear the stream's pollution without harming the organisms living in the river habitat. Luke also found that limestone sand would work more quickly than an equal mass of limestone rocks.

Write About It Be a keen observer. Research one environmental issue in your community. Identify a possible cause, and present one possible solution. Explain in a letter to your local newspaper how you would research the effectiveness of that solution.

◀ Acid runoff from mines caused dead zones, where the water in the Cheat River changed color.

vinegar

Pucker Up!

From West Africa, we have chicken yassa—seasoned with malt or cider vinegar. From Japan, we have sushi rice—seasoned with rice vinegar. From Italy we have grilled sea bass with anchovy dressing—seasoned with balsamic vinegar. All the world loves vinegar!

This sour-tasting ingredient is made from the oxidation of ethanol in a liquid. Most vinegar is 3 to 5 percent acetic acid by volume, which is why it curdles with basic ingredients that have a basic pH, such as milk.

Why does vinegar taste so sour? For a long time, scientists weren't sure. Then a team led by scientists at Duke University Medical Center identified two proteins on the surface of our tongues—PKD1L3 and PKD2L1. They also tracked the process that sends an electrical signal to your brain to pucker up. Another study showed that your genes may play a role in how sour something tastes to you.

Design It Work with a partner to design an experiment to find out more about people's taste for sour. How do different people respond to the same sour food and drink? Consider how you can test the way people taste. How many people would you need to test? Will repeated trials help you to draw a conclusion?

◀ PKD1L3 and PKD2L1 are two proteins on the surface of the tongue. They cause vinegar to taste sour.

Using a Laboratory Balance

The laboratory balance is an important tool in scientific investigations. You can use a balance to determine the masses of materials that you study or experiment with in the laboratory.

Different kinds of balances are used in the laboratory. One kind of balance is the triple-beam balance. The balance that you may use in your science class is probably similar to the balance illustrated in this Appendix. **To use the balance properly, you should learn the name, location, and function of each part of the balance you are using. What kind of balance do you have in your science class?**

The Triple-Beam Balance

The triple-beam balance is a single-pan balance with three beams calibrated in grams. The back, or 100-gram, beam is divided into ten units of 10 grams each. The middle, or 500-gram, beam is divided into five units of 100 grams each. The front, or 10-gram, beam is divided into ten units of 1 gram each. Each of the units on the front beam is further divided into units of 0.1 gram. What is the largest mass you could find with a triple-beam balance?

The following procedure can be used to find the mass of an object with a triple-beam balance:
1. Place the object on the pan.
2. Move the rider on the middle beam notch by notch until the horizontal pointer on the right drops below zero. Move the rider back one notch.
3. Move the rider on the back beam notch by notch until the pointer again drops below zero. Move the rider back one notch.
4. Slowly slide the rider along the front beam until the pointer stops at the zero point.
5. The mass of the object is equal to the sum of the readings on the three beams.

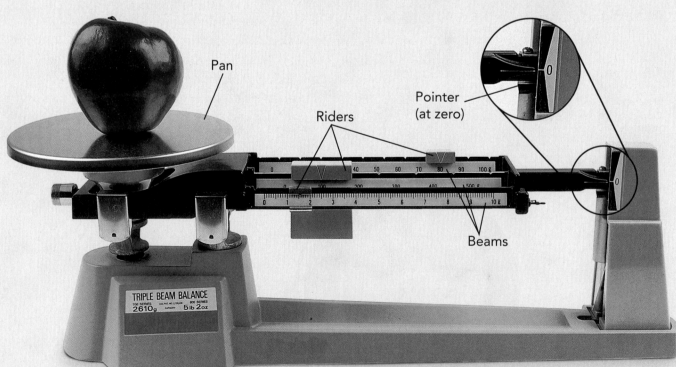

Pan

Riders

Pointer (at zero)

Beams

TRIPLE BEAM BALANCE
700 SERIES   800 SERIES
2610 g   CAPACITY   5 lb 2 oz

List of Chemical Elements

Name	Symbol	Atomic Number	Atomic Mass[†]
Actinium	Ac	89	(227)
Aluminum	Al	13	26.982
Americium	Am	95	(243)
Antimony	Sb	51	121.75
Argon	Ar	18	39.948
Arsenic	As	33	74.922
Astatine	At	85	(210)
Barium	Ba	56	137.33
Berkelium	Bk	97	(247)
Beryllium	Be	4	9.0122
Bismuth	Bi	83	208.98
Bohrium	Bh	107	(264)
Boron	B	5	10.81
Bromine	Br	35	79.904
Cadmium	Cd	48	112.41
Calcium	Ca	20	40.08
Californium	Cf	98	(251)
Carbon	C	6	12.011
Cerium	Ce	58	140.12
Cesium	Cs	55	132.91
Chlorine	Cl	17	35.453
Chromium	Cr	24	51.996
Cobalt	Co	27	58.933
Copernicium	Cn	112	(277)
Copper	Cu	29	63.546
Curium	Cm	96	(247)
Darmstadtium	Ds	110	(269)
Dubnium	Db	105	(262)
Dysprosium	Dy	66	162.50
Einsteinium	Es	99	(252)
Erbium	Er	68	167.26
Europium	Eu	63	151.96
Fermium	Fm	100	(257)
Fluorine	F	9	18.998
Francium	Fr	87	(223)
Gadolinium	Gd	64	157.25
Gallium	Ga	31	69.72
Germanium	Ge	32	72.59
Gold	Au	79	196.97
Hafnium	Hf	72	178.49
Hassium	Hs	108	(265)
Helium	He	2	4.0026
Holmium	Ho	67	164.93
Hydrogen	H	1	1.0079
Indium	In	49	114.82
Iodine	I	53	126.90
Iridium	Ir	77	192.22
Iron	Fe	26	55.847
Krypton	Kr	36	83.80
Lanthanum	La	57	138.91
Lawrencium	Lr	103	(262)
Lead	Pb	82	207.2
Lithium	Li	3	6.941
Lutetium	Lu	71	174.97
Magnesium	Mg	12	24.305
Manganese	Mn	25	54.938
Meitnerium	Mt	109	(268)
Mendelevium	Md	101	(258)
Mercury	Hg	80	200.59
Molybdenum	Mo	42	95.94
Neodymium	Nd	60	144.24
Neon	Ne	10	20.179
Neptunium	Np	93	(237)
Nickel	Ni	28	58.71
Niobium	Nb	41	92.906
Nitrogen	N	7	14.007
Nobelium	No	102	(259)
Osmium	Os	76	190.2
Oxygen	O	8	15.999
Palladium	Pd	46	106.4
Phosphorus	P	15	30.974
Platinum	Pt	78	195.09
Plutonium	Pu	94	(244)
Polonium	Po	84	(209)
Potassium	K	19	39.098
Praseodymium	Pr	59	140.91
Promethium	Pm	61	(145)
Protactinium	Pa	91	231.04
Radium	Ra	88	(226)
Radon	Rn	86	(222)
Rhenium	Re	75	186.21
Rhodium	Rh	45	102.91
Roentgenium	Rg	111	(272)
Rubidium	Rb	37	85.468
Ruthenium	Ru	44	101.07
Rutherfordium	Rf	104	(261)
Samarium	Sm	62	150.4
Scandium	Sc	21	44.956
Seaborgium	Sg	106	(263)
Selenium	Se	34	78.96
Silicon	Si	14	28.086
Silver	Ag	47	107.87
Sodium	Na	11	22.990
Strontium	Sr	38	87.62
Sulfur	S	16	32.06
Tantalum	Ta	73	180.95
Technetium	Tc	43	(98)
Tellurium	Te	52	127.60
Terbium	Tb	65	158.93
Thallium	Tl	81	204.37
Thorium	Th	90	232.04
Thulium	Tm	69	168.93
Tin	Sn	50	118.69
Titanium	Ti	22	47.90
Tungsten	W	74	183.85
Uranium	U	92	238.03
Vanadium	V	23	50.941
Xenon	Xe	54	131.30
Ytterbium	Yb	70	173.04
Yttrium	Y	39	88.906
Zinc	Zn	30	65.38
Zirconium	Zr	40	91.22

[†]Numbers in parentheses give the mass number of the most stable isotope.

APPENDIX C

Periodic Table of the Elements

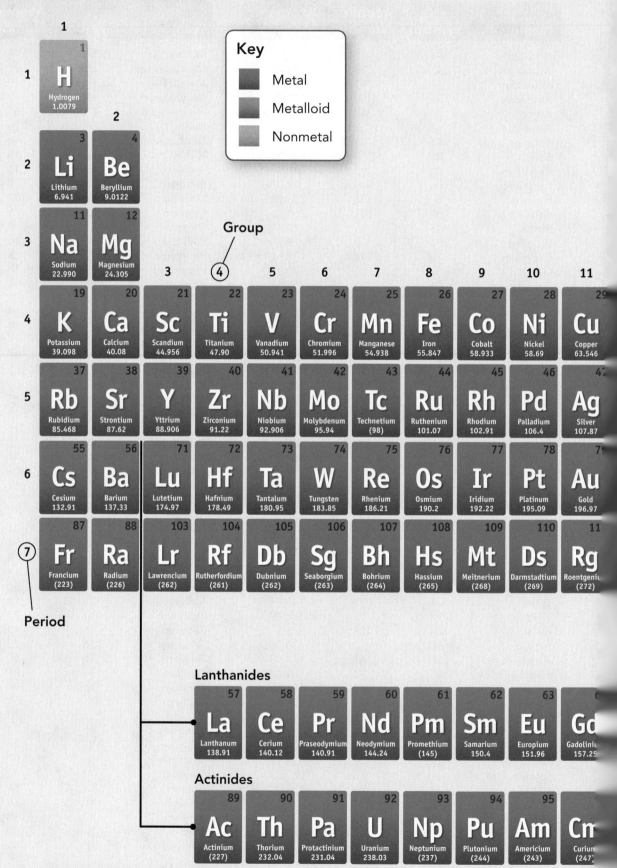

1

1		
1		
H		
Hydrogen		
1.0079		

Key
- Metal
- Metalloid
- Nonmetal

2

3	4
Li	**Be**
Lithium	Beryllium
6.941	9.0122

11	12
Na	**Mg**
Sodium	Magnesium
22.990	24.305

Group ④

Period ⑦

	3	**4**	**5**	**6**	**7**	**8**	**9**	**10**	**11**
4	21 **Sc** Scandium 44.956	22 **Ti** Titanium 47.90	23 **V** Vanadium 50.941	24 **Cr** Chromium 51.996	25 **Mn** Manganese 54.938	26 **Fe** Iron 55.847	27 **Co** Cobalt 58.933	28 **Ni** Nickel 58.69	29 **Cu** Copper 63.546

19 **K** Potassium 39.098	20 **Ca** Calcium 40.08
37 **Rb** Rubidium 85.468	38 **Sr** Strontium 87.62
55 **Cs** Cesium 132.91	56 **Ba** Barium 137.33
87 **Fr** Francium (223)	88 **Ra** Radium (226)

5: 39 **Y** Yttrium 88.906 | 40 **Zr** Zirconium 91.22 | 41 **Nb** Niobium 92.906 | 42 **Mo** Molybdenum 95.94 | 43 **Tc** Technetium (98) | 44 **Ru** Ruthenium 101.07 | 45 **Rh** Rhodium 102.91 | 46 **Pd** Palladium 106.4 | 47 **Ag** Silver 107.87

6: 71 **Lu** Lutetium 174.97 | 72 **Hf** Hafnium 178.49 | 73 **Ta** Tantalum 180.95 | 74 **W** Tungsten 183.85 | 75 **Re** Rhenium 186.21 | 76 **Os** Osmium 190.2 | 77 **Ir** Iridium 192.22 | 78 **Pt** Platinum 195.09 | 79 **Au** Gold 196.97

7: 103 **Lr** Lawrencium (262) | 104 **Rf** Rutherfordium (261) | 105 **Db** Dubnium (262) | 106 **Sg** Seaborgium (263) | 107 **Bh** Bohrium (264) | 108 **Hs** Hassium (265) | 109 **Mt** Meitnerium (268) | 110 **Ds** Darmstadtium (269) | 111 **Rg** Roentgenium (272)

Lanthanides

57	58	59	60	61	62	63	
La	**Ce**	**Pr**	**Nd**	**Pm**	**Sm**	**Eu**	**Gd**
Lanthanum	Cerium	Praseodymium	Neodymium	Promethium	Samarium	Europium	Gadolinium
138.91	140.12	140.91	144.24	(145)	150.4	151.96	157.25

Actinides

89	90	91	92	93	94	95	
Ac	**Th**	**Pa**	**U**	**Np**	**Pu**	**Am**	**Cm**
Actinium	Thorium	Protactinium	Uranium	Neptunium	Plutonium	Americium	Curium
(227)	232.04	231.04	238.03	(237)	(244)	(243)	(247)

Many periodic tables include a zigzag line that separates the metals from the nonmetals. Metalloids, found on either side of the line, share properties of both metals and nonmetals.

18

2
He
Helium
4.0026

13	**14**	**15**	**16**	**17**

5	6	7	8	9	10
B	**C**	**N**	**O**	**F**	**Ne**
Boron	Carbon	Nitrogen	Oxygen	Fluorine	Neon
10.81	12.011	14.007	15.999	18.998	20.179

13	14	15	16	17	18
Al	**Si**	**P**	**S**	**Cl**	**Ar**
Aluminum	Silicon	Phosphorus	Sulfur	Chlorine	Argon
26.982	28.086	30.974	32.06	35.453	39.948

12

30	31	32	33	34	35	36
Zn	**Ga**	**Ge**	**As**	**Se**	**Br**	**Kr**
Zinc	Gallium	Germanium	Arsenic	Selenium	Bromine	Krypton
65.38	69.72	72.59	74.922	78.96	79.904	83.80

48	49	50	51	52	53	54
Cd	**In**	**Sn**	**Sb**	**Te**	**I**	**Xe**
Cadmium	Indium	Tin	Antimony	Tellurium	Iodine	Xenon
112.41	114.82	118.69	121.75	127.60	126.90	131.30

80	81	82	83	84	85	86
Hg	**Tl**	**Pb**	**Bi**	**Po**	**At**	**Rn**
Mercury	Thallium	Lead	Bismuth	Polonium	Astatine	Radon
200.59	204.37	207.2	208.98	(209)	(210)	(222)

112	113	114	115	116	117	118
Cn	***Uut**	***Uuq**	***Uup**	***Uuh**	***Uus**	***Uuo**
Copernicium	Ununtrium	Ununquadium	Ununpentium	Ununhexium	Ununseptium	Ununoctium
(277)	(284)	(289)	(288)	(292)		(294)

*The discoveries of elements 113 and above have not yet been officially confirmed.

Atomic masses in parentheses are those of the most stable isotopes.

65	66	67	68	69	70
Tb	**Dy**	**Ho**	**Er**	**Tm**	**Yb**
Terbium	Dysprosium	Holmium	Erbium	Thulium	Ytterbium
158.93	162.50	164.93	167.26	168.93	173.04

97	98	99	100	101	102
Bk	**Cf**	**Es**	**Fm**	**Md**	**No**
Berkelium	Californium	Einsteinium	Fermium	Mendelevium	Nobelium
(247)	(251)	(252)	(257)	(258)	(259)

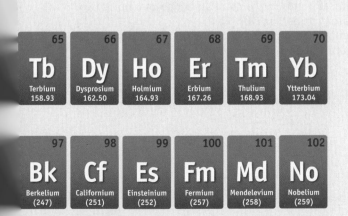

GLOSSARY

A

acid A substance that tastes sour, reacts with metals and carbonates, and turns blue litmus red. (213)
ácido Sustancia de sabor agrio que reacciona con metales y carbonatos, y que vuelve rojo el papel de tornasol azul.

activation energy The minimum amount of energy needed to start a chemical reaction. (183)
energía de activación Cantidad mínima de energía que se necesita para iniciar una reacción química.

alkali metal An element in Group 1 of the periodic table. (92)
metal alcalino Elemento en el Grupo 1 de la tabla periódica.

alkaline earth metal An element in Group 2 of the periodic table. (92)
metal alcalinotérreo Elemento en el Grupo 2 de la tabla periódica.

alloy A mixture of two or more elements, at least one of which is a metal. (151)
aleación Mezcla de dos o más elementos, uno de los cuales es un metal.

alpha particle A particle given off during radioactive decay that consists of two protons and two neutrons. (109)
partícula alfa Partícula liberada durante la desintegración radiactiva que tiene dos protones y dos neutrones.

amorphous solid A solid made up of particles that are not arranged in a regular pattern. (42)
sólido amorfo Sólido constituido por partículas que no están dispuestas en un patrón regular.

atom The basic particle from which all elements are made; the smallest particle of an element that has the properties of that element. (10, 73)
átomo Partícula básica de la que todos los elementos están formados; partícula más pequeña de un elemento, que tiene las propiedades de ese elemento.

atomic mass The average mass of all the isotopes of an element. (81)
masa atómica Promedio de la masa de todos los isótopos de un elemento.

atomic number The number of protons in the nucleus of an atom. (78)
número atómico Número de protones en el núcleo de un átomo.

B

base A substance that tastes bitter, feels slippery, and turns red litmus paper blue. (215)
base Sustancia de sabor amargo, escurridiza y que vuelve azul el papel de tornasol rojo.

beta particle A fast-moving electron that is given off as nuclear radiation. (109)
partícula beta Electrón de movimiento rápido producido como radiación nuclear.

boiling Vaporization that occurs at and below the surface of a liquid. (51)
ebullición Evaporación que ocurre en y bajo la superficie de un líquido.

boiling point The temperature at which a liquid boils. (51)
punto de ebullición Temperatura a la cual hierve un líquido.

Boyle's law A principle that describes the relationship between the pressure and volume of a gas at constant temperature. (60)
ley de Boyle Principio que describe la relación entre la presión y el volumen de un gas a una temperatura constante.

C

catalyst A material that increases the rate of a reaction by lowering the activation energy. (187)
catalizador Material que aumenta la velocidad de una reacción al disminuir la energía de activación.

Charles's law A principle that describes the relationship between the temperature and volume of a gas at constant pressure. (58)
ley de Charles Principio que describe la relación entre la temperatura y el volumen de un gas a una presión constante.

chemical bond The force of attraction that holds two atoms together. (10, 125)
enlace químico Fuerza de atracción que mantiene juntos a dos átomos.

chemical change A change in which one or more substances combine or break apart to form new substances. (23, 164)
cambio químico Cambio en el cual una o más sustancias se combinan o se descomponen para formar sustancias nuevas.

chemical energy A form of energy that is stored in chemical bonds between atoms. (27)
energía química Forma de energía almacenada en los enlaces químicos de los átomos.

chemical equation A short, easy way to show a chemical reaction, using symbols. (170)
ecuación química Forma corta y sencilla de mostrar una reacción química usando símbolos.

chemical formula Symbols that show the elements in a compound and the ratio of atoms. (11, 134)
fórmula química Símbolos que muestran los elementos de un compuesto y la cantidad de átomos.

chemical property A characteristic of a substance that describes its ability to change into different substances. (6)
propiedad química Característica de una sustancia que describe su capacidad de convertirse en sustancias diferentes.

chemical reaction A process in which substances change into new substances with different properties. (164)
reacción química Proceso por el cual las sustancias químicas se convierten en nuevas sustancias con propiedades diferentes.

chemical symbol A one- or two-letter representation of an element. (83)
símbolo químico Representación con una o dos letras de un elemento.

chemistry The study of the properties of matter and how matter changes. (5)
química Estudio de las propiedades de la materia y de sus cambios.

closed system A system in which no matter is allowed to enter or leave. (175)
sistema cerrado Sistema en el cual la materia no puede entrar ni salir.

coefficient A number in front of a chemical formula in an equation that indicates how many molecules or atoms of each reactant and product are involved in a reaction. (177)
coeficiente En un ecuación, número delante de una fórmula química que indica cuántas moléculas o átomos de cada reactante y producto intervienen en una reacción.

colloid A mixture containing small, undissolved particles that do not settle out. (201)
coloide Mezcla que contiene partículas pequeñas y sin disolver que no se depositan.

compound A substance made of two or more elements chemically combined in a specific ratio, or proportion. (11)
compuesto Sustancia formada por dos o más elementos combinados químicamente en una razón o proporción específica.

concentrated solution A mixture that has a lot of solute dissolved in it. (205)
solución concentrada Mezcla que tiene muchos solutos disueltos en ella.

concentration The amount of one material in a certain volume of another material. (186)
concentración Cantidad de un material en cierto volumen de otro material.

condensation The change of state from a gas to a liquid. (52)
condensación Cambio del estado gaseoso al estado líquido.

corrosion The gradual wearing away of a metal element due to a chemical reaction. (91)
corrosión Desgaste progresivo de un elemento metal debido a una reacción química.

corrosive The way in which acids react with some metals so as to wear away the metal. (213)
corrosivo Forma en que los ácidos reaccionan con algunos metales y los desgastan.

covalent bond A chemical bond formed when two atoms share electrons. (139)
enlace covalente Enlace químico que se forma cuando dos átomos comparten electrones.

crystal A solid in which the atoms are arranged in a pattern that repeats again and again. (136)
cristal Sólido en el que los átomos están colocados en un patrón que se repite una y otra vez.

crystalline solid A solid that is made up of crystals in which particles are arranged in a regular, repeating pattern. (42)
sólido cristalino Sólido constituido por cristales en los que las partículas están colocadas en un patrón regular repetitivo.

GLOSSARY

D

decomposition A chemical reaction that breaks down compounds into simpler products. (180)
descomposición Reacción química que descompone los compuestos en productos más simples.

density The ratio of the mass of a substance to its volume (mass divided by volume). (18)
densidad Razón de la masa de una sustancia a su volumen (masa dividida por el volumen).

diatomic molecule A molecule consisting of two atoms. (100)
molécula diatómica Molécula que tiene dos átomos.

dilute solution A mixture that has only a little solute dissolved in it. (205)
solución diluida Mezcla que sólo tiene un poco de soluto disuelto en ella.

directly proportional A term used to describe the relationship between two variables whose graph is a straight line passing through the point (0, 0). (59)
directamente proporcional Término empleado para describir la relación entre dos variables cuya gráfica forma una línea recta que pasa por el punto (0, 0).

double bond A chemical bond formed when atoms share two pairs of electrons. (140)
enlace doble Enlace químico formado cuando los átomos comparten dos pares de electrones.

ductile A term used to describe a material that can be pulled out into a long wire. (90, 149)
dúctil Término usado para describir un material que se puede estirar hasta crear un alambre largo.

E

electrical conductivity The ability of an object to carry electric current. (90, 150)
conductividad eléctrica Capacidad de un objeto para cargar corriente eléctrica.

electron A tiny, negatively charged particle that moves around the outside of the nucleus of an atom. (74)
electrón Partícula pequeña de carga negativa que se mueve alrededor del núcleo de un átomo.

electron dot diagram A representation of the valence electrons in an atom, using dots. (125)
esquema de puntos por electrones Representación del número de electrones de valencia de un átomo, usando puntos.

element A substance that cannot be broken down into any other substances by chemical or physical means. (9)
elemento Sustancia que no se puede descomponer en otras sustancias por medios químicos o físicos.

endothermic change A change in which energy is absorbed. (27)
cambio endotérmico Cambio en el que se absorbe energía.

endothermic reaction A reaction that absorbs energy. (168)
reacción endotérmica Reacción que absorbe energía.

energy level A region of an atom in which electrons of the same energy are likely to be found. (76)
nivel de energía Región de un átomo en la que es probable que se encuentren electrones con la misma energía.

enzyme A type of protein that speeds up a chemical reaction in a living thing; a biological catalyst that lowers the activation energy of reactions in cells. (187)
enzima Tipo de proteína que acelera una reacción química en un ser vivo; catalizador biológico que disminuye la energía de activación de las reacciones celulares.

evaporation The process by which molecules at the surface of a liquid absorb enough energy to change to a gas. (51)
evaporación Proceso mediante el cual las moléculas en la superficie de un líquido absorben suficiente energía para pasar al estado gaseoso.

exothermic change A change in which energy is released. (27)
cambio exotérmico Cambio en el que se libera energía.

exothermic reaction A reaction that releases energy, usually in the form of heat. (168)
reacción exotérmica Reacción que libera energía generalmente en forma de calor.

F

fluid Any substance that can flow. (43)
fluido Cualquier sustancia que puede fluir.

freezing The change in state from a liquid to a solid. (50)
congelación Cambio del estado líquido al sólido.

G

gamma rays Electromagnetic waves with the shortest wavelengths and highest frequencies. (109)
rayos gamma Ondas electromagnéticas con la menor longitud de onda y la mayor frecuencia.

gas A state of matter with no definite shape or volume. (45)
gas Estado de la materia sin forma ni volumen definidos.

group Elements in the same vertical column of the periodic table; also called family. (87)
grupo Elementos en la misma columna vertical de la tabla periódica; también llamado familia.

H

half-life The time it takes for half of the atoms of a radioactive element to decay. (111)
vida media Tiempo que tarda en decaer la mitad de los átomos de un elemento radiactivo.

halogen An element found in Group 17 of the periodic table. (101)
halógeno Elemento del Grupo 17 de la tabla periódica.

hydrogen ion A positively charged ion (H^+) formed of a hydrogen atom that has lost its electron. (219)
ión hidrógeno Ión de carga positiva (H^+) formado por un átomo de hidrógeno que ha perdido su electrón.

hydroxide ion A negatively charged ion made of oxygen and hydrogen (OH^-). (220)
ión hidróxido Ión de carga negativa formado de oxígeno e hidrógeno (OH^-).

I

indicator A compound that changes color in the presence of an acid or a base. (214)
indicador Compuesto que cambia de color en presencia de un ácido o una base.

inhibitor A material that decreases the rate of a reaction. (187)
inhibidor Material que disminuye la velocidad de una reacción.

International System of Units (SI) A system of measurement based on multiples of ten and on established measures of mass, length, and time. (16)
Sistema Internacional de Unidades Sistema de medidas basado en múltiplos de diez y en medidas establecidas de masa, longitud y tiempo.

inversely proportional A term used to describe the relationship between two variables whose product is constant. (61)
inversamente proporcional Término usado para describir la relación entre dos variables cuyo producto es constante.

ion An atom or group of atoms that has become electrically charged. (131)
ión Átomo o grupo de átomos que está cargado eléctricamente.

ionic bond The attraction between oppositely charged ions. (132)
enlace iónico Atracción entre iones con cargas opuestas.

ionic compound A compound that consists of positive and negative ions. (132)
compuesto iónico Compuesto que tiene iones positivos y negativos.

isotope An atom with the same number of protons and a different number of neutrons from other atoms of the same element. (79)
isótopo Átomo con el mismo número de protones y un número diferente de neutrones que otros átomos del mismo elemento.

L

law of conservation of mass The principle that the total amount of matter is neither created nor destroyed during any chemical or physical change. (25, 174)
ley de conservación de la masa Principio que establece que la cantidad total de materia no se crea ni se destruye durante cambios químicos o físicos.

liquid A state of matter that has no definite shape but has a definite volume. (43)
líquido Estado de la materia que no tiene forma definida pero sí volumen definido.

luster The way a mineral reflects light from its surface. (90, 148)
lustre Manera en la que un mineral refleja la luz en su superficie.

GLOSSARY

M

malleable A term used to describe material that can be hammered or rolled into flat sheets. (90, 149)
maleable Término usado para describir materiales que se pueden convertir en láminas planas por medio de martillazos o con un rodillo.

mass The amount of matter in an object. (16)
masa Cantidad de materia de un objeto.

mass number The sum of protons and neutrons in the nucleus of an atom. (79)
número de masa Suma de los protones y neutrones en el núcleo de un átomo.

matter Anything that has mass and takes up space. (5)
materia Cualquier cosa que tiene masa y ocupa un espacio.

melting The change in state from a solid to a liquid. (49)
fusión Cambio del estado sólido a líquido.

melting point The temperature at which a substance changes from a solid to a liquid; the same as the freezing point, or temperature at which a liquid changes to a solid. (49)
punto de fusión Temperatura a la que una sustancia cambia de estado sólido a líquido; es lo mismo que el punto de congelación (la temperatura a la que un líquido se vuelve sólido).

metal A class of elements characterized by physical properties that include shininess, malleability, ductility, and conductivity. (89)
metal Clase de elementos caracterizados por propiedades físicas que incluyen brillo, maleabilidad, ductilidad y conductividad.

metallic bond An attraction between a positive metal ion and the electrons surrounding it. (147)
enlace metálico Atracción entre un ión metálico positivo y los electrones que lo rodean.

metalloid An element that has some characteristics of both metals and nonmetals. (103)
metaloide Elemento que tiene algunas características de los metales y de los no metales.

mixture Two or more substances that are together in the same place but their atoms are not chemically bonded. (12)
mezcla Dos o más sustancias que están en el mismo lugar pero cuyos átomos no están químicamente enlazados.

molecular compound A compound that is composed of molecules. (141)
compuesto molecular Compuesto que tiene moléculas.

molecule A neutral group of two or more atoms held together by covalent bonds. (10, 139)
molécula Grupo neutral de dos o más átomos unidos por medio de enlaces covalentes.

N

neutralization A reaction of an acid with a base, yielding a solution that is not as acidic or basic as the starting solutions were. (222)
neutralización Reacción de un ácido con una base, que produce una solución que no es ácida ni básica, como lo eran las soluciones originales.

neutron A small particle in the nucleus of the atom, with no electrical charge. (77)
neutrón Partícula pequeña en el núcleo del átomo, que no tiene carga eléctrica.

noble gas An element in Group 18 of the periodic table. (102)
gas noble Elemento del Grupo 18 de la tabla periódica.

nonmetal An element that lacks most of the properties of a metal. (97)
no metal Elemento que carece de la mayoría de las propiedades de un metal.

nonpolar bond A covalent bond in which electrons are shared equally. (143)
enlace no polar Enlace covalente en el que los electrones se comparten por igual.

nuclear reaction A reaction involving the particles in the nucleus of an atom that can change one element into another element. (107)
reacción nuclear Reacción en la que intervienen las partículas del núcleo de un átomo que puede transformar un elemento en otro.

nucleus 1. In cells, a large oval organelle that contains the cell's genetic material in the form of DNA and controls many of the cell's activities. **2.** The central core of an atom which contains protons and neutrons. (75) **3.** The solid inner core of a comet.
núcleo 1. En las células, orgánulo grande ovalado que contiene el material genético de la célula, en forma de ADN, y que controla muchas de las actividades celulares. **2.** Parte central de un átomo que contiene protones y neutrones. **3.** Parte central sólida de un cometa.

O

open system A system in which matter can enter from or escape to the surroundings. (175)
sistema abierto Sistema en el que la materia puede escapar a sus alrededores o entrar desde ahí.

P

period A horizontal row of elements in the periodic table. (86)
período Fila horizontal de los elementos de la tabla periódica.

periodic table An arrangement of the elements showing the repeating pattern of their properties. (82)
tabla periódica Configuración de los elementos que muestra el patrón repetido de sus propiedades.

pH scale A range of values used to indicate how acidic or basic a substance is; expresses the concentration of hydrogen ions in a solution. (220)
escala pH Rango de valores que se usa para indicar cuán ácida o básica es una sustancia; expresa la concentración de iones hidrógeno de una solución.

physical change A change that alters the form or appearance of a material but does not make the material into another substance. (21, 164)
cambio físico Cambio que altera la forma o apariencia de un material, pero que no convierte el material en otra sustancia.

physical property A characteristic of a pure substance that can be observed without changing it into another substance. (6)
propiedad física Característica de una sustancia pura que se puede observar sin convertirla en otra sustancia.

polar bond A covalent bond in which electrons are shared unequally. (143)
enlace polar Enlace covalente en el que los electrones se comparten de forma desigual.

polyatomic ion An ion that is made of more than one atom. (132)
ión poliatómico Ión formado por más de un átomo.

precipitate A solid that forms from a solution during a chemical reaction. (166)
precipitado Sólido que se forma de una solución durante una reacción química.

pressure The force pushing on a surface divided by the area of that surface. (46)
presión 1. Fuerza que actúa contra una superficie, dividida entre el área de esa superficie. 2. Fuerza que actúa sobre las rocas y que cambia su forma o volumen.

product A substance formed as a result of a chemical reaction. (164)
producto Sustancia formada como resultado de una reacción química.

protons Small, positively charged particles that are found in the nucleus of an atom. (75)
protones Partículas pequeñas de carga positiva que se encuentran en el núcleo de un átomo.

R

radioactive dating The process of determining the age of an object using the half-life of one or more radioactive isotopes. (111)
datación radiactiva Proceso para determinar la edad de un objeto usando la vida media de uno o más isótopos radiactivos.

radioactive decay The process in which radioactive elements break down, releasing fast-moving particles and energy. (107)
desintegración radiactiva Proceso en el cual los elementos radiactivos se descomponen y liberan partículas y energía de movimiento rápido.

radioactivity The spontaneous emission of radiation by an unstable atomic nucleus. (108)
radiactividad Emisión espontánea de radiación por un núcleo atómico inestable.

reactant A substance that enters into a chemical reaction. (164)
reactante Sustancia que interviene en una reacción química.

reactivity The ease and speed with which an element combines, or reacts, with other elements and compounds. (91)
reactividad Facilidad y rapidez con las que un elemento se combina, o reacciona, con otros elementos y compuestos.

replacement A reaction in which one element replaces another in a compound or when two elements in different compounds trade places. (180)
sustitución Reacción en la que un elemento reemplaza a otro en un compuesto o en la que se intercambian dos elementos de diferentes compuestos.

GLOSSARY

S

salt An ionic compound made from the neutralization of an acid with a base. (223)
sal Compuesto iónico formado por la neutralización de un ácido con una base.

saturated solution A mixture that contains as much dissolved solute as is possible at a given temperature. (207)
solución saturada Mezcla que contiene la mayor cantidad posible de soluto disuelto a una temperatura determinada.

semiconductor A substance that can conduct electric current under some conditions. (103)
semiconductor Sustancia que puede conducir una corriente eléctrica bajo ciertas condiciones.

solid A state of matter that has a definite shape and a definite volume. (41)
sólido Estado en el que la materia tiene forma y volumen definidos.

solubility A measure of how much solute can dissolve in a given solvent at a given temperature. (207)
solubilidad Medida de cuánto soluto se puede disolver en un solvente a una temperatura dada.

solute The part of a solution that is dissolved by a solvent. (199)
soluto Parte de una solución que se disuelve en un solvente.

solution A mixture containing a solvent and at least one solute that has the same properties throughout; a mixture in which one substance is dissolved in another. (199)
solución Mezcla que contiene un solvente y al menos un soluto que tiene las mismas propiedades; mezcla en la cual una sustancia se disuelve en otra sustancia.

solvent The part of a solution that is usually present in the largest amount and dissolves a solute. (199)
solvente Parte de una solución que, por lo general, está presente en la mayor cantidad y que disuelve a un soluto.

sublimation The change in state from a solid directly to a gas without passing through the liquid state. (53)
sublimación Cambio del estado sólido directamente a gas, sin pasar por el estado líquido.

subscript A number in a chemical formula that tells the number of atoms in a molecule or the ratio of elements in a compound. (134)
subíndice Número en una fórmula química que indica el número de átomos que tiene una molécula o la razón de elementos en un compuesto.

substance A single kind of matter that is pure and has a specific set of properties. (5)
sustancia Tipo único de materia que es pura y tiene propiedades específicas.

surface tension The result of an inward pull among the molecules of a liquid that brings the molecules on the surface closer together; causes the surface to act as if it has a thin skin. (44)
tensión superficial Resultado de la atracción hacia el centro entre las moléculas de un líquido, que hace que las moléculas de la superficie se acerquen mucho, y que la superficie actúe como si tuviera una piel delgada.

suspension A mixture in which particles can be seen and easily separated by settling or filtration. (201)
suspensión Mezcla en la cual las partículas se pueden ver y separar fácilmente por fijación o por filtración.

synthesis A chemical reaction in which two or more simple substances combine to form a new, more complex substance. (180)
síntesis Reacción química en la que dos o más sustancias simples se combinan y forman una sustancia nueva más compleja.

T

temperature How hot or cold something is; a measure of the average energy of motion of the particles of a substance. (26, 47)
temperature Cuán caliente o frío es algo; medida de la energía de movimiento promedio de las partículas de una sustancia.

thermal conductivity The ability of an object to transfer heat. (90, 149)
conductividad térmica Capacidad de un objeto para transferir calor.

thermal energy The total energy of the motion of all the particles of an object. (26)
energía térmica Energía total del movimiento de las partículas de un objeto.

tracer A radioactive isotope that can be followed through the steps of a chemical reaction or industrial process. (112)
trazador Isótopo radiactivo que se puede seguir mediante los pasos de una reacción química o un proceso industrial.

transition metal One of the elements in Groups 3 through 12 of the periodic table. (93)
metal de transición Uno de los elementos de los Grupos 3 a 12 de la tabla periódica.

triple bond A chemical bond formed when atoms share three pairs of electrons. (140)
enlace triple Enlace químico formado cuando los átomos comparten tres pares de electrones.

V

valence electrons The electrons that are in the highest energy level of an atom and that are involved in chemical bonding. (125)
electrones de valencia Electrones que tienen el nivel más alto de energía de un átomo y que intervienen en los enlaces químicos.

vaporization The change of state from a liquid to a gas. (51)
vaporización Cambio del estado de líquido a gas.

viscosity A liquid's resistance to flowing. (44)
viscosidad Resistencia a fluir que presenta un líquido.

volume The amount of space that matter occupies. (17)
volumen Cantidad de espacio que ocupa la materia.

W

weight A measure of the force of gravity acting on an object. (15)
peso Medida de la fuerza de gravedad que actúa sobre un objeto.

INDEX

INDEX

Page numbers for key terms are printed in **boldface** type.

INDEX

Page numbers for key terms are printed in **boldface** type.

ACKNOWLEDGMENTS

Staff Credits

The people who made up the *Interactive Science* team—representing composition services, core design digital and multimedia production services, digital product development, editorial, editorial services, manufacturing, and production—are listed below.

Jan Van Aarsen, Samah Abadir, Ernie Albanese, Zareh MacPherson Artinian, Bridget Binstock, Suzanne Biron, MJ Black, Nancy Bolsover, Stacy Boyd, Jim Brady, Katherine Bryant, Michael Burstein, Pradeep Byram, Jessica Chase, Jonathan Cheney, Arthur Ciccone, Allison Cook-Bellistri, Rebecca Cottingham, AnnMarie Coyne, Bob Craton, Chris Deliee, Paul Delsignore, Michael Di Maria, Diane Dougherty, Kristen Ellis, Theresa Eugenio, Amanda Ferguson, Jorgensen Fernandez, Kathryn Fobert, Julia Gecha, Mark Geyer, Steve Gobbell, Paula Gogan-Porter, Jeffrey Gong, Sandra Graff, Adam Groffman, Lynette Haggard, Christian Henry, Karen Holtzman, Susan Hutchinson, Sharon Inglis, Marian Jones, Sumy Joy, Sheila Kanitsch, Courtenay Kelley, Chris Kennedy, Toby Klang, Greg Lam, Russ Lappa, Margaret LaRaia, Ben Leveillee, Thea Limpus, Dotti Marshall, Kathy Martin, Robyn Matzke, John McClure, Mary Beth McDaniel, Krista McDonald, Tim McDonald, Rich McMahon, Cara McNally, Melinda Medina, Angelina Mendez, Maria Milczarek, Claudi Mimo, Mike Napieralski, Deborah Nicholls, Dave Nichols, William Oppenheimer, Jodi O'Rourke, Ameer Padshah, Lorie Park, Celio Pedrosa, Jonathan Penyack, Linda Zust Reddy, Jennifer Reichlin, Stephen Rider, Charlene Rimsa, Stephanie Rogers, Marcy Rose, Rashid Ross, Anne Rowsey, Logan Schmidt, Amanda Seldera, Laurel Smith, Nancy Smith, Ted Smykal, Emily Soltanoff, Cindy Strowman, Dee Sunday, Barry Tomack, Patricia Valencia, Ana Sofia Villaveces, Stephanie Wallace, Christine Whitney, Brad Wiatr, Heidi Wilson, Heather Wright, Rachel Youdelman

Photography

All uncredited photos copyright © 2011 Pearson Education.

Cover, Front and Back
Matthew Donaldson/Photolibrary, New York.

Front Matter
Page vi, JTB MEDIA CREATION, Inc./Alamy; **vii,** Michael C. York/AP Images; **viii,** Tom Schierlitz/Getty Images; **ix,** Carsten Peter/Speleoresearch & Films/National Geographic/Getty Images; **x,** N A Callow/Science Source; **xi,** David Doubilet/National Geographic Stock; **xiii laptop,** iStockphoto.com; **xv girl,** JupiterImages/Getty Images; **xviii laptop,** iStockphoto.com; **xx,** Digital Art/Corbis.

Chapter 1
Pages xxii–1 spread, JTB MEDIA CREATION, Inc./Alamy; **3 t,** Nigel Hicks/Dorling Kindersley; **3 b,** John Shaw/Science Source; **4 t painting,** *The Head of Medusa* (ca. 1590), Michelangelo Merisi da Caravaggio. Oil on canvas glued to wood. Diameter: 21 5/8 in (55 cm). Pre-restoration. Uffizi Gallery, Florence, Italy/Photograph copyright © 2005 Nicolo Orsi Battaglini/Art Resource NY; **4 b painting,** Bridgeman Art Library; **4–5 bl,** Nigel Hicks/Dorling Kindersley; **5 br,** Katy Williamson/Dorling Kindersley; **6 br inset,** iStockphoto.com;

6 l inset, Wave RF/Photolibrary New York; **7 t inset,** Nicole Hill/Rubberball/Photolibrary New York; **6–7 bkgrnd,** ArabianEye/Getty Images; **7 b,** Andy Crawford/Dorling Kindersley; **8 b,** Courtesy of Prof. Mark Welland and Dr. Ghim Wei Ho, Nanoscience Centre, University of Cambridge, UK; **9 neon,** iStockphoto.com; **9 balloon,** Ashok Rodrigues/iStockphoto.com; **9 jewelry,** iStockphoto.com; **9 kettle,** Dorling Kindersley; **9 pan,** PhotoObjects.net/JupiterUnlimited; **10 bkgrnd,** Max Blain/Shutterstock; **11 r,** Steve Gorton/Dorling Kindersley; **11 b,** Mark A. Schneider/Photo Researchers, Inc.; **11 tl,** Tyler Boyes/Shutterstock; **13 ml,** Charles D. Winters/Photo Researchers, Inc.; **14 bkgrnd,** Patrick Robert/Corbis; **14 inset,** Juergen Hasenkopf/Alamy; **16–17 spread,** Mark Lennihan/AP Images; **18–19 miners,** Bettmann/Corbis; **19 figure 4C,** Dorling Kindersley; **19 figure 4A,** Albert J. Copley/age Fotostock/Photolibrary New York; **19 figure 4B,** Charles D. Winters/Photo Researchers, Inc.; **20 bkgrnd,** iStockphoto.com; **21,** Carolyn Kaster/AP Images; **22,** iStockphoto.com; **23 r,** GeoStock/Photodisc/Getty Images; **23 b,** iStockphoto.com; **24 t,** *Erasmus Weathervane* (2008), Rodney Graham. Copper and steel. Whitechapel Gallery, London. Reproduced by permission of artist. Photo: Anthony Upton/AP Images; **26 l,** Jonathan Hayward/AP Images; **26 r,** Umit Bektas/Reuters; **27,** John Shaw/Science Source; **28 arrowhead,** Matthew J. Sroka/Reading Eagle/AP Images; **28 single coin,** iStockphoto.com; **28–29 mummy,** Amr Nabil/AP Images; **28–29 t coins,** Jakub Semeniuk/iStockphoto.com; **29 clay pot,** iStockphoto.com; **30 t,** Nigel Hicks/Dorling Kindersley; **30 b,** Umit Bektas/Reuters.

Interchapter Feature
Page 34 bkgrnd, *The Alchemist* (ca. 1640), Hendrick Heerschon. Oil on canvas. The Fisher Collection, Pittsburgh PA/Alamy; **35 inset,** American Institute of Physics/Photo Researchers, Inc.; **35 bkgrnd,** Lawrence Berkeley National Laboratory/Science Photo Library/Photo Researchers, Inc.

Chapter 2
Pages 36–37 spread, AP Photo/Michael C. York; **39 b,** Charles D. Winters/Photo Researchers, Inc.; **39 m2,** SuperStock; **39 m1,** BC Photography/Alamy; **40 bkgrnd,** James M. Bell/Photo Researchers, Inc.; **40 hands with phone,** Ryan Pyle/Corbis; **42 l,** foodfolio/Alamy; **42 r,** Mark A. Schneider/Photo Researchers, Inc.; **44,** BC Photography/Alamy; **45,** Charles D. Winters/Photo Researchers, Inc.; **47,** Giovanni Mereghetti/Marka/SuperStock; **48,** Stocksearch/Alamy; **49,** SuperStock; **50,** Winfield Parks/National Geographic Society; **53 bkgrnd,** Neal Preston/Corbis; **53 inset,** Charles D. Winters/Photo Researchers, Inc.; **53 t,** Frank Greenaway/Dorling Kindersley; **54 r,** Andreas Kuehn/Getty Images; **54 l,** Wolfgang Weinhäupl/Westend61 GmbH/Alamy; **55 b,** epa European Pressphoto Agency creative account/Alamy; **55 t,** Photolibrary New York; **56,** Kat Fahrer/Middletown Journal/AP Images; **62 b,** epa European Pressphoto Agency creative account/Alamy; **62 t,** Mark A. Schneider/Photo Researchers, Inc.

Interchapter Feature
Page 66 bkgrnd, Sami Sarkis/Getty Images; **67 t,** Stephen Lockett/Alamy; **67 ml,** Ted Kinsman/Photo Researchers, Inc.

Chapter 3

Pages 68–69 spread, Photolibrary New York; **71 m1,** Tom Schierlitz/Getty Images; **71 m2,** NASA/Photo Researchers, Inc.; **72 l,** The Lighthouse/Science Source; **72 r,** Nano-Tex, Inc./AP Images; **73,** Daryl Solomon/Getty Images; **74 watermelon,** chevanon/Shutterstock; **75 t,** Lynx/Iconotec.com/Photolibrary New York; **75 b,** Martin Bond/Photo Researchers, Inc.; **76 clouds,** Milton Wordley/Photolibrary New York; **76 cotton ball,** Steve Gorton and Gary Ombler/Dorling Kindersley; **76 onion,** Steve Gorton/Dorling Kindersley; **76 bowling ball,** Corey Radlund/Brand X Pictures/Photolibrary New York; **78 elephant,** DLILLC/Corbis; **78 cat,** deepov/Fotolia; **80,** Portrait of Dmitry Ivanovich Mendeleyev (ca. 1865). Archives Larousse, Paris, France/The Bridgeman Art Library International; **81 l,** Richard Megna/Fundamental Photographs; **81 r,** Richard Megna/Fundamental Photographs; **81 m,** Richard Megna/Fundamental Photographs; **83,** Dorling Kindersley; **86 l,** Charles D. Winters/Photo Researchers, Inc.; **86 m,** Charles D. Winters/Photo Researchers, Inc.; **86 r,** Charles D. Winters/Photo Researchers, Inc.; **87 bl,** Charles D. Winters/Photo Researchers, Inc.; **87 br,** Kim Kyung Hoon/Reuters; **87 t,** PjrFoto/Studio/Alamy; **88 t,** snyfer/Fotolia; **88 b,** Lucato/iStockphoto.com; **90 tm,** László Rákoskerti/iStockphoto.com; **90 tr,** Charles D. Winters/Photo Researchers, Inc.; **90 tl,** Joel Arem/Photo Researchers, Inc.; **90 single penny,** Peter Spiro/iStockphoto.com; **90–91 rusty chain,** Tom Schierlitz/Getty Images; **90 pile of pennies,** Keith Webber, Jr./iStockphoto.com; **91 r,** Kai Schwabe/Photolibrary New York; **92 t,** Anastasia Novikova/Alamy; **92 bl,** Living Art Enterprises, LLC/Photo Researchers, Inc.; **93,** Science Source/Photo Researchers, Inc.; **94 t,** Juerg Mueller/Keystone/AP Images; **94 b,** Bullit Marquez/AP Images; **95,** Salvatore Di Nolfi/Keystone/AP Images; **96,** Rene Tillmann/AP Images; **97,** Digital Art/Corbis; **98,** Charles D. Winters/Photo Researchers, Inc.; **99,** Lawrence Lawry/Photo Researchers, Inc.; **100,** Jim W. Grace/Photo Researchers, Inc.; **101 t,** LWA/Dann Tardif/Photolibrary New York; **101 b,** Stockbyte/Photolibrary New York; **102,** Julian Baum/Photo Researchers, Inc.; **103 r,** NASA/Photo Researchers, Inc.; **103 l,** Rosenfeld Images Ltd./Photo Researchers, Inc.; **104 green creature,** Peter Galbraith/iStockphoto.com; **106,** European Space Agency (ESA)/AP Images; **108,** tci/MARKA/Alamy; **111,** Biophoto Associates/Photo Researchers, Inc.; **113,** David R. Frazier Photolibrary/Photo Researchers, Inc.; **114 t,** Lawrence Lawry/Photo Researchers, Inc; **114 b,** tci/MARKA/Alamy.

Interchapter Feature

Page 118 bkgrnd, Ed Register/Shutterstock; **119 body,** Cordelia Molloy/Photo Researchers, Inc.; **119 bkgrnd,** photobank.kiev.ua/Shutterstock.

Chapter 4

Pages 120–121 spread, Carsten Peter/Speleoresearch & Films/National Geographic/Getty Images; **123 b,** M. Claye/Photo Researchers, Inc.; **123 t,** Giordano Cipriani/SOPA/Corbis; **124,** Panorama Stock/Photolibrary New York; **125,** Andy Crawford/Dorling Kindersley; **127,** Ed Reinke/AP Images; **128–129 spread,** Charles D. Winters/Photo Researchers, Inc.; **129 t,** Edward Kinsman/Photo Researchers, Inc.; **130,** Jens Meyer/AP Images; **132 tr,** Charles D. Winters/Photo Researchers, Inc.; **132 tl,** Andrew Lambert Photography/

Photo Researchers, Inc.; **134,** Giordano Cipriani/SOPA/Corbis; **135,** Geoffrey Holman/iStockphoto.com; **136 l,** M. Claye/Photo Researchers, Inc.; **139 r,** Andrew Lambert Photography/Photo Researchers, Inc.; **138 t,** Peter Weber/Getty Images; **138 bkgrnd,** Ted Kinsman/Science Source; **138 b inset,** Frank Greenaway/Dorling Kindersley; **141,** JupiterImages/AP Images; **144 salt close-up inset,** Tom Pepeira/Photolibrary New York; **144–145 spread,** Eric Martin/Icontec/Photolibrary New York; **146,** OTHK/Getty Images; **147,** Stephen Oliver/Dorling Kindersley; **148–149 spread,** Damian Dovarganes/AP Images; **150 pan,** Dorling Kindersley; **150 horn,** Dorling Kindersley; **150 plug,** David H. Lewis/iStockphoto.com; **151,** Jeff Rotman/Getty Images; **152 t,** Eric Martin/Icontec/Photolibrary New York; **152 b,** Damian Dovarganes/AP Images.

Interchapter Feature

Page 156 bkgrnd, Pictor International/ImageState/Alamy; **156 b inset,** Steve Cole/Digital Vision/Getty Images; **157 tl,** Klaus Guldbrandsen/Science Photo Library/Photo Researchers; **157 turtle,** Chris Johnson/Alamy; **157 b,** Jet Propulsion Laboratory/NASA.

Chapter 5

Pages 158–159 spread, N A Callow/Science Source; **161 m1,** Martyn F. Chillmaid/Photo Researchers, Inc.; **161 b,** Kai Schwabe/Photolibrary New York; **162,** the food passionates/Corbis; **163 l,** Peter Spiro/iStockphoto.com; **163 r,** Charles D. Winters/Photo Researchers, Inc.; **164 untoasted bread,** Cole Vineyard/iStockphoto.com; **164 toasted bread,** Cole Vineyard/iStockphoto.com; **164 fresh apples,** Drew Hadley/iStockphoto.com; **164 can,** Harun Aydin/iStockphoto.com; **164 crushed can,** snyfer/Fotolia; **164 rotten apple,** Christopher Pattberg/iStockphoto.com; **164 leaf,** Wojtek Kryczka/iStockphoto.com; **166 curdled milk,** Martyn F. Chillmaid/Photo Researchers, Inc.; **166–167 effervescent tablets,** Gandee Vasan/Getty Images; **167 bread,** Olivier Blondeau/iStockphoto.com; **167–168 rotten food spread,** Kevin Summers/Getty Images; **168 l,** Daniel Loiselle/iStockphoto.com; **168 r,** Charles D. Winters/Photo Researchers; **170,** Ho New/Reuters; **171 stickie,** Blackpixel/Shutterstock; **172–173 r,** Mike Blake/Reuters; **174 tl,** Prisma Archivo/Alamy; **176–177 spread,** Kaminskiy/Shutterstock; **178–179 car,** Morgan/AP Images; **178–179 car engine,** GIPhotostock/Science Source; **178–179 astronaut,** NASA Johnson Space Center Collection; **180,** Kai Schwabe/Photolibrary New York; **182,** Philadelphia Public Ledger/AP Images; **185,** Stephen Morton/AP Images; **188 t,** Gandee Vasan/Getty Images; **189,** James Harrop/iStockphoto.com; **190 l,** iStockphoto.com; **190 r,** Amanda Rohde/iStockphoto.com.

Interchapter Feature

Page 192; Charles D. Winters/Photo Researchers, Inc.; **193 bkgrnd,** Dorling Kindersley.

Chapter 6

Pages 194–195 spread, David Doubilet/National Geographic Stock; **197 t,** Joe Scherschel/National Geographic Society; **197 m1,** Stew Milne/AP Images; **197 m2,** Eric Risberg/AP Images; **198,** Sony Pictures/Everett Collection; **200,** Joe Scherschel/National Geographic Society; **201,** Eric Risberg/AP

Images; **202–203 spread,** Stew Milne/AP Images; **204,** Kevin Schafer/Alamy; **207 b,** Jacqueline Larma/AP Images; **207 tr,** Dorling Kindersley; **208 bkgrnd,** RDE Stock/Alamy; **208 tl,** Sergei Kozak/Getty Images; **212 bkgrnd,** Gareth Mccormack/ Getty Images; **212 tr inset,** Niedersächsisches Landesamt für Denkmalpflege/AP Images; **212 bl inset,** Richard Ashworth/ Robert Harding World Imagery; **213 touchstone,** Christopher Cooper/DK Limited/Corbis; **213 bottle,** Dimitry Romanchuck/ iStockphoto.com; **213 necklace,** Jules Selmes and Debi Treloar/Dorling Kindersley; **214,** Cristina Pedrazzini/Photo Researchers, Inc.; **215 tr,** Dorling Kindersley; **215 lime,** iStockphoto.com; **215 muffin,** Shutterstock; **215 dish soap,** Shutterstock; **215 window cleaner,** Shutterstock; **217 r,** Kim Taylor/Nature Picture Library; **217 t,** Scott Camazine/Science Source **217 l,** Dorling Kindersley; **218 bkgrnd,** WaterFrame/ Alamy; **218 orange jellyfish inset,** Gregory Ochocki/Science Source; **221 antacid,** Jon Schulte/iStockphoto.com; **221 glass of water,** Susan Trigg/iStockphoto.com; **221 bananas,** LuxCreativ/iStockphoto.com; **221 lemons,** iStockphoto.com; **221 tomato,** iStockphoto.com; **221 soap,** Daniel R. Burch/ iStockphoto.com; **221 vinegar,** Comstock/JupiterUnlimited; **221 hydrochloric acid,** Radu Razvan/iStockphoto.com; **221 blood,** Timothey Kosachev/iStockphoto.com; **226 l,** iStockphoto.com; **226 r,** Daniel R. Burch/iStockphoto.com.

Interchapter Feature
Page 228 bl, Ron & Diane Salmon/Flying Fish Photography; **229 bkgrnd,** Daniel Sicolo/JupiterImages; **229 inset,** Anthony-Masterson/Digital Vision/Getty Images.

this is your book

you can write in it